D1562035

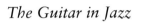

The Guitar in Jazz

University of Nebraska Press

Lincoln and London

Edited by James Sallis

The Guitar in Jazz
An Anthology

Acknowledgments for the use of copyrighted material appear on page 193, which constitutes an extension of the copyright page.

♾ The paper in this book meets the minimum requirements of American National Standard for Information Sciences—Permanence of Paper for Printed Library Materials, ANSI Z39.48-1984.

Library of Congress Cataloging-in-Publication Data

The guitar in jazz: an anthology / edited by James Sallis.
p. cm.
Includes index.
ISBN 0-8032-4250-6 (cl: alk. paper)
1. Jazz—History and criticism. 2. Guitar music (Jazz)—History and criticism. 3. Guitarists. I. Sallis, James, 1944–   .
ML3507.G85   1996
787.87'165—dc20   95-38563
                                                                    CIP
                                                                    MN

This book is dedicated,
quite simply,
to all musicians.
One does not want to think
of a world without them.

Contents

Illustrations

Introduction

It all began here in New Orleans, a couple of miles from where I sit in a circle of light at two in the morning writing this. It began with Johnny St. Cyr and Lonnie Johnson. St. Cyr played rhythm for King Oliver, Louis Armstrong, and Jelly Roll Morton; Johnson was a bluesman who played intricate, fluid lines. It began there—and it goes on beginning each time a player picks up his instrument. For one of the great paradoxes of jazz, the source of much of its power, is that jazz is at the same time the most innovative and most tradition-bound of musics.

In an earlier book, *The Guitar Players*, I took a long look at the parallel development of American musics—blues, country, jazz, rock—and the guitar as a solo instrument. The two, I found, were inextricably intertwined. I found also, as others had found before, that in American music all roads lead to jazz.

Afterwards, I had this sense of having spoken half a sentence and trailed off. Those sitting at the table with me were still leaning forward, into the ellipsis, waiting.

Maybe I should go on?

When in the early seventies I first began exploring American folk and popular musics, their histories remained largely unwritten. Coherent accounts of the sequestration of English ballads or banjo in America's mountain ranges, say, or biographical accounts of seminal players such as Lonnie Johnson, Eddie Lang, and Charlie Christian, were rare and sketchy. That's why I wrote *The Guitar Players*.

Now, some sixty years after the first jazz recordings, we know a little more. There are more books out there, dozens of magazines. And the general level of excellence—in guitar playing, in jazz and other improvisational music, in *all* the arts—is stunning.

I recall Roy Smeck remarking that Eddie Lang was playing Rachmaninoff's "Prelude" when everyone else was still just trying to pick out melodies.

Or Frederic Grunfeld's assertion that there's jazz guitar *before* Charlie Christian and jazz guitar *after* Charlie Christian, and they sound like two different instruments.

That's how many early cartographers of jazz's coastline feel today: My, how things have come along!

But in fact we don't know a *lot* more.

For all our accretion of savvy and skill, and for all the proliferation of music-oriented publications, documentation of the guitar's history in jazz and other American musics hasn't progressed far beyond initial efforts; in some respects it has regressed.

Partly this is due to changes in publishing: increased costs of production, allowing fewer limited-interest, low-return publications; consolidation of distributors and outlets into a scatter of megaliths; inevitable tolls of competition.

Partly it's simple demographics. Like that of science fiction, the readership of music magazines, particularly of guitar-based magazines, probably changes every five or six years, and, whereas a seventies readership may have come up on a diet of folk, bluegrass, and blues, current readers are almost exclusively the children of pop and rock.

Finally, that very escalation of skill itself has contributed to the failure to achieve any coherent, ongoing history of guitar and genre musics. For as playing grew ever more evolved, so the emphasis of guitar-based publications increasingly became technical—in regard to both actual playing techniques (hence columns on harmonics, on fine points of improvisation or comping) and to equipment (instruments, amplifiers, pickups, effects).

"The artist is like a millionaire," Cocteau wrote. "He travels ahead in a private car. The public follows behind in a bus."

On the American guitar scene, from the days of Lonnie Johnson and Eddie Lang, through Charlie Christian and Joe Pass, to John Abercrombie or Mike Stern today, it's always been the jazz guitarist who pushed far ahead and into new territories, leaving other players (pop, country, rock, or blues) to follow behind. As Leonard Feather writes in one of the pieces here, the guitar has seen an evolution, both in styles and in technical development, greater than any other instrument in jazz: "It has been a long and tortuous journey from the simple solos of Johnny St. Cyr to the vitality and complexity of today's electronic masters and pure jazz virtuosi."

Obviously I believe that this history, the mapping of its turns and augmentations, is important.

Yet there's more to this than hanging grandfather's portrait above the mantel. If all roads lead to jazz, and if you want to get there, or find out *how* you got there, then it helps to know the roads. Some are swift interstates, some local two-lanes. Although art never truly progresses in the way of most human enterprise, accruing knowledge and refining itself to an ever-sharper focus, it *does* advance, and does so by way of emendation, repetition, and recombination, forever looping back on itself, crossing genres, borders, and limits.

Which sounds, now that I write it (though it wasn't intended as such), very much like a definition of jazz.

I'll not attempt any summation of jazz guitar history here; Leonard Feather and Joachim Berendt do far better than I ever could. Nor will I address questions of fusion, or of jazz guitar's possible futures. See Bill Milkowski's Jim Hall–Mike Stern interview. They know a lot more about it, the three of them, than I do.

I *will* say that jazz may come as close to being the soul of America as anything we have.

Nietzsche said that without music, life would be a mistake. And with it—to take his words from another time—the world *is* transfigured, the heavens *are* full of joy.

James Sallis
February 1995
New Orleans

Four Jazz Choruses
by James Sallis

1.

Because the slave could not say what he meant
he said another thing. You know
how it is: one thing leads to another.
Soon he was saying all sorts
of things he didn't mean.

2.

We took his music (that's how it was meant
to be) but he didn't tell us the secret,
what he'd *really* meant by it. Meantime,
it was shuffling off to Chicago.

3.

Jazz floated up the river like a crocodile.
In New Orleans everyone ate oysters.
Bad notes were "clams."

4.

The horn's choked note rises from a dark club,
goes out over the city's long plain,
is there like air, never settles.

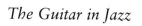

The Guitar in Jazz

The Guitar in Jazz

Leonard Feather

Leonard Feather died (on the eve of John Coltrane's birthday) a few weeks after I received his permission to reprint this piece. In a letter accompanying the permission form, he asked that I be certain to point out the fact that the piece was written many years ago and thus might seem out of date.

Well, yes. "Out of date" is another way of saying history. *And Leonard Feather's life was—from his early work as composer, arranger, and producer; his professional associations with Sarah Vaughan, Dinah Washington, and Duke Ellington; his authorship of seminal critical works such as* Inside Bebop *and* The Encyclopedia of Jazz; *and half a century of outstanding music journalism—a part of jazz history.*

The first book I turned to when I decided to find out more about this music was Feather's The Book of Jazz, *a portion of which appears below. I've since gone on to read most of the classic jazz studies, Berendt and Blesh and Hodeir, as well as Feather's other works. Another I found particularly helpful early on was* The Jazz Makers, *edited by Shapiro and Hentoff; among more recent works I greatly enjoyed Gary Giddins's* Riding on a Blue Note. *But at the time and for my needs, Feather's book proved a perfect primer, pulling a tremendous amount of material into focus. The bulk of the book, which follows a discussion of jazz origins and precedes one about improvisation, recounts, instrument by instrument, the development of jazz styles, thereby recapitulating the music's history again and again, each time from a different vantage point. The chapter on guitar, then, is a good place for us to begin.*

The guitar's role in jazz history has been overshadowed by the greater dominance in later years of the piano as a medium for ragtime. Yet long before the seeds of ragtime as a piano art were sown, primitive banjos and guitars were in use in the hands of itinerant folksingers deeply rooted in the blues. In homes that could scarcely afford furniture of any kind, let alone a piano, the heart of the musician, seeking a manual release, found its outlet not at the keyboard but on any plank of wood or metal across which a few wire strings could be arranged in simulation of the rough, vigorous sounds of the minstrel show's banjo and the wandering laborer's guitar.

The theory has been advanced that ragtime itself was a tributary of the early flow of banjo music. The piano, according to this hypothesis, was employed in ragtime to imitate one or two banjos; indeed, a very early published rag entitled "New Coon in Town" (1884) is significantly subtitled "Banjo Imitation." The use of the banjo among American blacks probably goes as far back as the American Revolution; Thomas Jefferson in 1781 referred to it as an instrument brought here from Africa.

The imitative process was eventually reversed: Huddie Ledbetter, a blues singer more generally known as "Leadbelly," tried to copy on his guitar the left hand of boogie-woogie piano when he heard it around Texas about 1910. Leadbelly represented, vocally and instrumentally, the folk-blues idiom that had a propulsive effect on early blues, ragtime, and jazz forms. As a young man in the last decade of the nineteenth century he was one of countless blacks who, in the postslavery years, were able to make their own living out of music. Leadbelly, who without urbanizing his style became a successful nightclub attraction in the North before his death in 1949, was one of the last survivors of an era in which the instruments that told a primitive and potent blues story grew side by side with ragtime and the brass band, interlocking more and more frequently until jazz was born.

In the earliest years of recorded jazz the two parallel forms, ragtime on the banjo and blues on the guitar, were preserved respectively in the work of Fred Van Eps, playing in the minstrel-show style typical of the early 1900s, and of Blind Lemon Jefferson, a contemporary and frequent associate of Leadbelly.

Little change was effected in jazz banjo during the early 1920s; the guitar for the most part was quiescent. Every band had its banjo man: Will Johnson or Bud Scott with Oliver, Charlie Dixon with Henderson, Freddy Guy with Ellington, Lew Black with the New Orleans Rhythm Kings, Johnny St. Cyr with the early version of Armstrong's Hot Five. Their four-to-the-bar strumming threaded the rhythm section together but added little or nothing of durable solo value. Lonnie Johnson, a guitarist who had played on the Mississippi riverboats with Charlie Creath, became a recording artist in 1925 and soon had to his credit the luster of disc associations with Duke Ellington and Louis Armstrong. With him came the first signs of melodic continuity and tonal depth, of a maturation beyond the metallic plunking that had characterized so many of his predecessors.

Eddie Lang was the first to elevate the guitar to the stature of horns and piano as an adult jazz voice. Lang could play the blues with an earthy feeling that, for some southern-oriented skeptics, belied his Philadelphia background; but he could also do for the guitar what Bix was doing for the cornet and Venuti for the violin, in the sense that all three combined unprecedented tonal purity with the gently swinging grace of an aerialist. In recording duets with Lonnie Johnson (under the pseudonym of "Blind Willie Dunn," presumably a more authentic name than Eddie Lang for the "race record" market), in duos and quartets with Venuti and innumerable sides with small jazz groups and large commercial orchestras such as Whiteman's and Goldkette's, Lang became one of the most accessible artists on wax; his early death in 1933 left a void that was never filled. At a time when guitarists were strumming simple, unaltered chords, Lang not only expanded the harmonic horizon, but also developed a single-string solo technique that was a decade ahead of its time, for not until 1939, with the advent of Charlie Christian and the electric amplifier, did the guitar step permanently out of the shadows of the rhythm section.

There were others who accomplished the difficult task of transferring the language of Lang to their own guitars: the late Carl Kress and Dick McDonough were among the most talented, devising well-meshed duets more noteworthy for their slickness than for intensity or depth; George Van Eps and others of that well-known plectrist family were early arrivals, but none quite captured the spark that had radiated from Lang.

In the six years that separated Lang's death from the so-called Christian era of the electric guitar, there were only half a dozen guitarists who left footprints still discernible. Two were strictly rhythm guitarists—Eddie Condon, whose banjo or guitar livened many a small-combo jam session but has never yet been heard in a solo role, and Freddie Green, whose imperative, rock-steady rhythm was tied like a tugboat to the Basie liner not long after it docked in New York. After nearly forty years with Basie, Green is still considered unique in his class and still has never taken anything more than a few brief, unamplified solos. The other four were solo guitarists: Teddy Bunn lent zest, humor, and a beat to the unique combo called the Spirits of Rhythm, featuring guitars and tiples (smaller instruments of the guitar family). Al Casey, a courier in the Fats Waller palace, stood in a corner while the leader played piano, sang, and clowned, but in his occasional short solos revealed an unprecedentedly smooth single-string solo style, and on his only solo record with Fats, the memorable "Buck Jumping," evidenced a mastery of both chord and single-string solos and deep-bred awareness of the blues.

Django Reinhardt, a Belgian-born Gypsy, burst on the scene with the formation in 1934 of the Quintet of the Hot Club of France (violin, three guitars, and bass), whose string-heavy sounds, novel and unprecedented though they were, seem in retrospect to suffer from much of the springlike swing of an overthick carpet. Reinhardt's Gypsy background was reflected in the capricious style, the sudden explosive use of passages in octaves, of flurries of too many notes too soon; very rarely did he manage to swing with complete ease. Yet he was the first foreign musician to have a profound influence in the United States; Les Paul and others listened to his records and copied his style. He visited the United States in 1946 and toured not too successfully with Duke Ellington, playing electric guitar with the air of one who had to keep up with the times, but the supple tone that had lent his work much of its charm for many listeners was coarsened as a result. Reinhardt, who died in 1953, left a bulky legacy of recordings, of which those taken at an easy ballad tempo seem the most viable.

Some observers in Paris in the late 1930s felt that a contemporary named Oscar Aleman could outswing Reinhardt and was a far superior jazzman, but the French spotlight was not large enough to accommodate two guitarists. Aleman, who made few records, was last heard of in Argentina.

Allan Reuss, with Benny Goodman, showed that the big swing bands had an important place for the rhythm guitarist. In general, however, the swing era was a period of transition for the guitar in jazz. As the spotlight concentrated more and more on large orchestras in which the strumming of the plectrist was as effectual as a swimmer battling a tidal wave, there were a few tentative attempts to solve the problem of inaudibility. One of these was a tin resonator, which helped to amplify in some small degree the guitar's sound.

One of the first musicians to use the resonator, later the first also to use the electric guitar, was Eddie Durham, the trombonist in Jimmie Lunceford's band who made a hobby of doubling on guitar. Durham was featured on the Lunceford record of "Hittin' the Bottle" in September 1935, probably the first recorded example of any form of guitar amplification. "Lunceford was crazy about the resonator," Durham recalls. "He used to bring the microphone right up to the

F hole of the guitar, so that between that and the resonator it was almost like having an electric instrument.

"A year or two later, after the people that made the resonator had gone out of business, I found somebody else who was manufacturing an electrically amplified instrument. I joined Count Basie's band in the summer of 1937 and stayed with him a little over a year. Toward the end of that time I made two sessions with the Kansas City Five and Six, just a few guys out of the Basie Band, with Freddie Green playing rhythm guitar and myself on electric.

"A lot of people thought that was a screwy idea, having an amplified guitar, and the ballroom managers were always afraid you'd blow out their lights. There was DC current all over the place, so I often had trouble finding electrical outlets while I was touring with Basie.

"Touring with the band I ran into Charlie Christian in Oklahoma City. He was playing piano when I first saw him, but I never in my life heard a guy learn to play guitar faster than he did. It was around the latter part of 1937, and I'll never forget that old, beat-up, five-dollar wooden guitar that he took to the jam session where I heard him play. I told Charlie the way to sound like an instrument, staccato, was to use all downstrokes. Most of the guys at that time played alternating up- and downstrokes across the strings. The downstrokes gave a sharper tone like a saxophone, but when you come back up, while the strings are bouncing back, it gives you a more legato effect.

"I don't think Christian had ever seen a guitar with an amplifier until he met me. It was a year before they got on the market generally, and then he got one for himself.

"I influenced Floyd Smith to get an electric guitar too. His mother didn't want him to buy an instrument, but one day I went downtown with him and talked him into getting one. I taught him how to tune it. The next time I saw him he was with Andy Kirk."

Both Floyd Smith and Durham experimented with two types of amplified instruments—electric Spanish and electrical steel guitars. Playing the latter, Smith made a record with the Kirk Orchestra, "Floyd's Guitar Blues," in March 1939. A minor sensation, it was a trigger for the whole fusillade of new guitar styles to be issued only months later by Charlie Christian's arrival in New York.

With the advent of Christian, the guitar came of age in jazz. As early as 1938, in small bands around North Dakota, he was using the single-note line of a guitar as a third part voiced with trumpet and tenor saxophone, thus removing it from the purely rhythmic function. On his solos he played with an utterly relaxed, even beat, mainly in eighth notes. Occasionally, he might play a Reinhardt solo taken note for note from one of Django's records, but basically his style was at an opposite pole, for Christian was the quintessence of swing. Harmonically, he was able to experiment with augmented and diminished chords, to weave his own web around some of the better standard tunes such as "You Go to My Head"—a practice beyond the harmonic scope of most other guitarists, indeed of most other jazzmen, in 1938. Rhythmically, according to observers who heard him at that time, his ideas were highly suggestive of what was to be known as bop. That his connection with bop was more than coincidental was confirmed when, after John Hammond had brought him to New York in the summer of 1939 to join the Benny Goodman Sextet, he spent many nights, after hours, jamming at Minton's in Harlem, where Gillespie, Monk, Kenny Clarke, and their fellow chemists held informal workshops.

Charlie Christian was only a "star," in the Hollywood sense, for two years (he contracted tuberculosis and died early in 1942), but it took only the first few months of this brief span to reorient the whole concept of jazz guitar. Every guitarist since then can be judged largely in terms of the debt he owes to Christian and how much of Christian's sublime facility he has acquired.

The true Charlie Christian spirit has been captured very closely by Barney Kessel, formerly of the Oscar Peterson Trio, now one of the more preoccupied denizens of the Hollywood recording jungle; by Irving Ashby and Johnny Collins, both sheltered from public view as unobserved members of Nat Cole's accompanying unit; by Mary Osborne, a young North Dakota girl who bought an electric guitar, sat in with Christian and studied his technique long before he became a New York cynosure; by "Jim Daddy" Walker, who made some remarkable records with Pete Brown in 1944 but has not been heard from since; and by Kenny Burrell, a Detroiter who in recent years has worked with such diverse performers as Jimmy Smith, Benny Goodman, and Astrud Gilberto.

These are the artists whose lineage goes directly back to Christian; others have evolved from Christian, adding new technical touches. The most agile of all is Tal Farlow (heard with the Red Norvo Trio off and on, 1950–55). Unlike most modern guitarists he is self-taught, in the sense that the phonograph and Christian were his only teachers.

Through the 1940s there were a few others who, without treading directly on Christian's territory, blended his innovations with their own personal qualities. Nat Cole's original trio in 1940 had an exceptional talent in Oscar Moore, who slipped from poll-winning eminence (first place every year in *Down Beat* and *Metronome*, 1945–48) to rhythm-and-blues obscurity. Billy Bauer brought some of his studies with Lennie Tristano to bear on a series of records with Tristano, Konitz, and company.

Though most of the Christian-influenced soloists have tended toward single-note horizontal lines in their solos, the potentialities inherent in the six strings of the guitar have not been neglected. The Lang-Kress-McDonough generation had its offspring in George Barnes, a brilliant studio musician whose duets with Carl Kress, in concerts and on records, offered a modern parallel for the Kress-McDonough work of the 1930s.

The guitarists of the bebop era were as much in Gillespie's and Parker's debt as in Christian's. Tiny Grimes played on Parker's first combo records; Remo Palmier and Bill De Arango distinguished themselves on early Gillespie sessions.

In the 1940s and 1950s guitar was a major voice, blended with piano, in the popular King Cole Trio. This led to the formation of the Page Cavanaugh Trio (with Al Viola on guitar), the Art Tatum Trio (with Tiny Grimes), and the Soft Winds featuring Herb Ellis, a Texan who displayed the peculiar beat and facility common to guitarists from the southwestern United States. From 1953 to 1958 Ellis was a galvanizing component of the Oscar Peterson Trio.

During the 1950s the piano-guitar-bass combo format receded from center stage. One superior guitarist, Johnny Smith, became a major jazz figure in 1952 when his recorded ballads, such as "Moonlight in Vermont," played in a relaxed chordal style, gained popular acceptance. From 1949 guitar (voiced with vibes and piano) was a cornerstone of the George Shearing Quintet. (Fifteen years later Chuck Wayne, Shearing's original guitarist, became the first plectrist to record modern jazz on the banjo, in a Focus album. He sounds like a man doing the twist in a waistcoat and spats.) The Red Norvo Trio of the fifties included such outstanding guitarists as Jimmy Raney, Tal Farlow, and Jimmy Wyble.

In 1962 bossa nova lent a badly needed impetus to the guitar in jazz. Almost abandoned by the few remaining big bands, and out of place in the hard-driving neo-bop and avant-garde combos, the guitar was a logical means of expression for this delicate, melodic music. The Brazilians helped to revive the unamplified Spanish concert guitar, played "fingerstyle." Jazz guitarists whose sounds had been standardized now could emerge from behind the electronic mask and play an occasional solo on a "real" guitar.

Most of the bossa nova guitarists (João Gilberto, Luis Bonfa, and Antônio Carlos Jobim) were not basically jazz-oriented; but at least one, Bola Sete, showed equal facility in every medium—electric and unamplified, Brazilian and modern jazz, and every stop along the way. His collaborations with pianist Vince Guaraldi, and his unaccompanied performances, confirmed that Bola Sete is the most gifted and versatile Brazilian guitarist.

Prominent also in bossa nova were Charlie Byrd, a classical and jazz guitarist from Washington, D.C., whose technique, taste, and adaptability are as remarkable as Bola Sete's; and Laurindo Almeida, a Californian since 1947 but a native of São Paulo, Brazil. Almeida was teamed with Bud Shank on some records in the early 1950s that foreshadowed the cultural alliance later represented by bossa nova. A superb fingerstyle concert guitarist, Almeida has worked successfully with many U.S. jazzmen to produce pop-jazz works.

Several countries besides Brazil enriched the guitar heritage of jazz: notably Belgium (Jean "Toots" Thielemans and the late René Thomas), Hungary (Gabor Szabo and Attila Zoller), and Switzerland (Pierre Cavalli).

Four outstanding guitarists gained acceptance in the late 1950s or early 1960s. Bill Harris of Washington, D.C., showed an impressive range of amplified and Spanish styles in his Mercury albums. Jim Hall's keen rhythmic and harmonic sensitivity were heard in fruitful collaborations with such hornmen as Jimmy Giuffre, Sonny Rollins, and Art Farmer. Joe Pass, first heard in the Gerald Wilson band and the Shearing Quintet, showed a stunning technique and a phenomenal capacity for swinging. Wes Montgomery, who died in 1968, was a self-taught performer whose admirable technique was often deployed in grass-roots reexaminations of the blues.

Montgomery's death roughly coincided with the guitar revolution that saw this instrument take on many new functions, as well as such electronic accouterments as the wah-wah pedal, echoplex, and fuzz tone. Many of these developments were due to the impact of rock, which enabled the guitar to surpass piano as the most played, most purchased instrument in contemporary society.

The guitar world was approximately split into four factions. There were the loyalists who adhered to the swinging Charlie Christian tradition; blues guitarists, among them a new generation of youngsters as well as such recently acclaimed veterans as B. B. King; ethnic specialists who brought to the instrument some of the characteristics of other cultures from the Middle East, India, Hungary, and, of course, South America; and, most conspicuously, rock and jazz-rock guitarists, many of whom distorted the original sound of the instrument for effect. However, many of the more skilled instrumentalists moved back and forth between these various interpretational areas.

George Benson, for instance, emerged in the mid-1960s as a disciple of the Charlie Christian school, but in recent years he has followed the example of Wes Montgomery by recording material in a rock- and soul-influenced vein.

Among the first group, Joe Pass has proved himself the most astonishing and exciting pure jazz guitarist of the 1970s. He is capable of incredibly fast and imaginative single-string lines, but has recorded many exquisitely chord-based ballads and is an accomplished artist on acoustic as well as electric guitar. Pass has been called the Oscar Peterson of the guitar and, in fact, has met some of his greatest challenges in successful recordings and tours with Peterson.

Herb Ellis, clinging with similar success to the traditions of the past, has brought empathy, beauty, and swing to a number of guitar duet albums and concert tours, first with Pass and later with Barney Kessel. It is interesting to note that Kessel in recent years has been in and out of the jazz-rock scene, but remains a traditionalist at heart, as his best records clearly demonstrate.

The blues guitarists are a breed apart. Many of them are equally well known as singers, and many scored their early successes with black audiences in the South and in Chicago. The reigning figure is B. B. King, who moved from Memphis and ghetto theaters and clubs to interracial acceptance. By the late 1960s his uncompromising performances had established him worldwide as the foremost artist in his field. His singing is functional and pleasant, more entertainment-oriented than his playing; his guitar sound is firm and strong and his lines reveal a natural ability to translate the values of early jazzmen into soulful blues terms.

Among King's admirers and contemporaries have been Muddy Waters, Buddy Guy, and the late T-Bone Walker. Mike Bloomfield is one of several white guitarists who has developed along similar lines, while the permanence of the blues has been determined through the work of such youngsters as Shuggie Otis. The latter, son of the pioneering rhythm-and-blues catalyst Johnny Otis, came to prominence on records as a teenager in the late 1960s.

In the rock field several guitarists have developed techniques and concepts of interest to jazz musicians. Among them are the strong, percussive Carlos Santana, the eccentric and unpredictable Frank Zappa [now deceased], the blues-jazz-rock father figure Eric Clapton from Britain, and an American who for a long time was based in England, the late Jimi Hendrix, of whom Joachim Berendt rightly observed that Hendrix "played 'on' electronics, and not as if he were playing an instrument . . . for him electronics was a new idea, something spiritual that radiated not only over his guitar, but over all instruments—in fact, over sound *per se.*"

Certainly the most influential, and perhaps the least classifiable, of all contemporary guitarists has been Britain's John McLaughlin, who for several years went by the name of Mahavishnu. First heard in the United States as a member of the Miles Davis group, McLaughlin has encompassed an extraordinary range of styles and idioms, from folk blues through rock, with occasional suggestions of Indian sitar.

Other musicians who have been able to span the spectrum of contemporary guitar sounds include Pat Martino, Larry Coryell, John Abercrombie, Ralph Towner, who has recorded on twelve-string and classical guitars, Al DiMeola (brought to prominence with Chick Corea), Joe Beck, and Jeff Beck. The two Becks are not related; Jeff is an Englishman and Joe an American, but both have adapted themselves to the multiple requirements of studio and combo work in the 1970s.

Among those who have brought the characteristics of their respective native cultures into the new world of jazz guitar, Gabor Szabo is the longest established. Leading a variety of small groups, Szabo not only has mirrored the impact of the Hungarian Gypsies, but also has experimented with Indian and other exotic influences. His work, however, has been inconsistent, and he seems, through trying to move in so many different directions at once, to have lost some of the personal touches he displayed during the early sixties.

The Brazilians have been generally successful in the incorporation of a jazz rhythmic feeling with the harmonic and melodic concepts of their native country. Since the advent of the bossa nova guitarists noted above, several others have come to prominence, among them

Oscar Castro Neves (featured recently with Sergio Mendes's group) and the highly original composer-guitarist Baden Powell.

Uncategorizable is Sonny Sharrock, a former member of the Pharoah Sanders and Herbie Mann combos. He has been described by Berendt as "the free jazz guitarist par excellence," though many of his recent recordings have incorporated rock elements and involve an ingenious interplay with his vocalist wife, Linda Sharrock. Norway's Terje Rypdal also has flowed back and forth between the worlds of free jazz and rock.

To sum up, the guitar family has seen a greater evolution, both stylistically and in technical development, than any other instrument in jazz. It has been a long and tortuous journey from the simple solos of Johnny St. Cyr to the vitality and complexity of today's electronic masters and pure jazz virtuosi.

Nick Lucas

Nick Lucas and Jas Obrecht

"A long and tortuous journey," Leonard Feather wrote —and the guitar has certainly come a long way. Yet until quite recently two of its first-generation American virtuosi, Roy Smeck and Nick Lucas, were still playing. What follows is directly from Mr. Lucas, and it gives a wonderful glimpse of the guitarist's life in the twenties, of early recording, and of the guitar's gradual ascendance over banjo. This piece was prepared for Guitar Player *magazine by one of its editors, Jas Obrecht.*

In Fats Waller, His Life and Times, *Joel Vance wrote of the era in which Nick Lucas, Roy Smeck, and Eddie Lang emerged as soloists: "The decades of the 1920's and 1930's were, arguably, the most productive period of distinguished and persuasive urban, literate popular music. The 1930's were a beneficiary of the adventurous and experimental music of the preceding decade, when pop music began to absorb and adapt jazz, classical and futuristic elements. . . . The latter decade kept the essence of the new elements but eliminated the silliness of the 'jazz age' and 'flaming youth.' "*

Studio and stage veteran Hy White in 1978 recalled the gradual shift from banjo to guitar as he saw it. He'd begun his career playing violin and would become an outstanding guitarist. "Little by little," White said, "the guitar overtook the banjo. It was decided by our band that I should have a banjo— since every other group had one—and I bought mine for somewhere around eight or ten bucks; the chord book was thirty-five cents. I must say that although I couldn't play well, I looked good! But then all of a sudden every banjo player started doubling on guitar. When a band played a waltz or a soft ballad, the banjo player typically switched to guitar."

Some players, such as Carl Kress, retained the banjo tuning when they made the switch. (Interestingly, studio players today, called upon for a banjo part, tune their banjos like the top four strings of their guitars.) But one by one the banjo players became guitarists. Duke Ellington's Freddy Guy was one of the last holdouts, finally making the change in 1933.

When I was in college here in New Orleans in the sixties the only banjo you ever saw was Manny Sayles's at Preservation Hall. A lot of tenors had been fitted with five-string necks, a lot more had been junked: you couldn't give them away. Then gradually, as the demand for vintage instruments spread from guitars to other stringed instruments, and as various kinds of traditional music gained new devotees, tenors began showing up again. Japanese players and collectors love them. On lists from dealers such as George Gruhn or Elderly Instruments, they're listed alongside pre-war Martins and Gibson F-series mandolins, and may go for much the same price. Walk around almost any of New Orleans's street festivals now and you'll see banjos, mostly played by young people, up there with the clarinets and brass. This year the city even hosted a convention of banjo bands. The playing of many of these new banjoists, drawn as they are by deep affection and little else to both the music and the instrument, is amazing—intricate, driving chord solos, mixed duple and triple meters, rapid tremolo, charged single lines. And they always smile while they're doing it.

First of all, before I started playing an instrument, my brother Frank, who was five or six years older than I, wanted me to study music without an instrument—*solfeggio.* I studied with a Sicilian maestro who taught me the fundamentals of music—timing and things like that. After I studied that for about a year, Frank put me on the mandolin because in those days it was the dominant instrument with Italians and the general public. It wasn't a commercial instrument; it was mostly for house entertainment. Frank was a very versatile, thorough musician who played accordion, and he wanted me to accompany him when he performed. My brother would take me along to perform in weddings, christenings, saloons, and streetcars. I'd pass the hat around—anything to make a dollar so we could help the family along.

Of course, this work I did with him gave me all the practice I needed, especially with getting the right-hand tremolo technique. I studied the mandolin under Frank's tuition, and he was very stern, and this helped me. He gave me all the musical education I ever needed. After that we parted because he went into vaudeville with an act called the Three Vagrants. After I graduated from high school I was on my own and got a job in Newark, New Jersey, at a nightclub called Johnson's Café. This was in 1915. In the interim my brother had me learn guitar so it could be used as more of a background, since the mandolin was primarily a lead instrument. I had become as good on guitar as I was on mandolin. Believe it or not, though, when I started at this club I was playing an instrument called the banjeaurine—a mandolin with a banjo head on it—because they wanted more volume than a guitar.

So I played with this big orchestra—piano, violin, and banjeaurine. We played the revues—like they had a soprano singer, a comic, a line of girls, and a male singer. The show lasted about two hours. Eventually they went haywire and put in a drummer. This was in Newark, and of course Newark is a short jump from New York. Naturally, I got all the work in town, because there were only a few musicians available who could qualify to play for these nightclubs. You had to be a good faker and read quick. They'd say—play it in C, or play it in D, put it up in F, and put it down a key. And if you couldn't do that, the music didn't mean a damn thing. When I went to the Musicians' Union I had to pass an examination so I could get my card. Of course, they don't do that today; you pay the initiation and you're in. I was at that club for two years, and this is where I got my experience. Toward the end there I started doubling on guitar for waltzes and things like that.

Then I went to another nightclub in Newark called the Iroquois, going with a combo with which I had a great experience. I played with one of the best jazz pianists of that era, Blanche Merrill, and Mose Mann, a violin player, and Joe Jigg, a drummer. Unbeknownst to me, this was giving me all the experience and qualifications for becoming a jazz musician. The salary that I got on that first job in Newark was twenty dollars a week, and I thought that was good then. Newark was a wide-open town in those days; they had nightclubs all over and everything went—gambling, prostitution. So when I got the job at the Iroquois, they gave me twenty-five dollars.

After that I formed a unit called the Kentucky Five, the original Kentucky Five. In those days they leaned on the South—the Dixieland jazz bands were very famous. I got the group together and toured the Interstate circuit as a backup for the Zeigler Twins; they were a vaudeville act. I had a violin, lead sax, alto sax, piano, drums, and myself. That was in the years 1919 and 1920. I had gotten married in 1917 and my daughter was born in 1918, and naturally I couldn't stay on the road too long. So I got myself a job in New York with Sam Lanin, the bandleader.

At that time Sam Lanin was the kingpin of New York, and he did most of the recording dates. I was working with him at the Roseland Ballroom. I got myself a tenor banjo and had the guitar alongside me at all times because when we played waltzes, it was very difficult to play the three-quarter beat on the banjo. The guitar came in handy; it blended better. We had two bands on the stand when we'd perform— one would stop and then immediately the other one would continue. Those were the days when it was five or ten cents a dance—way back.

You'd buy tickets and pick up a dame there and dance with her, and that's how she survived. The other band was led by Mel Hallett, who was very popular up around the Boston area.

I did all of Sam Lanin's recording dates. In fact, sometimes I did two a day. The sessions went from 9:00 in the morning until 1:00, and then from 2:00 to 5:00. I still did my job at night. I had a contract with Sam, getting ninety dollars a week. All they paid us for the phonograph dates was twenty dollars a session; that was the scale then. So I made forty dollars a day there, four or five days a week. With my salary I was making between two hundred dollars and three hundred dollars a week; that was a lot of money.

We always had trouble with the recording dates because in those days they had the old cylinder wax. They had a big box in the back where they'd keep all these waxes heated up. The wax was pretty thick. We only had one horn to catch all of the music into the cylinder to record; this was the days before microphones. We had the conventional combination, like three saxes, two trumpets, trombone, piano, rhythm banjo, and tuba—not bass. Guitar was unheard-of. The tuba player and myself had to sit way back in the studio because when you blow notes out of the tuba, if it's too loud, the needle would jump off the cylinder and they'd have to start all over again—very sensitive. Same thing with the banjo—it was penetrating.

So I thought up the idea one morning of bringing my guitar to the studio. Sam said, "What are you gonna do with that?" I said, "Well, Sam, I'm having so damn much trouble with the banjo, let me try the guitar." He told me they wouldn't hear it from where I was and put me right under the horn. Visualize the great big horn and dog you see advertised by the Victor phonograph company; well, that's what we had. He put me under the horn and the instrument was there. The rhythm was smoother, and we didn't have any trouble with the needle jumping out of the grooves. So he said, "Hey, Nick, that's all right! Keep it in." That was the beginning of me playing guitar on record dates. I would say that was around 1921. The next year I did "Pickin' the Guitar" and "Teasin' the Frets" for the Pathé phonograph company on Forty-second Street. I composed those tunes, and all I had in the studio were the musical director and the technicians—nobody else. I used a guitar made by Galliano; it was a small company located on Mulberry Street in New York. Now I haven't done any research on it, but I think that those solos were the first ones recorded. I worked with Lanin for a while longer, and then I worked for Vincent Lopez at the Pekin Café on Forty-fifth Street. In those days Lopez was very hot in New York.

When I left New York I went to join Ted Fiorito, who was an old friend from Newark. He had a band in Chicago called the Oriole Terrace Orchestra. He was at the Edgewater Beach Hotel and offered me $150 a week. This was in 1923. So my wife, my daughter, and I got in the car and drove out there. Took us about four days to get there because they didn't have route numbers; it was town to town. You couldn't drive at night because you'd get lost. At that time I still had my Galliano, and we were a big hit in Chicago. We were booked there for two weeks and stayed more than two years.

That was where I got my big break on radio. In those days radio was one of the only media of entertainment. Between sets with the band I used to go into the WEBH studio adjacent to our bandstand and fill in some time with my guitar and sing—kind of croon. That's when I started to get mail from all over the country. Now this wasn't a network broadcast by any means; it was just that people had crystal sets and would get me all through the night. I started to become very, very popular. So the Gibson instrument company approached me and wanted me to use their guitar. This was in 1924. I said, "Gee, I've got a great instrument now. I'm very happy with it, and it sounds good. However, if you make me a guitar to my specifications, I'll be glad to make the change." I had no ties or contract with the Gallianos because I had bought my guitar for thirty-five dollars. So Gibson said, "We'll do anything that'd make you satisfied, and if you're not satisfied, fine." At that time the guitar was practically obsolete. It was going out, and they had to do something.

The distinction about my guitar was this: The neckboard was a little wider because they used to make them—and still make them today—a little bit too narrow. You can't get a true tone out of some of your chords if the strings are so close together. I don't have an exceptionally big hand, but I wanted more room between the E and B strings especially, so when I played a G or C chord all the notes would come out distinct. I wouldn't get any interference from flesh on the fingers. I also said I wanted a little wider body than usual, and I wanted it black and unshiny so the spotlight wouldn't make it glare all around the people in the audience. So they came up with this Nick Lucas model, which was a beauty. I still have the original one, still play it. It's a gem. It's been fixed about forty times. I wouldn't part with it.

So while I was with the Oriole orchestra I was becoming very popular through the radio. I wasn't getting any money for it; it was all gratis. That was my first stepping stone to my success as a single performer. Then the Brunswick phonograph company, which was located in Chicago, heard me and signed me up to record. I made a record there called "My Best Girl" and "Dreamer Dreams." These were my first sides for them, all by myself singing into the old horn. It was a terrific seller, and then I left the band to go on my own in the latter part of 1924. The record was catching on all over, and they wanted me to make personal appearances all over the United States. My first big theater engagement was at the Chicago Theater. Then a friend of mine named Bert Wheeler heard me sing and told a New York agent to come out and catch my show. He did, and we didn't sign a contract. We just had a handshake and were together for about fifteen, twenty years. Then my next big break came when I played the Palace Theater of New York. That was the epitome of all; that was tops.

After I was a big hit there I went to England. At the Café de Paris the Prince of Wales and Queen of Spain were in to see my show one night, and then they had me entertain them privately about two weeks later. That's when I got publicity all around the world, and from then on I couldn't do anything wrong. When I came back to America, naturally I had all the work I wanted and continued to play in vaudeville because that was the only thing around. Vaudeville was it. I did all the circuits, making three thousand dollars a week; that's like thirty thousand dollars today, maybe more. I was all by myself, doin' a single. My wife and family were sure happy. This all came unexpectedly too, because in those days entertainers were few and far between; I could count them on my one hand. They were very famous: there was Eddie Cantor, Al Jolson, and Bing Crosby. See, I was in that era. I was before Bing Crosby, but I wasn't before Eddie Cantor. He was *way* before me. Al Jolson too—I was practically a schoolboy when they were around. My ambition was to be as good as they were. But I never tried to copy anybody. I try to be myself. When I record I use my own ideas, and back then I felt that I was a little unique due to the fact that my voice and guitar blended as one. I used to play a lot of solos too, but in those days they mainly wanted to hear me sing.

When I got to 1929 and played the Orpheum Theatre in Los Angeles, I got my biggest break. It was with *The Gold Diggers of*

Broadway. This was big time. I was on the same bill with Sophie Tucker and Jack Benny. That's pretty stiff competition, isn't it? But I was learning as I was going along, watching these performers. I was very observant. I learned how to get on and off the stage, and that wasn't easy. It took me fifteen years to learn how to take a bow. Today they do it overnight. My big song in the show was "Tiptoe through the Tulips." I never dreamed that a song would become synonymous with my name all these years, and still, no matter where I go, it's "Tiptoe through the Tulips." I only hope to write another one like it! You see, when you're in show business, you never know about a song until you sing it to the public. Every songwriter thinks that every song he writes is great, but this isn't true until the public buys it; they are the ones who decide.

I don't know whether this is wrong or right, but I think I helped a lot of these contemporary guys way, way back. Gene Autry says that without Nick Lucas he wouldn't be playing the guitar. Barney Kessel said I influenced him; same with Merle Travis—he's a fine guy. And even Roy Clark said that he learned from me. Now I'm ignorant of all this until they tell me. I'm not saying it in the spirit of conceit, but I feel that a lot of these contemporary guitar players studied from my books. I had two of them on the market; they came out around 1927. The first one was a beginner's text for ordinary musicians, and then I had a second one that was a little advanced. A lot of the knowledge back then was hearsay; guitar players didn't know from nothing. They picked up my books, and so the books became very popular. Well, today, as you know, every girl and boy wants to play the guitar. There's a big guitar school around the corner from where I live in Hollywood, and I see them every day walking around the neighborhood with cases. So I think I started something.

Until 1965 I performed steadily. I worked at Harrah's Club in Lake Tahoe and Reno for eight years with my own group, but that was too tough on my throat. My voice today is better than ever. I don't socialize enough to get acquainted with these good musicians today who have made it big—which I am happy for, because I had my turn. I had my success, and I thank the good Lord that I'm in good health and can still sing and work. I play a lot of fair dates and choice casuals. I just recently played three days at the Shrine Show in Indianapolis, and they want me back because they enjoyed it. I'm happy that I'm still able to do it. I'm in good shape physically and can still play "Pickin' the Guitar" and "Teasin' the Frets"—that's not easy! It takes a lot of fingering. As long as my health keeps up I'm still going to keep doing it until I can't do it any longer. I have a couple of things cooking: I think I'm going to grab myself a couple of good country and western tunes and record them. I think I could handle it very nicely and get the right background. It would thrill me to know it could be done.

People today mainly want to hear me sing. The guitar is part of my act, and nobody can play for me. I improvise, play little runs in between, do a little solo. Like I'll play "Baby Face" and play sixteen bars on the guitar. I feel that my voice is me; my guitar comes second. But the guitar is the one that made me. Without the guitar I wouldn't be what I am today because the two, as I said before, are one. Nick Lucas without a guitar wouldn't be Nick Lucas.

Eddie Lang

James Sallis

There are many explanations for the change from banjo to guitar: the guitar's superior adaptability to changing styles and trends; the advent of electronic recording and microphones that eliminated volume difficulties; the increasing popularity of string bass, with which the guitar blended better, over tuba, a natural partner for banjo. But more than anything the change resulted from the playing of Eddie Lang.

Roy Smeck said of Lang: "He was in a class by himself. He was so far ahead of everybody. He was playing Rachmaninoff's 'Prelude' when everyone else was trying to pick out melodies." You've already read Leonard Feather's assertion that Lang was the first to elevate guitar to the stature of horns and piano as a jazz voice. Writer Rich Kienzle has even suggested that Lang's use of a Gibson L-5, the first modern archtop acoustic, is probably responsible for connecting the jazz guitarist with that type of instrument—an image that has continued for over half a century.

When I taught guitar I had a short list of things students absolutely had to listen to. Bach was on the list, as were Bill Monroe and Hawaiian guitarist Bob Kaai. But what always brought students up in their chairs, even the most reluctant among them, were the Eddie Lang–Lonnie Johnson duets. I'd drop the needle onto "Hot Fingers" or "Have to Change Keys to Play These Blues" and, glancing over, could almost see lights flaring behind their eyes: My God, that was guitar playing, and it had a history!

This piece is from my book The Guitar Players, *which traces the parallel development of American music and the guitar as solo instrument. I've specially revised the piece for reprint here, deleting material covered by other writers or whatever seemed peripheral.*

Eddie Lang was born Salvatore Massaro in South Philadelphia either in 1902 (the year after Queen Victoria died) or in 1904 (the year after the Wright brothers made their first, twelve-second flight). Fats Waller was born in 1904, and Bix Beiderbecke by comparison lived from 1903 to 1931. Lang died at about age thirty in 1933, the year Prohibition was repealed, Franklin Roosevelt came into office and Bob Wills left the Light Crust Doughboys to form his own western swing band.

Lang's stage name apparently was taken from a boyhood baseball hero. His father was a banjo and guitar maker with a taste for classical music, and Eddie's own first instrument was the violin, which he began studying at age seven. Eddie seems to have inherited from his father a love of classical forms; he later transcribed Rachmaninoff's "Prelude in C♯ minor" for solo guitar, and several musicians recall his playing other pieces such as Debussy's "Maiden with the Flaxen Hair" (never recorded). Lang also had a profound admiration for Segovia. There are echoes not only of classical guitar but of flamenco as well in his playing over the years.

Eddie's early training almost certainly began with traditional Italian *solfeggio*, or sight singing. Joe Venuti, a lifelong friend and musical partner to Lang whose own training began at age four, explained *solfeggio* to a *Down Beat* interviewer many years later as "the Italian system under which you don't bother much about any special instrument until you know all the fundamentals of music. It's the only way to learn music right."

We can't say with any authority when Lang made the change to guitar; possibly, exposed to banjos and guitars at home, he'd been playing them since childhood. When he and Venuti got their first paying job with Bert Estlow's quintet at Atlantic City's L'Aiglon restaurant in 1921, he was still playing violin but may have been experimenting seriously with fretted instruments too. The following season found him playing banjo with Charlie Kerr's orchestra. He also played and worked casually with Red Nichols, the Dorsey brothers, and Russ Morgan during this time. Lang played a regular four-string tenor banjo for a while, then a six-string "banjo-guitar." This hybrid instrument, essentially a banjo with a guitar neck and tuned like the guitar, was popular with several of the older jazz players. Johnny St. Cyr played one for a time, and New Orleans's Danny Barker made it his regular instrument. In recent years both bluesman Reverend Gary Davis and country fingerpicker Sam McGee have recorded on the banjo-guitar.

By 1923 Lang appears to have settled on the guitar, though presumably he was still required to play banjo on some jobs. A photo of Adrian Rollini's band at the Club New Yorker in 1927 shows Lang holding a tenor banjo, his guitar resting on the floor before the band.

He was playing guitar behind Venuti in 1923 when Red Nichols first heard the duo playing "concert music" at the Knickerbocker Hotel in Atlantic City. Lang and Venuti had been working out duets since childhood, first playing standard mazurkas and polkas, eventually starting to improvise: "I'd slip something in, Eddie would pick it up with a variation. Then I'd come back with a variation. We'd just sit there and knock each other out."

Lang's first professional break came in the summer of 1924 when the Mound City Blue Blowers were booked into Atlantic City's Beaux Arts Café.

The group—Dick Slevin on kazoo, Jack Bland on banjo, and Bill McKenzie who sang jazz choruses with a comb and tissue paper—had teamed in 1922 as the Novelty Jazz Trio, but for their debut recording on Brunswick, they had become the Mound City Blue Blowers in celebration of St. Louis, where they (and, incidentally, ragtime) originated. That initial session produced "Arkansas Blues," a hit for them. Frankie Trumbauer, soon Bix Beiderbecke's musical confrere, also recorded a number called "San" with the group that year, and his solo on the record became a set piece imitated almost universally by jazz saxophonists. McKenzie went on to become an influential talent scout for the Okeh company, where he was instrumental in getting recording contracts for a number of jazz artists, Bix among them.

The Mound City Blue Blowers were an uptown version of the Negro jug bands being recorded sporadically at about the same time by Ralph Peer and others. Using various stringed instruments, a hodgepodge of harmonicas and kazoos and the near-ubiquitous jug for bass lines, these groups offered straight blues, string-band music, nonsense songs, and covers of popular tunes. Later city musicians such as Tampa Red and Georgia Tom mimicked the sound of these bands by adding kazoos and the like to their own music; this came to be known as hokum and, in Paul Oliver's description, "imitated country bands but with urban sophistication."

As Lang jammed with the Blue Blowers in casual sessions, McKenzie was impressed with his playing and with the substantial contributions Lang's guitar made to the Blowers' rather tenuous sound. By August Eddie was a regular member, remaining in Atlantic City but going up to New York whenever he was needed for theater or record dates.

As Richard Hadlock points out in his fine essay on Lang in *Jazz Masters of the Twenties*, recordings with the Blue Blowers contain in germ many of Lang's characteristics. His tone is full; he tends to vary his rhythm playing far more than customary by using a different chord position, inversion, or substitution on each beat; he employs vibrato and artificial harmonics uncommonly associated with popular guitar at the time. "In contrast to the monotonous chopping of most banjoists of the day," Hadlock writes, "Eddie's ensemble guitar sparkled with passing tones, chromatic sequences, and single-string fills."

Lang continued to appear with the Mound City Blue Blowers through most of 1925, also playing with Venuti at various Atlantic City clubs, but it was obvious that the group's popularity was declining while Lang's was steadily rising. "From late 1924 on," Hadlock notes, "the guitarist was more in demand than perhaps any other jazz musician in the country."

Lang became in effect the first ace studio guitarist. Electronic recording microphones easily allayed volume problems, and in some sessions with Ross Gorman's studio band (drawn largely from Paul Whiteman's orchestra) Lang's guitar was utilized as a solo instrument while a banjo played conventional rhythm behind the group. Singers found Lang's mutable chords, single-string fills, and rippling arpeggios valuable to their performances, and during this period the guitarist worked as studio accompanist to a number of singers, including Cliff Edwards ("Ukulele Ike") and Al Jolson. Lang and Venuti drifted individually and rather randomly through various bands but generally wound up playing together.

Working with the Gorman Band, which also included Red Nichols, Miff Mole, and Jimmy Dorsey, seems to have given Eddie just the opportunity he needed to mature along his own lines. His harmonic sensibilities deepened; his solos and command of the instrument grew ever more sure. One Gorman number, "Sleepy Time Gal," featured Lang's guitar in a duet with baritone sax, a startling combination that prefigures Charlie Christian's ensemble playing years later. On other numbers he and Venuti would contribute "hot" duet parts.

The musical partners developed a considerable reputation. In October 1926 producer Eddie King brought them in for a session with the Jean Goldkette Orchestra because "People know who they are, and they'll help sell the records." The session did not go well. King, disliking hot jazz, had little in common with the orchestra musically, and there was bitterness between the producer and Bix Beiderbecke. King's refusal to allow Bix to play on a Goldkette side two years earlier had led indirectly to Bix's dismissal from the band he'd just rejoined.

The session did initiate a lengthy if somewhat loose association of Lang and Venuti with the fourteen-piece Goldkette group. It also led to a working partnership with Beiderbecke, and the duo recorded frequently with the group centering around Bix and Frank Trumbauer's orchestra. Lang's utility on these recordings has been recalled emphatically, though peripherally, by jazzman Max Kaminsky: "When I think of those twenties bands with that dreadful twenties beat that Bix was usually trapped in (except when Eddie Lang was on guitar), it's no mystery to me that he drank himself to death."

Many of the Goldkette sides are memorable. "Singin' the Blues" from a February 1927 session quickly became a jazz classic, chiefly due to Bix's solo. Directly supporting the cornetist, Lang used the arpeggio style usually reserved for singers; his rich chords and inversions in other passages were no doubt picked up by Bix's unfailing ear and transformed into fresh lines. For "I'm Coming, Virginia," another hit from a May 13 session, arranger Irving Riskin voiced Lang's guitar lead over supporting horns, an extremely novel approach.

The same session that produced "I'm Coming, Virginia" also found Bix on piano playing in trio with Trumbauer and Lang. Lang's solo here is among his best, supported and no doubt fueled by the modern chords for which Bix had a decided taste. A reworked version of "I'd Climb the Highest Mountain," the tune was issued as "For No Reason at All in C." On the final chorus Bix picked up his cornet.

The Goldkette Orchestra disbanded for financial reasons on September 18, 1927, three days after a final recording session had produced "Clementine." Resulting from a carefully worked-up head arrangement and separate section rehearsals, this tune contained the longest Bix solo on any Goldkette record (a full chorus over sustained chords) and was, according to trombonist Bill Rank, "undoubtedly the best record we ever made." It was quite unlike other Goldkette performances, as though the band wanted to leave one final piece of hard evidence that it not only existed, but truly flourished. "By any standard," the authors of *Bix: Man and Legend* observe, " 'Clementine' is an extraordinary record. . . . The band, lifted by Lang's guitar, sings along with a freshness and rich tonal balance rare on any recording of the 1920s and a rhythmic relaxation looking a good decade into the future."

Two days after the "Clementine" session Trumbauer, Bix, and Lang returned to the studio as a trio and cut "Wringin' and Twistin'," written by Trumbauer and Fats Waller, probably at one of the daily

Harlem jam sessions hosted by Fletcher Henderson. Again Bix played out the last chorus on cornet; Lang echoed his final flourish and ended on a harmonic.

In the same 1926–27 period Lang was recording with Red Nichols and the Five Pennies, a popular group that carried Lang's name to an ever greater audience. Experimental and often uneven, this group produced some highly original music and provided the setting for several excellent solos from Lang on pieces such as "Washboard Blues" and "That's No Bargain." Eddie's solo on "Get a Load of This" is reminiscent of Bix and was later developed by Lang into a specialty he called "Eddie's Twister." It became his first recorded solo piece.

Also in 1926 Lang and Venuti began cutting the duets that are certainly among their most influential work. The first, from the fall of that year, was a thinly disguised "Tiger Rag" issued as "Stringin' the Blues," backed with "Black and Blue Bottom." Venuti's skittering violin is clearly the feature of these recordings; still, Lang's command of dynamics and accompaniment modes is everywhere evident.

In his autobiography, *Jazz Band: My Life in Jazz*, Max Kaminsky writes about those duets:

> The records Venuti made in the late twenties with the marvelously gifted Eddie Lang were uniquely beautiful, and they were way ahead of their time. . . . [Lang] was one of the rare two or three musicians with whom Beiderbecke recorded who was equal in musicianship to Bix. For instance, on the Okeh record of "Singin' the Blues," made in 1925, Lang not only plays magnificent ensemble and counterpoint to Bix's cornet; he is the only one in the band who is keeping time. I have never understood how Django Reinhardt could have been so highly praised—except, of course, that he lived some twenty-five years longer than Lang—and Eddie Lang's genius so neglected.

Following dissolution of the Goldkette Orchestra, in which Venuti and Lang had really been but occasional members, the duo lodged for a while with a new band just coming together under Roger Wolfe Kahn. Kahn had bought out the Arthur Lange Orchestra and was restocking it with some of the best New York talent. He had little trouble getting that talent because the band spent the majority of its time in town, paid very well, and worked only from 11:00 P.M. to

1:00 A.M., thus permitting lots of outside recording, radio, and theater work. Arthur Schutt, pianist with the band, remembers everybody averaging $400 to $500 a week, and says in one seven-day period he made $1,250.

We have memoirs from two jazz giants who heard Lang and Venuti with the Kahn Band. The first is from George Van Eps, the son of virtuoso banjoist Fred Van Eps, who would himself become a titan of jazz guitar, approaching the instrument as a "lap piano" on which he simultaneously played bass line, chords, and melody.

"As a very young fellow," Van Eps told Ted Greene for a *Guitar Player* article, "I was in the habit of building crystal radios, and one day I happened to get the cat's whisker in the right place and I picked up WEAF in New York. There was a live broadcast from the Pennsylvania Hotel of the Roger Kahn Big Band featuring the wonderful Eddie Lang on guitar. When I heard him, I said, 'That's it—that's what I want!' But I couldn't afford a guitar then—it wasn't until a year and a half later, while playing banjo in a little group with my brothers, that I was able to scrape up the money. . . . And that was the end of the banjo for me."

In his autobiography, *The Kingdom of Swing* (written with Irving Kolodin), Benny Goodman tells of his first trip to Harlem in 1927, accompanied by Glenn Miller and Harry Greenberg:

> Then, too, before we opened we went around to the Perroquet, where Roger Wolfe Kahn had his band at the time, with Lang, Venuti, Miff, Tommy Gott, Leo McConvell, and several other good men. I liked this band a lot, because the kind of guitar that Eddie Lang played was absolutely new at the time, and his use of the instrument was pretty much responsible for its taking the place of the old banjo. In all the kid bands I had played with, and for a while after that, the banjo was always the thing. Then Lang came along on those old records of the Mound City Blue Blowers (around 1924–1925) and it was something so different that musicians took notice of it right away.

In 1934 George Van Eps was guitarist with the Benny Goodman Band, though he remained but a single year. And of course it was Goodman who from 1939 to 1942, as a vessel for Charlie Christian, introduced modern jazz guitar to the world.

While continuing their heavy commercial recording schedules in 1927–28, Lang and Venuti also began paying more attention to their own music, putting out an array of duet, trio, and quartet recordings. Lang made his first solo records at this time too, beginning with "Eddie's Twister" and going on to "April Kisses," "A Little Love, A Little Kiss," "Melody Man's Dream," "Church Street Sobbin' Blues," and others. On several of the earlier cuts he is supported by pianist Arthur Schutt from the Kahn Band; on later cuts, Frank Signorelli replaces Schutt. Altogether there are about fifteen sides on which Lang is solo or primary performer. Some are readily available on Yazoo Records' *Eddie Lang: Guitar Virtuoso* (Yazoo 1059).

Steve Calt contributes excellent notes for the Yazoo album:

> His most memorable ensemble recordings of the late twenties were the seventy-odd sides he produced as part of Venuti's Blue Four and Blue Five groups; together they pioneered a medium that has been termed "chamber music jazz" for its emphasis on pure sound, rather than dance music or extra-musical effects. The same phrase could describe Lang's own featured recordings, most of which were made with the backing of pianist Frank Signorelli, a member of the Trumbauer Orchestra who coauthored such works as "I'll Never Be the Same" [a solo recorded by Eddie in 1928 with Rube Bloom on piano]. By composing many of his own pieces (such as "Rainbow Dreams," which was written for his wife Kitty), Lang parted company with other top-notch guitarists of the decade, like Roy Smeck.

Every signature of Lang's style is manifest in the solo pieces: the strong attack and fluent, bluesy lines with intriguing use of smears, glissandi, and harplike artificial harmonics; unusual intervals, particularly the pianistic tenth and Bix-like parallel ninth; sequences of augmented chords and whole-tone passages; the relaxed, hornlike phrasing. Although primarily a plectrum player, Lang would periodically tuck the pick away in his palm and perform fingerstyle, especially when playing arpeggios and fills behind a vocalist.

Guitarist and Lang student Marty Grosz has described one of the Lang solos, "There'll Be Some Changes Made," recorded in 1928, as "a journey from Naples to Lonnie Johnsonville (New Orleans, Natchez, South Side Chicago) in two and a half minutes. After a cadenza right out of the bagnios of old Italy and a few F. Scott Fitzgerald chords from pianist Signorelli, Lang proceeds to play a slower than expected 'Changes' in the simplest and yet most eloquent manner . . . blue and melancholy as hell. It is a very difficult matter to play a lead as simply and directly as that and to make it come to life, especially on guitar. Here is the real genius of Sal Massaro. This is the honest bread stick. How Eddie Lang found out I don't know."

Lang in fact had become, in addition to his regular work with jazz bands and vocalists, something of a blues specialist, recording with singers such as Bessie Smith, Victoria Spivey, and Texas Alexander, also doing instrumental sessions with older jazzmen like Joe "King" Oliver and Clarence Williams. He recorded more than two dozen sides with black blues artists, certainly more than any other white musician of his time. For these interracial recordings—"mixed bands" were uncommon well into the forties—he generally used the pseudonym Blind Willie Dunn.

One session with Lang, Hoagy Carmichael, Lonnie Johnson, King Oliver, and Clarence Williams was released by Okeh as from "Blind Willie Dunn's Gin Bottle Four." Another, a 1929 jam among Oliver's protégé Louis Armstrong, Jack Teagarden, Joe Sullivan, and Lang, a simple, straightforward blues, came out as "Knockin' a Jug."

But Lang's finest essays into the blues idiom were his ten instrumental duets with Lonnie Johnson.

Johnson, like Lang an ex-violinist, had much the same reputation and influence in black music circles as did Lang in his. Just as jazz guitarists find their roots in Lang, so contemporary blues guitarists like B. B. King bridge directly back to Lonnie Johnson. The man's technique was astonishing, his taste and originality constant. A highly developed guitar stylist, he linked modern blues to the older forms, in his lengthy career recording everything from Delta-style acoustic blues to Chicago rhythm and blues, working also as a sideman on records by Louis Armstrong, Duke Ellington, and others. Johnson sat in as a casual accompanist to some of the same singers as did Lang, among them Texas Alexander and Bessie Smith, which is presumably how the guitarists met. Considering Lang's taste for blues and inclination to jam pretty much at the drop of a guitar case, it couldn't have been long before they were trading licks. Unfortunately, no details of their association survive.

"Eddie could lay down rhythm and bass parts just like a piano," Johnson is reported as saying. "He was the finest guitarist I had ever heard in 1928 and 1929. I think he could play anything he felt like." Johnson later referred to the duets with Lang as his "greatest musical experience."

The duets were loosely arranged blues in which, according to guitarist Richard Lieberson, the two musicians "transcend their disparate backgrounds to create a two-guitar sound that has rarely been equaled for sheer excitement." For the most part Lang stayed in the background, playing his unique rhythm and feeding Johnson changes, while Lonnie played high-register, fingerpicked blues lines remarkable for their fluency, variety, and shifting rhythmic base. Lang did come out front for occasional leads, as in the introduction and third verse of "Blue Guitars," second and third verses of "Midnight Call," and the intro and first verse of "Blue Room." These duets are infectious, provocative music, as fresh and vigorous today as when they were recorded. Several of Lang's own solo pieces, such as "Melody Man's Dream" and "Perfect," seem to exhibit Johnson's influence in their timing and emphasis on high-register lines.

"He didn't tell me what to do," Johnson said. "He would ask me." And Johnson does seem to have been the driving force of the duets, with Lang quite content to give him rhythmic and harmonic support. It is probable that Lang recognized Johnson's superior facility in the idiom; still, comparison with Lang's own blues leads discloses more similarities than differences, shared strengths above relative debility. The two had considerable common ground.

"Lang was the finer musician," Sam Charters wrote in *The Country Blues*, "and had probably more knowledge of the guitar's harmonic possibilities than any musician of his period, but Lonnie had an emotional sense and emotional intensity that shaded Lang's brilliance. Their duets were always marked with a careful respect for each other's abilities."

At the time of the duets with Lonnie Johnson, Lang was already a featured soloist in the prestigious twenty-nine-piece Paul Whiteman Orchestra. Whiteman was practically the monarch of popular musical entertainment in the period that stretched between declining interest in "hot" jazz and the arrival of the swing bands; and he paraded, in the words of Frank Tirro from his *Jazz: A History*, "an endless supply of popular songsters, semiclassical arrangers and composers, vaudeville tricksters, and name jazz musicians before the public." Whatever his aesthetic shortcomings, Whiteman seems to have had genuine feeling for his musicians; he was a good manager and an honorable man. He provided a shelter for many fine musicians, Bix, George Gershwin, Lang, and Venuti among them, and probably did more to promote general acceptance of jazz than anyone else of his period.

Lang had worked with Whiteman in the past. He and Venuti joined the orchestra briefly in 1927, and throughout that year Whiteman called upon Lang for special recording needs, often bringing in Carl Kress when Lang was not available. He and Venuti rejoined Whiteman in 1929 and remained a year, featured on many recordings, concerts, and radio broadcasts, even in *The King of Jazz*, the first all-Technicolor movie. Lang also played frequently behind Whiteman vocalists Mildred Bailey and Bing Crosby.

Frank Trumbauer remembers Lang carrying the entire Whiteman library in the form of cues on the back of a small business card. Whiteman himself, ten years after, had this to say in *Down Beat*:

> Eddie played with our band over a long period of time during which I had less trouble with rhythm than at any other time. . . . No matter how intricate the arrangement was, Eddie played it flawlessly the first time without ever having heard it before or looking at a sheet of music. It was as if his musically intuitive spirit had read the arranger's mind and knew in advance everything that was going to happen.

Lang and Crosby became close friends during their Whiteman days, Eddie eventually marrying a friend of Crosby's wife Dixie Lee. Kitty Lang had been with the Ziegfeld Follies and was Eddie's second wife, remaining with him for the few years he had left. It was for Kitty that Lang wrote his solo piece "Rainbow Dreams," recorded in 1928.

By 1930 the Whiteman Orchestra was having trouble meeting its nine-thousand-dollar weekly payroll and began trimming sails. Crosby left the organization in the spring of that year, Lang and Venuti departing shortly thereafter.

"Singers replaced big bands as the chief purveyors of popular songs," Russel Nye comments in *The Unembarrassed Muse: The Popular Arts in America*, and in 1931 Lang became full-time accompanist to Crosby. Crosby had called Eddie Lang "the best musician I know." Now Lang dedicated the majority of his time and professional activity to supporting the rapidly rising Crosby, working four theater shows a day, nightly radio broadcasts, and frequent Crosby record dates. When Crosby went to Hollywood with a three-hundred-thousand-dollar contract for five films, Eddie went along, even making a brief appearance in *The Big Broadcast of 1932*.

Lang did find time to work other dates during this period. He recorded with a jazz-oriented vocal trio, the Boswell Sisters, displaying on releases such as "Mood Indigo" and "There'll Be Some Changes Made," according to Richard Hadlock, "a new feathery touch, combined with the steadfast four-four rhythmic flow, that was signaling the coming of swing music and the end of the 'hot' era." He also recorded with his pal Venuti as part of the Venuti-Lang All-Star Orchestra, which included Benny Goodman and Jack Teagarden. The four sides cut by this band are generally considered classics, a fair summation of the past decade's achievements and a preview of music soon to come.

In 1932 Lang recorded, with Carl Kress, his only guitar duets aside from those with Lonnie Johnson. The two sides, "Pickin' My Way" and "Feelin' My Way," exhibit Lang's characteristic strengths and demonstrate, too, that he was still developing as a guitarist. Kress would be instrumental in extending the guitar duet as a recognized jazz form into present times, pairing with Dick McDonough from 1934 to 1937 and, after McDonough's death, with Tony Mottola; then again, in 1961, with George Barnes.

Eddie Lang died at about age thirty, on March 26, 1933. Hitler established the Nazi dictatorship in Germany that year, and a favorite song on the radio and in musical shows was "I've Got the World on a String." Lang's chronic sore throat had worsened and begun to affect his general health. He entered the hospital for a routine tonsillectomy and, while still under anesthetic, developed an embolism from which he died without regaining consciousness.

Lang of course left a gargantuan legacy. Almost single-handedly he legitimized the guitar and created roles for it in solo, accompaniment, and ensemble settings. His novel use of chord voicing and arpeggio figures alternated with single-string lines formed the basic vocabulary of jazz guitar, and other techniques appropriated elsewhere (the glissando and gruppetto from classical music, the smear and bent string from blues, artificial harmonics) built on that foundation, setting guitarists' future directions. He had earned a great deal of respect for his instrument and, among other musicians because of his professionalism and complete musicianship, for jazzmen as well.

A recurrent criticism has been that Lang did not swing, and his playing does seem stiff by today's standards, but little more so than that of contemporaries; contentions that Lang's playing did not survive its time certainly seem unfounded. Marty Grosz says:

The Chicago guys felt that Lang didn't really swing, and I'm inclined to go along to an extent. . . . But I think we can overlook that for the nonce. In his way he did so much, and it sounds so damn natural and easy. And he was first; he had to think the whole thing out for himself. It's always more difficult to lead the way. Hence modern bass players can play rings around Jimmy Blanton—but Blanton was first and had the soul. Same with Lang.

Joel Vance summed things up nicely in a review of jazz reissues for *Stereo Review*:

It has been said that Lang didn't "swing," and he probably didn't possess the rhythmic feeling inherent in many jazzmen. But he was not unduly concerned about this—nor should we be. Lang was more interested in the harmonic and compositional potential of the guitar and, in an almost atavistic sense, in the *honor* of the instrument. He thought like an Italian and played like an American, and while his music may not always have been "pure jazz," it was always successful as music in ways that antedate and transcend jazz.

And *that*, finally, is the genius of Sal Massaro.

From Blues to Jazz Guitar

Dan Lambert

 *Every serious musician in a sense recapitulates the whole history of music, and of his or her chosen instrument, in his or her personal development. And Dan Lambert over the past couple of decades has followed this familiar course. Like most younger guitar players, his earliest musical experience was with rock. But Dan described in a letter to me his first exposure to the music that really got him going as a guitarist: "I was at a party late at night in Champaign, Illinois. The campus radio station was on and this amazing music was on. Mostly one guy playing and singing and sounding so full but still intricate. For a white boy who had been playing guitar for less than a year and thought all there was in the world was lead and rhythm, this music was a religious experience. I was hooked. To this day I don't remember any of the musicians I heard in that couple of hours, but what an impact it had on me."*

Soon he was playing acoustic guitar in a strong folk style reminiscent of Leo Kottke (whom he still admires), and much of what was on his first album, Hot Time on the Old Town Tonight, *shows that influence. With* Fancy Guitar *he began to move farther afield; it was a folk album, but one underscored with the influence of classical guitar, jazz,* R&B. Down the Highway *and subsequent albums, almost as a kind of homage, have shown the influence of Chicago blues, especially that of Robert Nighthawk, and of jazz guitarists from Django to Joe Pass.*

That said, it should be no surprise that when we were discussing this book Dan suggested a piece on the guitar's evolution from blues to jazz. That evolution was occurring, in its own way and at its own pace, in what seems to me a peculiarly American form of synthesis, in Dan's playing. Who better, then, to speak of it?

Readers with no music theory may first want to turn to the appendix following this piece.

Joe Pass is the musical descendant of Lightnin' Hopkins, considering both these players as solo guitarists and as representatives of their particular genres—Hopkins the primitive country bluesman, Pass the sophisticated jazzer. Tracing strains of evolution is simplified in players whose unaccompanied styles contain melody, harmony, and rhythm in a single instrument, with the ideas coming from one musician. Obviously, Hopkins didn't wake up one morning to find himself a bald-headed white boy with a mustache and a Gibson ES-175: there's a gradual line of development that can be followed.

Where is the border, assuming there *is* a border, between blues and jazz? Both are highly improvised forms. Both require profound emotional commitment and dedication to the ongoing process of rethinking the music each time, and while, it is played: new harmonies, new rhythms, rephrasings, elaborations. The best blues and jazz alike has always that sense of "Now what's going to happen?"

The blues are vocal-oriented. Rhythmically rich, certainly, but the central element is the vocal or voicelike quality of the instruments. When someone points out a "bluesy" guitar line, he means the crying/talking nature of the notes. This is important, possibly a major point of separation between blues and jazz. Jazz, in its leaning toward sophisticated harmonies, can lose that vocal quality; blues never does.

A bluesman looks at blues for its basic emotional content, the jazzman more academically (twelve measures, I–IV–V harmonic structure with variations). Lightnin' Hopkins changed chords when he felt like it. Maybe he'd keep that E chord thumping away, or he'd stretch the vocal line or play one of those trademark runs of his that may go on for half a measure or take two measures. Billy Gibbons recalled for *Guitar Player* the first time he played with Hopkins:

> We were playing a traditional blues and we came up to where you would think the second change would normally be, and we all went to the second change. Lightnin' was still in the first change. He stopped and looked at us. Dusty said, "Well, Lightnin', we all went to the second change. That's where it's supposed to be, isn't it?" Lightnin' looked back and said, "Lightnin' change when Lightnin' want to change."

So did Blind Lemon Jefferson, about whom Mike Bloomfield once said: "He was really a great player, very fast, very strange. Blind Lemon didn't play with a beat—you couldn't dance to his music." Actually, there is a beat there, though zany and difficult to follow. On "Matchbox Blues" from the 1927 Chicago sessions, for example, following a five-measure intro the verses range somewhere between sixteen and seventeen measures in length, with the voice entering often in midmeasure and twisted guitar lines that go on forever.

Blind Lemon improvised by his own rules, Hopkins by his. They were both unschooled (what I prefer to call "natural") musicians and cared only about what sounded good. Blind Lemon didn't know he was playing an A-diminished chord after the seventh in the intro to "Matchbox Blues," but he knew that sliding the A7 shape down a fret while keeping that fifth string chugging away sounded pretty hot. Alan de Mause recognized the importance of this primitive style in the study of jazz guitar when he began his book *Solo Jazz Guitar* with a discussion of Hopkins's style, "a ferocious one, rough and tumble, and very intense."

Other players sharing that "ferocious" style were Son House, Charley Patton, Bukka White, and Robert Johnson, all relying heavily on bottleneck guitar to produce that voicelike sound so indicative of blues guitar. Monotonic bass patterns would get slugged out on lower strings while the bottleneck worked on the high strings. Rhythmic invention was the goal here, with melodic improvisation taking place more or less incidentally, filling up spaces left by the vocal and rhythm. This is not to say that these players didn't come up with some infectious, funky riffs. Charley Patton didn't even bother to change chords in "Mississippi Bo Weavil Blues"; that upper-register bottleneck riff was all he needed.

Of course, there's a lot of distance, stylistically, between Charley Patton and Charlie Christian even if they are both using riff styles. And one player who fits into this gap is Blind Arthur Blake.

Overall, Blake's playing had a much more "refined" sense of rhythm, not the intense kick of Lightnin' Hopkins or Charley Patton but more of a swing: Blake's playing made you tap your foot, not stomp it. The monotonic bass figures became bass lines outlining sophisticated chord progressions. Sometimes the chord sequences were based on the circle of fifths, a typical progression moving up a perfect fourth each successive chord (E–A–D–G and ending in C, for example). Other tunes were based on standard twelve-measure blues progressions. In "Black Dog Blues," for instance, Arthur Blake transformed the twelve-bar format into an elaborate guitar part full of chromatic movement and passing chords.

Blake plays the root note of the chord in the bass except in measures three and seven, where he uses the B note for the bass of the G7 chord. In measure eight he uses chromatic bass movement to connect the C and A7 chords (the bass moving C–B–B♭–A), also in measure ten to connect the A-diminished to the C in measure eleven (the bass moving A–B♭–B–C).

These harmonic variations were a major stylistic step in the evolution of jazz guitar. Whereas Blind Lemon's melodies may have been every bit as elaborate as Arthur Blake's, the harmonic background Jefferson used was much simpler. This gave Blake's playing a slicker, more "uptown" sound. His pieces in fact were orchestrated affairs with as much movement in the middle voices (generally considered the harmony) as in the treble (melody) and bass. Blake gave a lot of attention to those middle, supporting voices.

Traditional Twelve-Bar Harmony

C	F	C	C^7
F	F	C	C
G^7	F	C	C/G^7

Arthur Blake's "Black Dog Blues"

C	F/F$^\sharp$DIM.	C/ $^{\text{G}^7}_{\text{B BASS}}$	C/C^7
F	F$^\sharp$DIM./G	C/ $^{\text{G}^7}_{\text{B BASS}}$	C/A^7
G	A DIM.	C/G^7	C/G

The melodies in Blake's playing were still riff-type, but now these phrases would change with every chord. This was another important step: the idea of improvising over a set of chord changes and changing the melodic center with the chords is at the foundation of jazz guitar. But Arthur was definitely a blues player. While his chord progressions had reached a new level of sophistication, the melodies played over those changes remained for the most part bluesy, vocal-inflected lines. When Blake played a tune with lyrics, his guitar melodies rarely strayed from the melodies being sung and then only to introduce a "pet lick" turnaround or chord-connecting run. He relied heavily on pet licks, using, like many bluesmen, the same accompaniment for several tunes.

The guitarist who most clearly straddled the blues/jazz fence was Lonnie Johnson. His recorded output provides an excellent opportunity to compare and contrast blues and jazz guitar styles. Even when accompanying a straight-ahead country blues singer like Texas Alexander, Lonnie managed to take the song uptown. He would behave himself during the vocal choruses, waiting to slip in some razzle-dazzle on the instrumental breaks. Take, for example, Alexander's 1927 recording of "Cornbread Blues." Johnson's playing during the vocal accompaniment sounds like a not so erratic Blind Lemon, staying with a I–IV–V harmony and weaving intricate lines around the vocal. It's not until Lonnie takes an instrumental chorus on the last verse that he gives himself away. Below we have an example of what he does with the twelve-bar harmony in the key of E.

Lonnie Johnson begins this break with the traditional harmonic scheme, continuing the country blues feel from the previous verses. However, he's not doing that Blind Lemon arpeggio/single note/run style—he's playing block chords with sophisticated voicings, not unlike a piano player.

"Cornbread Blues"

Lonnie Johnson—Guitar

Note: The diminished chords appearing in the Lonnie Johnson pieces are all voiced with the root on top.

In the first measure the D note (the seventh of the E7 chord) goes down a half-step to become the C♯ in the second measure (the third of the A-add-nine chord). All the chords in the first four measures share a common B tone, the B serving as the fifth of the E and E7 chords and the ninth of the A-add-nine. So these first four measures are an effective tie between what Lonnie has been doing in the song and what he's about to play. He has kept the harmony fairly basic but contrasts the style in which he executes it. Measures five and six are a continuation of the traditional harmony. In fact, he slips back into that Blind Lemon style, riffing around a straight A chord.

Then comes measure seven. Lonnie Johnson loved those descending diminished chords; he used them not so much as passing chords but as coloration devices, much the same way Django Reinhardt treated diminished and augmented chords. Measure eight finds Lonnie playing a chromatic run that links the sixth of the E chord (C♯) to the third of the F♯ chord (A♯) in the ninth measure. Using the F♯7 chord (II7) in the key of E to lead to the B7 (V7) chord was another thing he often repeated. One can visualize what Lonnie plays in measures eight and nine as a I–VI–II–V turnaround substituting a chromatic run for the VI chord and C♯ dim–E dim for the V chord. He goes back to a basic A chord (IV), then to chromatically descending diminished chords to end the song. The high notes of these chords provide a smooth means of connecting the fifth and third of the E chords found on either end of the diminished cadence: B, the fifth of the E chord, goes to A♯ goes to A goes to G♯, the third of the E chord.

With all this, and with his always-smooth delivery, Lonnie was able to accompany a singer like Texas Alexander and lend an overall sound of sophistication to the project without destroying Alexander's country roots. Lonnie took the blues sound and the jazz sound, put them together and made it work. Another dynamic example of this marriage is his solo-guitar instrumental "Playing with the Strings."

The basic structure here is an intro, seven choruses of varying length, a bridge, three more choruses, and the bridge again to wrap it up. The choruses range in length from roughly eight measures to roughly thirty—"roughly" because Lonnie frequently ignores the bar lines, changing chords at will, and any attempt to chart what he's doing rhythmically is at best an approximation. These irregular measures, the general rushing of the cut time, the quick, upper-register melodies and descending diminished chords, all add up to give this tune a hot, zany feel. I've charted the intro, first and seventh (longest) chorus, and the bridge.

The intro is a typical Lonnie Johnson diminished-chord sequence with a tumbling, triple-meter feel. As in a good part of the tune, Lonnie shows little regard for bar lines. From the outset the listener is kept at bay as to what is going to happen next and when. The odd, seven-measure length of the intro also contributes to this. He ends the section with one of his favorite techniques: the F♯7 to B7 progression.

"Playing with the Strings"

Introduction   Lonnie Johnson—Guitar

E DIM	D♯ DIM	C♯ DIM	B DIM
F♯ 7	F♯ 7	B 7	

Main Theme (First Chorus)

The main theme (first chorus) is a snappy melodic figure over an E chord, going to an arpeggio-type run over a B7 chord, then back to an E chord. Again the length of this section is an odd nine measures.

Seventh Chorus

This transcription is of the longest chorus of the tune: a thirty-measure blues. Lonnie begins with an eight-measure blues motif (E to E minor back to E) that gets repeated, accounting for the first sixteen measures of the section. Next comes the IV chord being played with a funky F♯-to-E figure—a "boogie-woogie" riff often heard both in jazz and blues. Lonnie moves on to his favorite F♯7 chord, then executes a chromatically descending diminished-chord sequence (from E dim to A♯ dim), again with that tumbling, 3/4-time feel. This section also ends with the F♯7 to B7.

The bridge to "Playing with the Strings" starts off with an upper-register run over an E chord, similar to the melody at the beginning of the first chorus. Then, however, Lonnie plays a four-measure melody built on the A and G♯ chords. This motif is played twice and is instantly recognizable, even among the myriad variations that occur during this tune. It's simple but it works.

Bridge

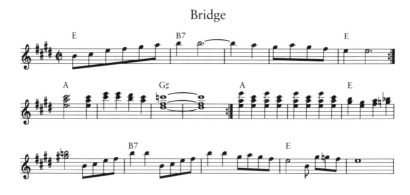

Lonnie Johnson here has taken the abandon of primitive country bluesmen insofar as meter is concerned, adding the melodic variation and harmonic sophistication of a jazzman and playing it all over a hot 1928 rhythm. It's a tune that stylistically bridges the gap between blues and jazz, containing strong elements of both.

Lonnie Johnson and Eddie Lang recorded a number of guitar duets with titles like "Two Tone Stomp," "Handful of Riffs," and "Midnight Call Blues." One interesting example of these is a slow, swinging blues entitled "You Have to Change Keys to Play These Blues." On this tune Lonnie is using his nine-string guitar (as he did on all the Lang-Johnson duets) tuned down somewhere between E♭ and D; he is playing out of E-chord shapes. Eddie Lang plays backup throughout the tune except on the fourth chorus, during which he plays the melody. (His solo, incidentally, is note for note the same break, though transposed, that he plays on Louis Armstrong's "Knockin' a Jug.") Lonnie's playing here is very loose, very "off the cuff"—lots of smooth, bluesy flatted-third bends and descending chromatic scales. His guitar sustains nicely, giving his playing a distinctly human, singing tone. Lang's break, on the other hand, seems perfectly conceived and tight, and so the styles contrast to good effect—Lang's polished gem in the middle of Johnson's funk. The string bends in this tune are also of interest: Lonnie bends notes to make them "cry," wringing every last drop of emotion from a note, while Eddie bends notes to give them a slightly "off," out-of-tune sound. Lonnie's is the more emotional (bluesy) approach, Eddie's an intellectual (jazzy) approach.

"You Have to Change Keys to Play These Blues"

Second Chorus   Eddie Lang—Guitar

E	E	E	E7 F7 F♯7 G7 G♭7
A	A	E	E
B7	A	E	E6 E7

"You Have to Change Keys to Play These Blues" actually does change keys. Since Lonnie is playing out of E-chord shapes, I've written out the progressions in E and A. The choruses are arranged E–E–A–E–A. Chords given here are for the second and third choruses.

Notice the fourth measure of each chorus, both with interesting chromatic seventh-chord progressions from the I chord to the IV chord. While playing the E chord in the chorus in the key of E, Lang emphasizes the G♯ note, giving the chord a smooth, harmonized sound. He also performs a simple but effective modulation between the two choruses, going from an E6 chord to an E7 chord to an A chord. The last three measures of the chorus in E contain some beautiful middle-voiced runs that tie the chords together nicely. When Lang plays the backup for the chorus in A the second time, he gets from the A chord in measure eight to the E7 in measure nine by performing a descending seventh-chord progression: G7 to F♯7 to F7 to E7. Lonnie Johnson plays an A-minor chord in measure six of the chorus in E when he plays backup. The chords support the solos perfectly, with Lang giving special attention to subtle shadings in his voicings. Also, the occasional chromatic movement has the effect of shifting this otherwise relaxed tune into the next gear.

Third Chorus

A	A	A	A7 B♭7 B7 C7 C♯7
D⁷	D⁷	A	A
E⁷E⁶E⁷ E	E⁷	A	A

Jazz guitarists who were contemporary or nearly so with Lonnie Johnson and who played good blues were Teddy Bunn, Oscar Aleman, Django Reinhardt, Tiny Grimes, Eddie Durham, and Oscar Moore. All made their livings playing standards and pop tunes, but blues was an important part of their repertoires. Moving further to the jazz side of things, rhythms become more subtle, chord progressions generally more complex, melodies scalar and less imitative of the human cry; in fact, often the harmonic complexity is supplied by the soloist's suggesting (or stating) a set of changes with his lines and arpeggios.

Current jazz guitarists playing fine blues include Joe Pass, Herb Ellis, Barney Kessel, and Jim Hall. All these players, when they want to inject some drive, some extra *push*, into their blues, tend to get down to basics—to put a little more Lightnin' Hopkins in their playing. Melody lines get more vocal-oriented, harmonies more straightforward, rhythms more direct. In 1968, when Barney Kessel recorded the rough and tumble blues "Watch the Birds Go By," I doubt that he was thinking about Blind Lemon, but the ferocity, that basic, primitive power, is there. In his own way Barney takes the listener full circle in the evolutionary development from blues to jazz guitar.

Appendix to Blues and Jazz Guitar

With the thought that a working knowledge of music theory, in particular chord structure, would be helpful to the reader of this article, here's a quick primer.

The granddaddy of all scales in Western music is the twelve-tone chromatic scale. One octave, from C to C, looks like this:

The interval between any two adjacent notes is a half-step. The *major scale* (do, re, mi, etc.) is built from notes of this chromatic scale, using half-steps between the third and fourth notes of the scale, also between the seventh and eighth, but whole steps everywhere else:

These are the notes in the key of C major. Giving each of these notes a corresponding number makes it possible to transpose (or transfer to a different key) and to discuss chord theory:

C D E F G A B C
1 2 3 4 5 6 7 8

Chords, then, are built from groups of these notes:

Major chord	1, 3, 5	C major	C, E, G
Seventh chord	1, 3, 5, b7	C7	C, E, G, Bb
Minor chord	1, b3, 5	C minor	C, Eb, G
Minor 7 chord	1, b3, 5, b7	Cm7	C, Eb, G, Bb

Diminished chords are built on sets of notes each a minor third (one and a half steps) apart. A C diminished would be spelled C, Eb, Gb, A.

Augmented chords are built on sets of notes each a major third (two steps) apart. Django Reinhardt liked to add a flatted seventh to this triad, spelling it C, E, G♯, Bb—making it a C7 augmented fifth.

A *whole-tone scale* has consecutive intervals of one whole step, a C whole-tone scale thus being C, D, E, F♯, G♯, A♯, C. A melody derived from a C whole-tone scale works perfectly when played against a C7aug5, since all notes of the chord are contained in the scale. (A♯ and Bb are "enharmonic," meaning that they are two names for the same flat sign pitch; this is true of all the sharp/flat pairs in the chromatic scale.)

This idea of what notes are in what chord and which scale to play against which chord is the basis of jazz improvisation. Harmonic substitution—using chords that relate obliquely to the standard "changes"—is also extremely important, the goal being always the creation of a certain sound or feel.

The Jazz Guitar Duet

A Fifty-Year History

Richard Lieberson

The guitar, as everyone recognized early on, is an ideal instrument for accompaniment: its warm tone blends well with other instruments or the voice, and it can provide not only bass lines and a broad range of harmonic support but also an almost percussive drive. The guitar's melodic potential was obvious in the music of country bluesmen like Charley Patton and Robert Johnson, though not until Lonnie Johnson and Eddie Lang was it finally realized. Also with Lang began an investigation of the instrument's harmonic potential that continues into the work of George Van Eps, Jimmy Wyble, Ted Greene, and Ed Bickert.

Jazz guitar duets, as Richard Lieberson demonstrates here, have become something of a standard form in jazz, a kind of sub-genre that allows the guitar the fullest expression of its harmonic, melodic, and rhythmic potentials.

Once a student of George Barnes, Richard Lieberson has been a part of the New York music scene, as player, teacher, and writer, for over thirty years. In the seventies he was a ringleader of the acoustic country-swing quintet The Central Park Sheiks (recorded by Flying Fish). He has played Western Swing with Bob Wills alumnus Tiny Moore, twenties jazz with Vince Giordano's Nighthawks, and currently holds the guitar chair in the seventeen-piece George Gee Orchestra. Richard was a contributor to Miller-Freeman's The All Music Guide and is author of Old-Time Fiddle Tunes for Guitar (AMSCO).

This article, which first appeared in Guitar Player, was considerably revised and expanded by its author for inclusion here. It's an honor to be able to provide a venue for such outstanding work. This is a kind of scholarship one rarely encounters—and it is also one musician's deepest tribute to those who came before.

[I] am now looking forward to the time when a team of guitarists, such as Carl Kress and myself, can find a spot on the air to replace some of the many piano teams. There are great possibilities in guitar teams, and I predict they will be coming along in the future.

—Dick McDonough interviewed by
Frank Victor, Metronome, November 1933

The jazz idiom has undergone considerable transformation since Dick McDonough expressed his hopes for the guitar duet in 1933. In the ensuing years leading guitarists with roots in swing, bop, and contemporary jazz styles have occasionally formed partnerships that enabled them to fully exploit the wide variety of lead and accompaniment devices at their disposal. The guitar duet offers unlimited possibilities in the combination of single-string melody, chord solo, fingerpicking, and flatpicking styles. Guitarists have often used the duet format to develop their composing and arranging talents as well as their instrumental abilities.

The jazz guitar duet presents a particularly formidable challenge— the participants must take on the rhythmic and harmonic functions of the absent bass, drums, and piano. The guitarist who shines in a band situation may lack the versatility and sensitivity required in the duet context.

The guitar as a solo voice was a latecomer to jazz, and the jazz guitarist has always faced the difficult task of assimilating the innovations of pianists and horn players. The two-guitar format came more naturally to blues and country musicians, for theirs was a music more strongly rooted in the guitar. Memorable guitar duets were recorded by the blues teams of Big Bill Broonzy and Frank Brasswell, Charley Patton and Willie Brown, Frank Stokes and Dan Sane, Memphis Minnie and Joe McCoy, and Willie Walker and Sam Brooks. In the old-timey country field, Roy Harvey (of Charlie Poole's North Carolina Ramblers) teamed with Leonard Copeland and Jess Johnson for duets that drew upon turn-of-the-century parlor guitar styles as well as blues techniques borrowed from black musicians. Throughout the 1930s and 1940s, Alton and Rabon Delmore set standards for country guitarists with their tenor-guitar/standard-guitar arrangements.

The history of the jazz guitar duet begins, appropriately enough, with Eddie Lang (1902–1933), the man who first seriously explored the guitar as a solo instrument in jazz. Lang was *the* jazz/pop guitarist of the twenties and early thirties, recording with Joe Venuti, Paul Whiteman, Bix Beiderbecke, and innumerable vocalists. In 1928 and 1929 Lang, taking the pseudonym Blind Willie Dunn, teamed up with bluesman Lonnie Johnson (1894–1972) for a series of duets on the Okeh label.

Born Salvatore Massaro into an Italian family in 1902 and trained in the European musical tradition, Lang might appear to be an unlikely partner for a black folk-bluesman. Johnson, however, was among the most sophisticated and jazz-oriented of blues stylists; he ventured beyond blues circles to record as a sideman with Louis Armstrong and Duke Ellington.

On such numbers as "Hot Fingers" and "Two Tone Stomp," Johnson and Lang transcend their disparate backgrounds to create a two-guitar sound that has rarely been equaled for sheer excitement. Performing on a guitar with two or three of the top strings doubled in the manner of a twelve-string, Johnson spins out long lines (played fingerstyle) behind which Lang demonstrates his distinctive accompaniment style. It is Lang's backup, with its runs, bass lines, and unusual accents, as well as Johnson's advanced lead, that gives these pieces their unique quality. Recognizing Johnson's greater authority as a blues player, Lang steps out for only an occasional solo. Johnson's backup behind Lang, on the other hand, is rather basic. "Eddie could lay down rhythm and bass parts just like a piano," recalled Johnson. "He was one of the greatest musicians I ever worked with."[1]

In 1932, a year before his death, Lang recorded two duets with Carl Kress (1907–1965), a pioneer of the chord-melody style and one of jazz's great rhythm guitarists. Originally a banjoist, Kress tuned his guitar in fifths (Bb–F–C–G–D–A, low to high). This arrangement borrowed the tenor banjo's tuning on the top four strings (although Kress tuned his A string down an octave) and extended the standard guitar's range in the bass by a diminished fifth, giving Kress access to fuller chords and bass lines.

Whereas Lang's collaborations with Johnson are loosely arranged blues in which he functioned primarily as an accompanist, the Lang-Kress duets are more structured compositions featuring Lang's clear and restrained single-string work. Both pieces contain trio sections in addition to the main thirty-two-bar AABA themes. "Feeling My Way," a pretty melody taken at a medium-slow tempo, is kicked off by a deftly picked flamenco-style run by Lang. As the changes go by two to the bar, Kress outlines the underlying harmony by picking a bass note before each chord, creating a moving bass line in the manner of a stride pianist. Kress plays a chord solo on the trio theme while Lang supports him with arpeggios, runs, and bass lines. "Pickin' My Way" is more on the hot side. Kress abandons the moving bass style for a strong four-to-the-bar rhythm, and supplies a

---

1. Richard Hadlock, *Jazz Masters of the Twenties* (New York: Collier, 1974), p. 249.

great deal of movement in his accompaniment by approaching many chords chromatically. Lang's rendering of the theme is followed by a swinging chord solo from Kress, under which Lang plays a bass line. Something of the widespread influence of Lang can be gauged by the later transformation of "Pickin' My Way" into "High Flyer Stomp," recorded in 1937 by the High Flyers, a western swing group.

The two-guitar concept reached a new level of sophistication in Kress's work with fellow studio guitarist Dick McDonough. Mc-Donough soloed in single notes and double-stops as well as chords and played all the single-string lead on the duets. Recording together in 1934 and 1937, Kress and McDonough produced four classic duets, three of which were originals, the other being a stylization of Irving Berlin's "Heat Wave." Their duets are more structurally, harmonically, and rhythmically complex than the Kress-Lang pieces. These are not loosely arranged pieces based on blues or standard chord changes, but true compositions for guitar, with modulations, tempo changes, and rubato interludes. The guitarists play syncopations in imitation of band arrangements and, by combining a melody in double-stops or triads on one guitar with a lower single line on the other, create three- and four-part harmonies. This device is employed effectively on "Chicken à la Swing."

The evocative "Danzon" offers a contrast to the hot chord solos of "Stage Fright," "Heat Wave," and "Chicken à la Swing." This piece is primarily a vehicle for Kress, who creates impressionistic harmonies by suspending chords over his open F and C strings while McDonough fills in with single-string lines.

Aspiring jazz guitarists treasured the Kress-McDonough duets, which contain some of the best recorded examples of the chord-lead style of the thirties. The late George Barnes recalled going to a fellow guitarist's house and excitedly listening to the just-released duets, which they played over and over.

The Kress-McDonough duets were transcribed and published by Robbins Music.[2] Kress's parts were edited so as to be playable in standard tuning, or (on "Danzon") by raising the fifth string a whole step. The transcriptions are somewhat more syncopated than the

2. The Lang-Kress, Victor-Volpe, and Mastren-Harris duets were also published by Robbins, but none of this material is currently available.

recordings, and the editor's voicings occasionally more cluttered than those of the composers.

Guitarists Frank Victor and Harry Volpe recorded four duets for Decca in 1936, and at least two other titles appeared on Radiola in 1942. The Victor-Volpe pieces not only reflect the thirties jazz guitar vocabulary but seem to draw on ethnic dance music, parlor guitar styles, and "semiclassical" sources as well. Accomplished guitar work and clever arranging touches can be heard here (especially on "Easy Like" and "Fretted Harmony"), but it must be conceded that the Victor-Volpe pieces lack the substance of the various Kress collaborations.

Six duets were recorded in 1937 by studio/radio guitarists John Cali and Tony Gottuso. Not as delicately assembled as the Kress-McDonough pieces, the Cali-Gottuso sides are exciting, swinging guitar music in their own right. "They were head arrangements," recalls Gottuso, who did much of the arranging and single-string lead work. The highlight of the Cali-Gottuso sessions is "A Study in Brown," an ingenious adaptation of the Larry Clinton big-band hit. Here the guitarists use a number of imaginative devices to capture some of the variety of a full-band arrangement. In the course of the tune one hears chord solos supported by bass lines, full chords divided between the two guitars, single-line melody backed by straight rhythm, and upper-register chordal riffs combined with lower-register melodic figures. Another standout is Cali's original "Hittin' on All Six," which features some Langish single-string work. The duo also recorded two nonjazz pieces, "Violetta" and "Cariña-Bolero."

In 1938, while working at NBC studios, Dick McDonough collapsed and died. His death is attributed to pneumonia brought on by alcoholism. "Afterthoughts," a guitar solo in three parts, was composed by Kress in memory of his partner. Kress soon joined forces with the young Tony Mottola, who was just getting started in the studio world.

The Kress-Mottola duets, recorded as radio transcriptions, probably date from 1941. Taken as a whole, they are in a lighter vein than the Kress-McDonough pieces, and are not without humor, a point underscored by such titles as "Blonde on the Loose" and "Sarong Number." The ten tunes run the gamut from swinging romps ("Squeeze Box Swing," "Fun on the Frets") to the mildly exotic ("Sarong Number") and a waltz melody ("Serenade"). Although Mottola's is the lead instrument most of the time, one feels that the older and more seasoned Kress is the dominant force. The trademarks of the Kress-McDonough duets are all here: tempo changes, modulations, three-part harmonies, ballad interludes. Mottola sticks almost exclusively to single-string work, executing long, crisp lines over Kress's relaxed rhythm. The duo re-recorded some of these tunes in 1947, adding clarinet, bass, and drums.

Four duets by Carmen Mastren (1913–1981) and English guitarist Albert Harris were published (but not recorded) in 1942. Mastren had arranged as well as played guitar for Tommy Dorsey and was well versed in harmony and composition. Using triads and double-stops in different combinations, Mastren and Harris create four- and five-part chords. The wistful Mastren-Harris "Lament in E," with its harmonies reminiscent of Bix Beiderbecke's piano music, was recorded in 1977 by Marty Grosz and Wayne Wright. Harris also recorded a series of duets, including one dedicated to Eddie Lang, with fellow Englishman Ivor Mairants in 1935 and 1936.

In 1961, after a stint on TV's *Garry Moore Show*, Carl Kress formed a duo with the late George Barnes (1921–1977). Among the first to adopt the electric guitar, Barnes was one of the most underrated of jazz guitarists. Behind the scenes as a studio man for much of his career, he stepped into the limelight on his recordings with Kress. The Barnes-Kress duets offer the best recorded examples of Barnes's gorgeous way with a melody, buoyant, inventive lines, and overall command of the instrument.

This was the first guitar duo to employ electric instruments, and the first since Lang and Johnson to feature improvised choruses, at which Barnes excelled. By this time Kress had modified his tuning (now Bb–F–D–G–A–D, low to high, according to the liner notes of *Guitars, Anyone?*) and had become more adventuresome in his rhythms. Unlike previous guitar duos, which emphasized originals, the bulk of the Barnes-Kress repertoire consisted of standards. A typical number would include arranged in- and out-choruses, an improvised chorus or two by Barnes, and a Kress chord solo supported by a muted Barnes bass line.

Up until Barnes and Kress, jazz guitar duos had performed only on recordings and radio. Barnes and Kress went out into the clubs and concert halls, playing to enthusiastic audiences. While working with Barnes in Reno, Nevada, in 1965, Kress suffered a fatal heart attack.

In addition to producing two albums as a duo, Barnes and Kress recorded albums accompanying tenor-sax great Bud Freeman and singer Flo Handy. The duo also recorded a play-along album for Music Minus One, which gives the student the opportunity to play Barnes's arrangements backed by Kress's marvelously full rhythm guitar.

The Barnes-Kress duo had its finest moment in *Guitars, Anyone?*, recorded for the Carney label. Dazzling arranged passages are complemented by what may well be Barnes's finest soloing on record. Richard Carney recalls that the guitars were not amped but recorded directly through the console.

In 1969 Barnes began an association with Bucky Pizzarelli that was to last three years. One of the busiest studio men in New York, Bucky was eager to work with his recently purchased seven-string guitar. First made for George Van Eps by the Epiphone company in 1938, the seven-string has an additional bass string tuned an octave below the standard A (fifth) string. Working with Barnes, Bucky developed an original accompaniment style that was played fingerstyle on the seven-string. Occasionally switching to a pick, he also played swinging chord solos *à la* Kress and McDonough.

Playing a heavy schedule of club dates, Barnes and Bucky became familiar with each other's moves and developed a remarkable rapport, which is evident on their one album. Bucky recalled his association with Barnes in a June 1974 *Guitar Player* interview:

> Nothing was ever written. We even rehearsed separately, because we both had such busy daytime schedules so could just play together at night. I would learn the chords to a song and George would learn the melody. Then usually when I soloed, I did so in chords while George would play the bass line. When he soloed single-string, I played the chords behind him. And when he put a fancy tag ending on a song, I'd try imitating it there on the spot. . . . We had a couple of hundred songs in our repertoire, but from playing together every night for three years we became so familiar with it that we thought as one guitarist.

When Bucky left the duo, he was replaced by Art Ryerson, who also performed on a seven-string. Ryerson excelled at hot chord solos out of the Kress-McDonough bag. On ballads such as "Two Sleepy People" he sometimes accompanied Barnes with whole chords played in harmonics. Regrettably, Ryerson and Barnes never recorded together.

The guitarists discussed up until this point recorded highly structured and arranged duets. Subsequent guitar duos of the seventies have favored a more spontaneous approach that permits each player to stretch out at length.

While Barnes and Pizzarelli were polishing their swing stylings, bop guitar aces Chuck Wayne and Joe Puma began an association that lasted from 1972 to 1977. Abandoning the four-to-the-bar rhythm guitar of the swing era, Wayne and Puma preferred to "comp" behind each other as a pianist might. The highlights of the Wayne-Puma duets were choruses of simultaneous improvisation during which both guitarists launched into complex single-string excursions. Wayne recalled for *Guitar Player* a particularly exciting on-the-gig experience with Puma:

> Once we did a tune and at one point when we were improvising simultaneously we fell into the harmony of the particular chord. I was playing thirds and he was playing thirds. We wound up playing the full four-part chord, not accidentally or intentionally, but it just happened that at that point we were so attuned to what was happening that the whole section came out in four-part harmony, and it was exquisite. I almost fell off my chair. It was spontaneous, and just remarkable.

Two of jazz's most seasoned guitarists, Herb Ellis and Joe Pass, got together for the excellent *Two for the Road* album in 1974. Pass and Ellis seemed to bring out the best in each other as they traveled from swing standards to blues and bossa novas. There's an effective contrast of styles here, Ellis coming out of the Charlie Christian–Lester Young bag, Pass more influenced by the boppers. Especially noteworthy is the interplay between the two. Ellis has done occasional club work with Barney Kessel as well, and the two cut a 1977 album with a rhythm section. The Ellis-Pass duets emphasized interplay and included a good deal of simultaneous improvisation, while Ellis's duets with Kessel were more arranged and featured the guitarists trading hot choruses.

In the late seventies the acoustic, thirties-style jazz guitar duet had a small renaissance in the work of Marty Grosz and Wayne Wright. When Grosz moved to New York in 1976 to join the Bob Wilber–Kenny Davern Soprano Summit, he hooked up with Wright, a veteran of the George Barnes–Ruby Braff Quartet. Tuning his instrument Bb–F–C–G–B–D, a variation of the tuning used by Kress, Grosz played chord solos (and sang) while Wright handled the single-string chores.

The duo's repertoire included Kress-McDonough, Kress-Mottola, and Mastren-Harris pieces as well as original tunes and arrangements of swing classics.

The freer jazz and modern harmonies of the sixties and seventies also lend themselves to the two-guitar format. In 1976 Ralph Towner and John Abercrombie joined forces on an album of absorbing original compositions that utilized both acoustic and electric guitars for a variety of tonal colors. Jazz/fusion guitarist Larry Coryell has explored modern jazz standards and original material in recorded duets with Steve Khan and Belgian guitarist Phillip Catherine.

George Van Eps has often commented that he envisions the guitar as a miniature piano. In the hands of gifted players, two guitars can become a veritable jazz orchestra, replete with involved rhythms, complex harmonies, and soaring improvisations. Fifty years after Lang and Johnson got together for "Two Tone Stomp," the duet form continues to call upon the jazz guitarist's fullest creative resources.

Charlie Christian

Bill Simon

"His few treasured recordings constitute the great divide of the jazz guitar: there is the guitar before Christian and the guitar after Christian, and they sound virtually like two different instruments."

That's Frederic V. Grunfeld expressing, *in* The Art and Times of the Guitar, *sentiments you'll find echoed a hundred different ways in the literature. Charlie Christian was a jazz phenomenon. He came out of Oklahoma playing guitar as no one had ever imagined it* could *be played, had a few years on top, and then suddenly was gone, at age twenty-three. Tal Farlow, Herb Ellis, Barney Kessel—they all traced their lineage back to Christian. Wes Montgomery got his first job just by playing Charlie's solos, which he'd taken off records. He'd play one of the solos, then lay out. That was all he knew, and all he needed.*

We don't know much about Charlie, finally. We have his amazing music, as fresh and compelling today as it was fifty years ago, and we have—will have always—his boundless legacy. Like Mozart, like Robert Johnson, Charlie Christian was a miracle, one of the great originals. Like them, too, at times he seems less a musician than a vehicle, a channel for Music itself, allowing it to inhabit us.

The guitar had some history in jazz before Charlie Christian, but there's little evidence, if any, that Charlie was particularly aware of it.

He had his own ideas about the function of the instrument—as a solo voice, in a small combo, and in a big band. But he never talked about these ideas, he just played them—and they became the accepted, the ideal for an entire generation of guitarists.

There hasn't been more than a handful of musicians of whom it may be said that they completely revolutionized, then standardized anew the role of their instruments in jazz—Louis, Bird, Dizzy, Blanton, Chick Webb, Lester Young, perhaps a few more, but especially Charlie Christian.

Let's first take a look at the guitar-in-jazz prior to Charlie's sudden emergence, full grown, on the big time scene in 1939. . . . Going way back to the New Orleans beginnings, only one "name" guitarist survives in memory—Bud Scott (1890–1949) began early enough to join Robichaux's orchestra in 1904 and to participate in streetcorner "battles" with the first jazz "King," Buddy Bolden, around 1904.

Scott was a good musician, who later studied with legit teachers and was able to alternate on fiddle and even to play symphony and theater jobs. He claimed in his later years to have been the first guitarist to play all four beats with a downstroke. Scott's influence may have reached Charlie indirectly at least, since he was the unidentified guitarist on hundreds of recordings made with blues singers and early combos, including those of Richard M. Jones, King Oliver, Jimmie Noone, and many others.

From New Orleans days on until the late twenties, the guitar fought for its place on the scene with the jangly banjo, whose metallic ring may have been less inspiring to jazz feeling, but which carried better in the days before clubs and dance halls used amplifying systems. And, of course, before guitars themselves were amplified. The guitar, except in more intimate blues and ballad interpretations, was designed more to be felt by musicians than to be heard by the audience. Electric recording helped change that, and consequently, in the late twenties, we began to hear from such guitarists as Lonnie Johnson and Eddie Lang. As these men appeared on discs, their influence spread rapidly.

Johnson came first. He began to record around 1925, mainly backing blues singers, and musicians began to notice that, more than just voice with accompaniment, he was beginning to make each side a partnership. Single-string obbligato figures, interesting chord changes and voicings, and occasional solo passages by Johnson took the guitar a giant step from the primitive rolling rhythm backings of the cotton-field pluckers, and introduced the first virtuoso elements.

Johnson was far too sophisticated to be labeled strictly a bluesman: he eventually recorded with Louis Armstrong, and was guest star with Duke Ellington's band on such significant early sides as "The Mooche" and "Misty Morning."

A Philadelphia-born white musician, an ex-fiddler who went under the professional name of Eddie Lang (he was born Salvatore Massaro), was the next important voice on the fretted instrument. He was a Johnson follower, and was to bring the idea of the guitar-as-a-voice into the public consciousness through his key position with such bands as those of Jean Goldkette, Paul Whiteman, Roger Wolfe Kahn, Red Nichols, and later as accompanist for his sidekick, Bing Crosby.

Lang patterned his full tone after Johnson's, but he also introduced new expressive elements, new chord inversions, new subtlety and sensitivity. It was his kick to sneak off to jam with Johnson and some of the colored combos in days when this generally wasn't done. In fact, he even recorded several duets with Lonnie, and other sides in a combo with Johnson and King Oliver, using the *nom-de-disque* of "Blind Willie Dunn."

It has been said that Lang was the first man to make his fellow guitarists conscious of using the proper bass notes and the best possible chord voicings.

His chordal ideas were picked up, varied, and expanded by the next group of guitarists to hit the big time—men like George Van Eps, Carl Kress, the late Dick McDonough. Van Eps developed a style on guitar that might be likened to the "locked-hands" chordal style of some of the more modern pianists.

Then, when the single-string, one-note-at-a-time style of jazz guitar came into its own, it was an import—all the way from France. Its proponent was the Belgian-born Gypsy Django Reinhardt (1910–1953). While he had little if any influence on Christian, he did more than any other guitarist to create an acceptance for a solo virtuosic guitar, and to destroy the concept of the instrument as a device purely for rhythm. As a rhythm guitarist, in fact, Django was sadly deficient by jazz standards. With only three working fingers on his left hand, he was, of necessity, more of a single-string man than a chord man. And he was the fastest.

But Django's folk origins were Gypsy, not slave or sharecropper. He brought new, exotic, and showy elements into jazz; still, he himself never came close to the core of jazz. One has only to compare his frothy, though fertile, inventions with the driving, earthy improvisations of young Christian to understand the difference.

Django's role in a jazz combo was also limited by his instrument, which was still the unamplified Spanish guitar. Some years later, after Christian had established the electrified box in jazz, Django converted and by this time he had lost much of his old authority via attempts to adapt himself to the new jazz sounds of the mid-forties.

Once Django had attuned the public's ear to the notion of an audible guitar (but still had left much to be desired as far as jazz people were concerned), the stage was set for the new six-string messiah, and he emerged in the shape of that awkward, friendly, impossible rube of a kid named Charlie Christian.

If Charlie *had* been influenced by anyone directly, he never let on. Little is known of his formative years. It hardly makes sense, still. To anyone who knew him from 1937 on, it appeared that Charlie was the mature, original genius and had never been anything but. It was thus with Louis and Bird and maybe Tatum. Teddy Hill, who was Charlie's best friend after he hit New York, still scratches his head when he tries to explain the phenomenon.

"Where did he come from?" he'll ask, of no one in particular. "When we were kids growing up here in New York, we watched Benny Carter grow from a squeaky beginner to a master musician. Or take Dizzy. When he joined my band after Roy [Eldridge] left, he played just about like Roy. Then he was influenced a lot by Bill Dillard, who played lead trumpet for me and who, incidentally, was one of the best I ever had. Then Dizzy began to work out those new things with Monk and Klook [Kenny Clarke]. . . . The point is, we could see him grow. But what about Charlie. . . . Where did he come from?"

We do know that Charlie was born in Dallas, Texas, sometime in 1919, and that he was brought up in Oklahoma City. This was guitar country and, to a fair extent, blues country. Blues singers or country and western singers—they all played guitar in those parts.

Oklahoma City also was fertile ground for the stomp bands—particularly the Kansas City units that invented a happy, danceable approach to the blues—free-flowing, four-even-beats-to-the-bar blues. And the combos that developed riffing to a fine, forceful art—all in the process of doing as many different things as they could conceive to dress up that self-same twelve-bar blues progression. In the late twenties in Oklahoma City there had been Walter Page, the great bass man, with his Blue Devils, who included the late Dallas-born trumpeter Oran "Lips" Page, blues singer Jimmy Rushing, and pianist Bill "Count" Basie. This band had a rival in that of Bennie Moten out of Kansas City, and it was a historic day for jazz when they merged, and another historic day in 1935, when Basie picked up the baton where the lately deceased Moten had laid it down.

And the dominant sounds in jazz in that region, besides the good-rockin' blues shouters and the blues-'n'-boogie pianists, were those of the saxophonists. This was the breeding ground for many of the distinctive sax styles. Coleman Hawkins came out of St. Joseph, Missouri, though his development into a major stylist took place after he hit New York. But Ben Webster, Lester Young, Herschel Evans, Buster Smith, Harlan Leonard, Jack Washington, the late Dick

Wilson, and the more recent Charlie Parker, all came out of K.C. and vicinity, and all blew their way through the Southwest.

The fluidity and freedom and individual expressiveness these men brought to their music had its effect on the way other men approached other instruments. Longer lines, shifting accents, more notes per bar, harmonic explorations, even within a single solo line. Trumpet men, trombonists, and even drummers began to play more like saxophonists. And when Charlie Christian played solos on his guitar, that's how he played them—like a modern jazz saxophonist, but always as a guitarist.

Charlie, then, I believe, was a product of his region and his time. John Hammond, who brought him into full public view, is certain that he was influenced by Lester Young's tenor, and it's established that he was fond of Lester's playing, but apparently no more so than of many others'. Hammond also advances the theory that he was indebted to Floyd Smith, the one-time Andy Kirk guitarist, also out of that general region; and there could be something to this. But Smith's influence may have been more mechanical than musical. He was the first capable jazzman to exploit an electrified instrument. His choice happened to be the Hawaiian guitar—a slippery monster with which, however, he was able to cope without sacrificing jazz feeling. It may have been from Smith that Charlie got the idea of amplifying his Spanish-style box.

Whatever influences, Charlie, as we said, never mentioned them, and when they were suggested to him in conversation, he, apparently, just liked everybody and just about everything musical, and that was about all that could be gotten out of him—in conversation.

Charlie didn't have much education. By 1934, when he was fifteen, he was a professional musician. He was playing guitar, but he had big, strong fingers, and for a time he also played bass, with Alphonso Trent's band. Then he toured the Southwest with Anna Mae Winburn's aggregation. By 1937, he was playing electric guitar, and he organized his own little combo in Oklahoma City.

Soon he was back on the road, hitting such towns as Minneapolis and Bismarck, North Dakota, but none of the big jazz centers. He may have been with Al Trent again at that time, and Oscar Pettiford, who jammed with him in 1938, recalls vaguely that he was with Lloyd Hunter or Nat Towles.

In the program notes for a Columbia album, Al Avakian and Bob Prince tell of the time in Bismarck when a young guitarist, Mary

Osborne, went to hear Charlie play. "She recalls that on entering the club she heard a sound much like a tenor sax strangely distorted by an amplification system. On seeing Charlie, she realized that what she was hearing was an electric guitar playing single-line solos, and voiced like a horn in ensemble with the tenor sax and trumpet. She says, 'I remember some of the figures Charlie played in his solos. They were exactly the same things that Benny [Goodman] recorded later as "Flying Home," "Gone with 'What' Wind," "Seven Come Eleven," and all the others!' "

At the same period, the annotators recall, "Christian's prominence was established locally to the extent that a Bismarck music store displayed 'the latest electric guitar model as featured by Charlie Christian.' "

Oscar Pettiford was playing with his father's band in Minneapolis in 1938, when he met Charlie at a place called the "Musicians' Rest." Here the local and visiting bandsmen would come to juice and jam. "We had a wonderful time blowing with Charlie," Oscar reminisced. "I never heard anybody like that, who could play with so much *love*—that's what it was, pure *love of jazz*, and great happiness just to be a part of this thing called music.

"We exchanged instruments: he'd play my bass, and I'd try his electric guitar. I hadn't heard about him yet, but Charlie told me, 'You'd better watch out for a guy named Jimmy Blanton' [Charlie may have played with Blanton for a while in the Jeter-Pillars Band out of St. Louis]. I never forgot that."

Two people in Charlie's life made it their personal business to see that he found the recognition and fulfillment he deserved. Both John Hammond and Teddy Hill remain warmly proud of their roles and their friendship with this warm, generous—and grateful—boy. Both remain bitter to this day toward the newer "friends" who actually killed him with their own peculiar brand of "kindness."

Hammond's total contribution to jazz has been positively staggering. He has been mentor for Benny Goodman, Count Basie, Billie Holiday, and benefactor for countless others. . . . While he himself has not always been in sympathy with the new jazz trends of the forties and fifties, one of his "discoveries," Charlie Christian, was a prime influence in shaping these trends.

John first heard about Charlie from Mary Lou Williams in 1939. The fine pianist-arranger had heard Christian herself in Oklahoma City, when she had played the town some weeks earlier with the Andy

Kirk Band. Hammond's now brother-in-law, Goodman, was playing in San Francisco, and he had just signed with the newly reorganized Columbia Records. John was flying to Los Angeles to attend the first Columbia sessions.

He located Charlie in Oklahoma City, and wired that he'd be stopping off en route and would appreciate an audition. The plane landed at 1:00 P.M. after a much-delayed, steaming-hot summer flight, and Hammond got off, as he put it, "beat and bedraggled." To the "horror" of his fellow passengers, an old wreck of a car drove up to the airport, jam-packed with six young Negroes. One of them asked for Mr. Hammond, introduced himself as Christian, and reeled off the names of the others, all the members of his band.

Charlie thoughtfully had made a reservation for John at one of the "nicer" hotels, where his mother was working as a chambermaid.

But by three, the audition was on at the Ritz Café. This is the place where Charlie and his buddies were working about three nights a week at the nightly rate of $2.50 per man. Somehow, on a weekly paycheck of $7.50, the boys all looked presentable, if not prosperous.

Charlie possibly had the impression that Hammond was interested in the combo, or more likely, as with most friendly kid musicians, he just hoped this important man would like his pals too. As Hammond recalls now, the band was "simply horrible. Charlie was the only one who could play. But he was almost unbelievable."

The next day Hammond left for Los Angeles, and found Benny in no mood to expand his organization. In addition to the band, he still had the Quartet, with Lionel Hampton, and occasionally he would add the bass, Artie Bernstein, from the band to form a Quintet. John insisted that Christian was "essential" and pointed out that Benny might take him on without jumping the budget. . . . The band was still playing the Camel Caravan shows, and these provided a "guest fee," which could be used to take care of Charlie.

BG agreed to such an arrangement, and Hammond wired Charlie the money to fly in, ostensibly in time for one of that first series of recording dates for Columbia in August 1939.

This particular date had been going for two hours, and the band was cutting Fletcher Henderson's arrangement of Mendelssohn's "Spring Song," with "Smack" himself on piano, Bernstein on bass, Nick Fatool on drums, and others like Ziggy Elman, Chris Griffin, Vernon Brown, Toots Mondello, and Jerry Jerome in the band.

Suddenly, in walks this vision, resplendent in a ten-gallon hat, pointed yellow shoes, a bright green suit over a purple shirt, and, for the final elegant touch—a string bow tie. One man in the band, who happened to be color-blind, noticed that this character also toted a guitar and amplifier.

"There he is," Hammond prodded Benny. The King of Swing took one look and shivered visibly. "Wait till you hear him play," Hammond pleaded, but BG would have no part of it.

After the date, Goodman stayed around just long enough to hear Charlie play one chorus of "Tea for Two" without the amplifier. Then he rushed out to keep a dinner engagement.

Artie Bernstein, who had observed the whole bit, felt real compassion for Charlie, who really didn't know how to interpret the course of events. He enlisted Lionel Hampton and they conspired to sneak Charlie into the Victor Hugo, where the band was playing, that night. Normally, the band would take a break and vacate the stand, while Benny and the Quartet would stage a short concert.

Later, while Benny was off the stand, Artie and Hamp got Charlie in through the kitchen and set up his amplifier. Goodman strolled back into the room, spotted that awkward pile of bones on his stand, and did a quick double-take. There wasn't much he could do without creating a scene, so he signaled resignedly for "Rose Room."

They played "Rose Room" for forty-eight minutes!

Hammond had been in on most of Goodman's triumphs since he had persuaded him to stay with jazz in the early thirties, but he "never saw anyone knocked out as Benny was that night." Apparently, Charlie just kept feeding Benny riffs and rhythms and changes for chorus after chorus. That was Benny's first flight on an electronically amplified cloud.

In future months that "impossible rube" was to inspire and frame the most fluid, fiery, interesting, and human sounds that Goodman has ever produced.

A few days later, October 2, 1939, Benny set up the first Sextet recording session. This was the one where they recorded "Flying Home," a riff opus whose writer credits go to Eddie De Lange, Goodman, and Hampton. No one ever has denied that most of the riffs that have become standard on this otherwise slight concoction were Charlie's, and the same was to apply to most of the other Sextet "specials."

Charlie was in. Benny had to agree with Hammond that Charlie was "essential." From $7.50 a week, he was now making $150, as a regular member of the Goodman organization.

But Benny still didn't like an amplified guitar with the big band, and his colored stars still were restricted to the "chamber music" group. He did use Charlie on many of the band recordings, but most of the time the band chair was held down by Arnold Covarrubias or Mike Bryan.

Anyway, Charlie was "living." He had gone from the back-shack to the big time in one giant step. He was bright enough, and certainly not illiterate, but he apparently had just two great interests—music and chicks. Now he could indulge his tastes until satiated, and life became one big ball. When the warning signals sounded, Charlie refused to stop the party.

When he didn't seem to be feeling right, Benny sent him to his own doctor in Chicago who spotted the t.b. scars. Charlie knew he had been afflicted, but had never let on to his new boss.

The doc warned him to get his rest, and to take care of himself generally, but Charlie was having too much fun up in the stratosphere.

It was in October 1940 that Minton's was opened, in the Hotel Cecil, up on 118th Street in Harlem. Teddy Hill, one-time saxophonist and popular bandleader, was installed as manager. Teddy had been around for years, grown up with jazz in New York, but he was and is an insatiable fan. When Mr. Minton gave him a free hand, he opened the doors wide to the "guys" and announced that this would be the one place in town where they could come and play just what they wanted to play.

Teddy knew what was good and could tell when some of his boys began to lead jazz in new directions. He extended his hospitality to all musicians, but he took special care of the good ones. This friendly, generous, understanding man is credited with a major assist in the invention of modern jazz.

Dizzy Gillespie and Roy Eldridge before him had played with Hill's band; so had the adventurous drummer Kenny Clarke. In the twenties Hill, still in his teens, had toured the Midwest and South with Bessie Smith. He took his own band to France in the thirties and played for some weeks at the Moulin Rouge. Nearby in Montmartre, the Harlem émigré Bricktop—one-time benefactor of Duke Ellington—had a place, and her featured attraction was Django Reinhardt. Teddy was in the place every night to listen, and to him, Django was the greatest, until he heard Charlie Christian.

When one of the big colored bands would come to town to play the 125th Street Apollo, the sidemen would make it a point to fall into Minton's for some unfettered after-hours blowing. Teddy would cook up a big batch of food and supply free drinks, and usually the place would be packed with musicians, leaving little or no room for customers.

Monday nights were a special ball for any jazz fans who were able to spoon their way into the place. Most of the musicians with steady jobs were off that night, and they would flock in from Fifty-second Street, from Harlem clubs, and from some of the name bands downtown. On Mondays Hill would invite some special guests, and make certain that these weren't crowded off the stand.

Minton's became Charlie Christian's home. As far as the manager was concerned, Charlie owned the place.

Goodman was getting ready to open up at the Pennsylvania (now the Statler), and was holding rehearsals every afternoon. The boys had some free time, and the pianist, Mel Powell, brought Charlie up to Minton's. If you sincerely liked music, you were Charlie's friend, and Teddy Hill became his best friend. Charlie came up every night. After the band opened at the hotel, Charlie would finish his last set, hop in a cab, and speed up to Minton's where his seat on the stand was being held for him. He wouldn't take the time even to change his uniform, and oftentimes he was still wet with downtown-type perspiration when he arrived. Minton's stayed open until four, which gave him about two and a half hours to wail all of the high-band jimmies out of his soul.

As long as there was somebody on the stand to play music with, Charlie never got up out of that chair. There were always chicks around waiting for Charlie, but they couldn't get more than a nod from him until the last note had been blown at four. But they always waited.

And on Monday nights, when the Goodman band was off, Charlie was in his usual chair at Minton's from note one. Musicians, good and bad, battled on every instrument, crowding each other on and off the stand. But Charlie never budged. Guitarists came to listen to him, not to cut him. That would have been impossible and everyone knew it.

Jerry Newman, a young jazz fan and then amateur engineer, became a regular at the place and night after night would record the happenings with his own semipro equipment. He recalls that Charlie most of the time would electrify the crowd with his riffing and his long-lined solos and his powerful drive, but that sometimes the stand would become jammed with battling no-talents, and Charlie would simply sit there and strum chords.

Hill himself went out and bought Charlie an amplifier—the best one he could find—so that he wouldn't have to lug his own heavy box up there every night. It cost $155, which was a lot of money for an amplifier in those days. Charlie would put his lighted cigarettes down on the thing and forget about them while he was playing, and they'd burn all the way down. The box is at Teddy's home now, burns and all, and it will probably stay there until some official jazz museum or Hall of Fame has been established. Its owner has turned down dozens of offers for it.

Celebrities got word of Charlie's jamming habits, and began to flock in. Ella and Billie came and sang with him. Newman would take down his recordings, and after closing time, Charlie, Teddy, and Jerry would listen to the playbacks over and over and over.

One night, Lena Horne and Fats Waller joined the select company. Fats, who traveled in different jazz circles ordinarily, would sit and listen to Charlie with his arms folded, for once completely ignoring the bottle in front of him. . . . This one night, Newman was playing the records back and the second time around Fats sat down at the piano. Between each number he'd improvise an interlude, and everybody was gassed.

When Dizzy would fall by, that's when the musical sparks would fly. Diz and Charlie would "battle" for forty to fifty minutes at a time. It was the same on rarer occasions when Charlie Parker would drop around. And Christian loved it.

"It's like that back room was made for him." Hill undoubtedly heard more Charlie Christian than did any other person.

Everybody loved Charlie. The chicks mothered him, and the musicians kidded him good-naturedly. He was the Willie Mays of jazz. Teddy would tease him with, "We're going to bring that Django over here, and he'll blow you right off that stand." Charlie would break into a big grin and answer with a couple of slippery, typical Django phrases on his box.

He would discuss another musician, but only while the man was right there playing, and never in a derogatory way. He obviously loved Monk's piano, and Klook's drumming, and Diz. He even tolerated Joe Guy's trumpeting.

Guy was an Eldridge imitator whose biggest claim to fame was to be his later association with Billie Holiday and the mess he got into with her. On more than one occasion he was heard to grouse about the attention Charlie was getting. "If I was playing at the Pennsylvania with Benny Goodman, everybody would think I was great too." But he never got in Charlie's way and he never had it as good as when Charlie was riffing in back of his mediocre inventions. Charlie could make a midget feel like a giant.

Both of Charlie's mentors, Hill and Hammond, have told us that Charlie was increasingly interested in and moving toward more "classical" ideas, though he never considered himself other than a driving four-beat musician. In the Minton's days he was just twenty or twenty-one, and he was getting better all the time, was evidently far short of his potential peak.

And so life continued to be one big ball for Charlie until spring of 1941, when he got really sick. He was sent to Seaview, a New York City-operated sanitarium on Staten Island. He was getting routine care there until Count Basie's physician, Dr. Sam McKinney, took an interest in his case and began making weekly trips out to see him.

Teddy Hill was his other faithful visitor, making the long journey every Sunday. He tells about "Mom" Frazier, who had a restaurant uptown at 121st Street and Seventh Avenue where all the musicians hung around, and how this lady would mother them all, but her special favorite was Charlie. Every week that Charlie was away, she'd bake a chicken—especially prepared without spices—and a chocolate layer cake for him. When Hill would try to pay her, she'd shrug him off with, "Now you take this to my boy and tell him to hurry up out of that hospital."

Hammond was out in California most of those months, but he did arrange to have a guitar sent to Charlie in the hospital.

Charlie, in his newfound "high-life," had acquired another set of friends, and that's how he happened to die at the tender age of twenty-two; t.b. was only part of it.

There are stories of some of the boys from the Goodman and other bands dropping over to the Island for visits and spiriting Charlie out of the hospital for "parties" with combustible tea and chicks. These parties had their comic moments—if one can forget their tragic consequences.

There was the time, for example, when the Germans had just begun to overrun Western Europe. This one bass player, who was more concerned than most of his colleagues with current events and politics, buttonholed Charlie for an intense one-way discussion. Charlie was "stoned," and he loved everybody and would agree with anybody about anything.

"And, Charlie, those German planes roared over and dropped all those bombs and leveled just about every building in Rotterdam. And thousands of people—women and children—got wiped out. How about that, Charlie?"

Charlie cut through his haze and answered emphatically—"Solid!"

He had a couple of other "friends"—a guitar player and a tap dancer; the latter a well-known character around the bands. They brought over the "pot" and they also brought chicks. Charlie was getting better—in fact, it looked as though he would be getting out soon, and he was feeling his oats. But it was winter, and Charlie sneaked out late one special night and got excited and overheated.

Dr. McKinney learned of these extracurricular activities and made sure they were stopped, but it was too late. Charlie had pneumonia.

It was early in February 1942 when Hammond returned from California and received a call from a nurse at Seaview that Charlie was in bad shape. He rushed out to see him, and could tell that it was hopeless. He called Benny.

The next day Hill made his regular call, and that night Somebody turned off Charlie's "juice" for the last time.

And so, most of the jazzmen Charlie was to influence—just about every jazz guitarist in the years since his death—have had to learn their lessons from his all-too-few phonograph records. I don't think anybody had ever asked Charlie to be leader on a disc date, and if they had, it's doubtful that he would have accepted—it might have taken time and attention from his playing. He was content to play what Benny wanted him to play, apparently, but when he got up to Minton's, his release was almost feverish. As some of those Jerry Newman recordings show, he would play dozens of choruses on end. If he ran out of ideas temporarily, he'd simply riff rhythmically for a few bars until he caught his muse again.

Although the man came from the segregated South, there was no evidence that he carried any prejudices or any resentment against any person or group. He had no regional restrictions in his makeup. He had one home—music. He was meek and humble, but never an Uncle Tom.

Even today, young guitarists hearing his recordings for the first time are convinced immediately that this is the master. Jimmy Raney, one of the top guitarists of our modern day, didn't arrive in New York until 1944, or two years after Charlie had died. He had been about fifteen when he first heard "Solo Flight," the number Charlie cut with Benny's full band. "Jesus, I flipped!" was the typical reaction. "The only other time I felt something like that was the first time I heard Bird." Raney, like the others, believes that Charlie still stands on top of the heap, even when judged by the more modern standards. It was his sense of time, and of harmony—his way of outlining his chords without actually running them. The same observation has been made of Parker's playing on the alto sax.

Naturally, one is curious about the personal relationship between Charlie and his boss, Benny Goodman. One must look hard for any evidence that he interested Benny as a person. Charlie never discussed Benny. Benny came up to Minton's several times, but when he did, the boys played Benny's jazz, not Charlie's or Monk's or Klook's. That stuff didn't interest BG then or now. Charlie's $150 per from Benny was more money than he had ever seen before, and he could sit there at the Pennsylvania with the juice turned off most of the evening and play rhythm for Benny, because he had Minton's.

If Charlie were alive today, he'd probably be spending most of his working time in recording studios, but in the two years of his big-time activity, jazz dates were few and far between. He did cut twenty-five sides with the Benny Goodman Sextet or Septet, which in its best moments included Count Basie on piano, Jo Jones on drums, Cootie Williams on trumpet, Artie Bernstein on bass, and Georgie Auld on tenor sax. He also was on a flock of full-band sides, but was rarely featured. "Solo Flight"—which was strictly Charlie's showpiece—and "Honeysuckle Rose" are the only band numbers still available that offer any satisfying amount of Christian guitar.

Charlie also got in on two of the Lionel Hampton all-star combo sessions at Victor, cutting seven sides in a company that also included Dizzy Gillespie, Benny Carter, Coleman Hawkins, Ben Webster, Chu Berry, Milt Hinton, Cozy Cole, and the late Clyde Hart—on one date! And Red Allen, J. C. Higginbotham, Earl Bostic, Hart, Bernstein, and the late Sid Catlett on the other. There wasn't much "blowing" room for Charlie, obviously.

Teddy Wilson used him in October 1940 on a Columbia date in the backing for a set of four standards sung by the pop singer Eddy

Howard, along with such other positive stylists as Bill Coleman, trumpet; Benny Morton, trombone; Ed Hall, clarinet (the Café Society clique); and Bud Freeman, tenor sax.

There were two dates—they were J. C. Higginbotham's—backing the blues singer Ida Cox for Columbia's subsidiary label, Vocalion. James P. Johnson was pianist on one, and Henderson on the other. Lips Page, Ed Hall, Hampton (on drums), and Bernstein were in on these also.

There were the Metronome All-Star sessions of 1940 and 1941. Charlie had little trouble winning the polls once his first recordings with Benny had hit the market.

Charlie had one rather strange but quite successful session for Blue Note, the first of the independent jazz labels, in February 1941. This resourceful outfit had Edmond Hall assemble a quartet that consisted of clarinet (Hall), celeste (Meade Lux Lewis), bass (Israel Crosby), and guitar (Christian). They cut four sides for twelve-inch 78-rpm. discs, thus permitting the men more than the usual blowing time for those days. But Blue Note producer Alfred Lion wouldn't tolerate an amplified guitar, and that's how Charlie happened to record, in quite traditional company, his only unamplified solos on discs.

Easily the most important, revealing work of Christian on records is the material gleaned from Jerry Newman's well-worn acetates. It was this writer's privilege to arrange for the release of several of these Minton's cuttings in a Vox album in 1947. One was an original based on "Topsy" and the other was "Stompin' at the Savoy." The group was Charlie on guitar, Kenny Clarke on drums, Thelonius Monk on piano, Joe Guy on trumpet, and Nick Fenton on bass—the Minton's house band.

Apart from the poor balance, extraneous crowd noises, and some irritating Guy trumpet, this is the biggest and best sample of jazz guitar on discs. Charlie "wails" on chorus after chorus with those long, full-blown lines, those simple riffs, and those complex strung-out changes. Here was the beginning of "bop," with Clarke dropping "bombs" in unorthodox places behind Charlie's own shifting accents, and Monk beginning to play his own strange harmonics and "comping" for the soloists.

Newman himself took over these masters again when he started his Esoteric label, and brought them out on a ten-inch LP. Later he followed up with some additional gleanings, which he coupled with some early Gillespie sides, also cut at Minton's. Neither of these sets currently is in print, although there are plans to bring them out on one new twelve-inch LP coupling.

Aside from these, the most valuable Christian is to be found in the Goodman Sextet and Septet sides, many of which remain unavailable today. During 1956 Al Avakian, brother of Columbia's George Avakian, undertook the assignment of putting together a sort of Christian memorial mainly from unreleased studio material. Fortunately, some of the test acetates cut before and during several of the Goodman sessions had been retained. By transferring everything to tape, Avakian was able to do a brilliant editing and reassembling job. From bits, scraps, and rejected takes, he was able to put together what, next to the Newman material, is the best, least adulterated Christian obtainable.

Through these cuttings, one may study the evolution of the Goodman combo classics and Charlie's key role in their creation.

Charlie Christian probably is the only jazz figure who would have been able to serve as the model stylist on his chosen instrument as long as fifteen years after his disappearance from the scene. There isn't an important guitarist playing today who does not recognize him as the all-time best, and who does not credit him as a prime influence. In most of the better modernists, the strain has crossed with that of a saxophonist, Charlie Parker, but basically, it's Charlie Christian. The best thing anybody can say about a guitarist today is that he could be "the closest thing to Christian."

The album annotators and the critics have said it about Barney Kessel, Tal Farlow, Sal Salvador, and some of the others.

They've all been grateful.

Django's Blues

Dan Lambert

 *Jazz guitarists as a group, I think, tend to be mavericks, and many of the greatest players—musicians like Charlie Christian, Wes Montgomery—seem to drop out of nowhere, playing things no one had ever really thought about playing before. One of the great quantum leaps in jazz guitar, his work remaining today as amazing and sinuous as when he first recorded in the twenties and thirties, was Django Reinhardt.*

There are any number of sidestreams in jazz guitar, pockets of activity that remain vital, produce their own lineage, and, while accommodating themselves to general patterns, nonetheless remain discrete. In our own time we've seen South American styles, everything from the rapidly co-opted bossa nova to outlaw music like Bola Sete's, move into mainstream jazz. Another sidestream consists of a pantheon of gypsy guitarists beginning with Django and passing on to Christian Escoudé, Boulou Ferré, and Bireli Lagrene. In recent years the emergence of such eclectic, original players as Philip Catherine and Pierre Bensusan—who exist on their own plane somewhere between acoustic and electric, with strong folk elements, fine jazz instincts and technique, and an instrumental voice all their own—suggests that another sidestream may be forming.

Like that of his subject's here, Dan Lambert's playing is highly individualistic—sometimes relaxed and in a groove, often full of stabbing odd turns—and immediately recognizable. He easily accommodates himself to any playing situation, but anyone playing with him who goes in thinking bluegrass, blues, country, or whatever (instead of just music) is going to have problems. Part of his ability to accommodate comes from the historical enthusiasm he demonstrates in this piece: Dan's always listening to what's been played before on his instrument, tearing it down to see what's in there that he can use. One week it's Don Rich with Buck Owens, the next it's Robert Nighthawk, then a month of Eric Clapton and a few days of Oscar Aleman, some Joe Pass, some John Fahey. And of course it's just such synthesis that goes to make a strong personal style. Individual style does not reject tradition but embraces it—even if the line is jagged, not straight.

His name won't appear on a critics' choice "ten best blues players" list, but Django Reinhardt was a great blues player. He recorded a wealth of blues material from straight twelve-bar progressions to twelve-bar progressions with unexpected heads or bridges—a Django trademark also characteristic of Duke Ellington's writing. (As far as "writing" goes, it should be noted here that Django was composer of much of the blues material he performed.) He also played pop tunes and standards of the day with a dash of the blues thrown in, and the blues format seems to have been a favorite form of expression.

But what he did with those blues! Augmented and diminished chord sequences coming out of nowhere, abrupt key changes, a little Gypsy minor-chord funk—imagination: the flow never stopped. Nothing was sacred, either. Musical rules meant little to him. He did anything he could to get the sound he heard in his head onto the guitar. With his sense of melodic invention and ear for musical drama, Django could transform the most familiar song into a musical adventure.

Consider his 1937 duet version (guitar and bass) of "You Rascal You," not a twelve-measure blues but a standard for bluesmen and early jazzmen in familiar form: I–IV–V harmony, sixteen measures. The tune is twelve choruses long with a couple of bass solos in the middle. It is not my intention to write out Django's solos note for note (there's been enough of that sort of thing published already) but to dig deeper to get inside his thought processes. Why did he play the notes he did? What effect did these notes achieve?

The fifth chorus of "You Rascal You" is a mixture of chords and single-note lines. Django was fond of mixing chords and single notes (also octaves) all in the course of a single verse. He begins this chorus with two measures of a Bb minor six chord. This minor chord superimposed over the major chord harmony is a technique found in the most primitive blues and the most sophisticated jazz—almost a cliché. With Django's erratic, angular rhythm chops, however, it sounds anything but overused. He could get the greatest sound out of two-, three- or four-note high-string chords by doing either a quick fluttering strum or an upstroke rhythm chop. He uses both these techniques during the first eight measures of the chorus, then contrasts these chords in the next four measures with a lilting, descending chromatic single-note run from the D note on the high string to the G note on the same string. For the next three measures he plays a phrase based on a Bb6 arpeggio, taking a breather in the last measure to introduce Louis Vola's bass solo. Django's comping during the bass solo consists basically of rhythm accents every couple of measures on the standard I–IV–V harmony. He throws in an interesting chord progression during the last half of the second bass chorus beginning on measure nine.

"You Rascal You"

B♭6	B♭6	B♭6	B♭6
B♭6	B♭6	F7	F7
B♭6	B♭7	E♭7	E♭m7
B♭6	F7	B♭6	B♭6

CHORDS BEHIND LAST HALF OF SECOND BASS CHORUS

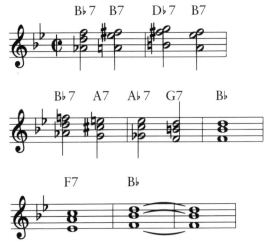

This progression is a particular voicing of a seventh chord (beginning with the tonic Bb 7) found on the second, third, and fourth strings being moved up and then down the neck. The sequence resolves to a basic Bb triad at the third fret, on to an F7, then back to the Bb. Django executes the turnaround with a smooth, straight half-note rhythm. This contrasts perfectly with the aggressive, slashing chord figures found in the rest of the tune. It's a beautiful way to swing out of the bass solo back into the guitar section.

Something humorous takes place during the next two choruses: Django drops a half-measure. Vola doesn't pick up on the loss for about a verse and a half, so from the middle of chorus eight to the end of chorus nine Django steams away a half-measure ahead of the bass. It happens in the middle of the sixth measure of the eighth chorus when Django executes a descending trill based on the F7 chord. Problem is, he puts it in a half-measure early and then doesn't compensate for it. This makes for some interesting changes over the next chorus or so. One half-measure early, Django starts chorus number nine with a series of four-note runs based around a Bb arpeggio. The schematic goes like this: taking the fifth of the chord (an F note), begin on the next scale tone higher (G), down to the chord tone (F), one half-step lower (E), then back to the same chord tone. Django plays this series changing the chord tone like this: F, Bb, F, Bb, D, F, Bb, and ending on an Eb note.

Next comes a descending octave run going chromatically from an F to a Bb. Incidentally, it is during this chromatic movement that Django and Vola meet again. Django loved drama in his music: arpeggios that built tension as they traveled (usually raced) up the scale; chromatic passages (either single notes, octaves, or chords) that traveled from one end of the fingerboard to the other; choppy rhythm passages that suspended chords in the most bizarre places. He would follow a section like that with the sweetest melody you ever heard or the most subtle, smoothly flowing chord progression: that's where the drama comes in. Any study of Django's music is a study of arranging and composition as much as a study of guitar.

On to his recordings of "Swing de Paris"—a blues with a bridge. It is in typical AABA arrangement with the A sections being twelve-measure blues in the key of C and the bridge (B section) being eight measures modulating to the key of A. (Standard A sections in the AABA form are usually eight measures long.) So here is Django playing a blues, arranging it in a form common to popular tunes of the day and slapping a bridge in the middle.

I've heard two versions of this tune, one on acoustic guitar, the other on electric. Both have the same intro figure and chord progressions, but there the similarity ends. The original melodies to the two versions bear no resemblance to each other. At first this surprised me, because the melody to the first chorus of the earlier (acoustic) version sounds so perfect. It doesn't sound improvised at all, it sounds composed. Either Django got bored with playing the original melody and got into the habit of winging it from the start, or the original melody to the earlier version was an improvised chorus too. The first explanation seems to fit Django's Gypsy character better. Whatever the case, I've transcribed the intro and that first chorus.

"Swing De Paris"

"Swing 48" is blues with a typical Django twist. The head, with the melody carried by clarinet, features a repeated four-measure run played over a G-minor chord followed by a whole-tone melody (with some half-step slides) played over E7 augmented, G7 augmented, and Bb7 augmented chords. The entire head is repeated, after which Django takes over the lead and swings into some hot G-minor blues. Several choruses of twelve-bar blues follow, with Django relying heavily on minor-chord arpeggios and chromatic passages. He executes a half-step trill at the beginning of one of the later choruses by fretting a G note on the fifteenth fret of the first string and a Gb on the twentieth fret of the second string and strumming them together vigorously. These two notes played together create an instantly recognizable, startling effect. The Gb note is neither in the G-minor scale nor G-minor arpeggio over which it is being played. This "wrongness" helps create the tension so characteristic of Django's music.

Django's novelty tunes are also beautiful studies in composition and arranging. Tunes like "Mystery Pacific" and "Rhythm Future," for instance, have angular "hot" sections that contrast nicely with smoother, swinging sections. And whether on ballads, blues, standards, or novelty tunes, Django's playing is always instantly recognizable, intensely his own. Biographical material, especially Stéphane Grappelli's recollections, suggests that Django's sometimes peaceful, sometimes bizarre playing fit his character perfectly; that the man was the music and the music the man.

Oscar Moore

Michael H. Price

 *Here's my short list of great guitarists no one's ever heard of: Allan Reuss, Snoozer Quinn, Buddy Fite, Bill Harris, Oscar Aleman, Teddy Bunn. Oscar Moore isn't unknown, but then he's not very well known either. "He was actually comping at a time when Charlie Christian was still chunking away," Barney Kessel has written, pointing out that Moore created almost single-handedly the role of electric guitar in small combos.*

The first time I heard Oscar Moore (on a Cole Trio recording) I had to know who the guitarist was. Such easy, quiet playing, floating to the top of the music for a minute, then sinking back into it. Really fine, distinctive guitar.

Mike Price is film critic for the Fort Worth Star-Telegram, a cartoonist and frequent writer on movies, comics and cartoons, and music. He plays piano and guitar with deranged Texas groups doing blues, fiddle tunes, Jimi Hendrix numbers, hokum, redneck ballads, and straight jazz, he puts together an album or two a year, and he's still wondering what he wants to be when he grows up.

"If you want to hear jazz guitar," said hot fiddler Stuff Smith, who played with many fine guitarists, "there's only one that gets my vote. That's Oscar Moore of the Nat 'King' Cole Trio." This order from headquarters is of course misleading and dated; the community of worthwhile guitarists could never be narrowed to one, nor is Moore's output all that readily available these days. But it is also instructive: Moore's reputation still hinges upon the adjective phrase "of the Nat 'King' Cole Trio."

But a symbiotic relationship is implicit here. Even as Nat Cole's phenomenal popularity drew attention to Moore, it was Moore's commitment to personal growth within the ensemble that boosted Cole, a derivative pianist and reluctant vocalist better acquainted with hustling bar gigs than with economic stability, to world acclaim.

Scrapper Blackwell's and Leroy Carr's smoothing of the blues in Depression 'Naptown had anticipated combo jazz, but it was Moore and Cole (then teenaged) who began pulling it together in the autumn of 1937. A light-touch blues player from Chicago, church-reared and fluent in both the stride style of Fats Waller and Teddy Wilson's heap-o'-treble leanings, Cole wanted to land a seventy-five-dollar-a-week job at the Swanee Inn on La Brea Avenue in Los Angeles, but needed a band. He first enlisted a drummer, Lee Young, then contacted Lionel Hampton, who was about to dissolve his own outfit and join Benny Goodman. Hampton steered Cole onto his bassist, Wesley Prince, and his electric guitarist, Oscar Moore. Any ensemble might have suited Cole, weary of scrambling for five-dollar-a-night piano-bar slots along the spine of California and longing for house-band security. An equal partnership in its early years, the combo brought him that security and, more significantly, nurtured his own artistic growth. The black-ink bottom line of Prince's playing freed Cole's left hand to punctuate rather than underpin his right hand; Moore's seductive tone and touch challenged Cole to match him for delicacy of phrasing if not for melodic intricacies. When Cole, Prince, and Moore arrived to open at the Swanee Inn and Young failed to show, no one carped at the absence of percussion. The act was a trio for keeps.

Oscar Frederic Moore was born on Christmas Eve, 1916, at Austin, Texas. The family soon relocated to Phoenix, where Oscar and his brother Johnny began private guitar lessons as grade-schoolers. By their teens the brothers had become professional musicians and settled in the Los Angeles area. Anticipating R&B, Johnny held faster to a blues basis, while Oscar took his cue from fellow Texan Charlie Christian. Lionel Hampton soon sensed Moore's spirit of innovation and offered him a chair; Moore's distinctive touch is heard in its formative stages on the Hampton recording of "Jack, the Bellboy," which boasts one of the guitarist's first long-line solos.

Springy is an apt adjective, denoting both tension and release, for the style Moore brought to the Cole combo. Nat Cole's piano work is often likened to that of Earl "Fatha" Hines but was in fact more Heinz 57 than Hines—an amalgam, borrowing all but the Fatha's trumpet-attack punch, as old-fashioned as early Waller, as contemporary as Wilson. It was in fact Moore who, mutating popular standards and traditional blues into a gently compelling, almost orchestral sound, gave the act its vision and direction.

Though superfluous, vocals proved the turning point for the trio—and for Cole in particular. Jazz historian Mary Lee Hester has doc-umented that one night a tipsy patron of the Swanee Inn insisted upon Cole's singing "Sweet Lorraine." Cole protested that none of the three was a singer (the tune, incidentally, has a fine structure for improvisation and a sappy-sentimental lyric) but the customer persisted, complaining at length to the manager.

"The proprietor told Nat to go ahead and give it a try," Moore told Hester. "It was a good thing that Nat knew the number. It was one of about four tunes [whose lyrics] he knew." Cole, an inveterate hummer who lacked confidence in his voice, proved in fact a capable crooner. Moore added: "From that point, Nat continued to sing and brought us into the act too. It ended up with us singing novelty tunes in unison."

Sensing by 1939 that more fertile ground lay on the East Coast, where the John Kirby Sextet was originating a program for CBS, the trio moved to New York City. There Decca Records signed them in 1940. Releases sold well, but the contract (renewable per session) was characteristically small change, geared in part to artist vanity. Decca often paid its neophytes with a suit of clothes or an overcoat, and New York Club dates, like those in California, paid at best only a living wage. With the combo's mounting popularity, however, the newly organized Capitol Records offered greener money in 1943 on condition that Cole sing. The second Capitol release, "Straighten Up and Fly Right," was the first star in Nat "King" Cole's crown.

Fame on record, though, need not translate into fame in person. The trio had landed a gig at Kelly's Stable in New York, its performances sandwiched between spots by Henry "Red" Allen's band and the brilliant Art Tatum, another of Cole's role-models. Neither the Stable's newspaper advertisements nor its playbills of this period mention the trio. In Cole, Moore, and Prince, however superior, lay the equivalent of a present-day "happy hour" act, and then as now, management viewed such an ensemble as simply making music to sip by. Patrons were drawn, though, by the trio's elemental approach to swing tempo and by Cole's developing artistry and Moore's impassioned, carefully conceived embellishments upon both challenging material (they were fond of jazzing the classics) and pedestrian standards. Despite the records' success, onstage singing remained a secondary consideration.

Critical attention was inevitable, and jazz commentators hungered to name a successor to Charlie Christian, who had died in 1942. Oscar Moore won pollsters' recognition during 1945–47 from both *Down Beat* and *Metronome*, also landing *Esquire* magazine's Silver Award for 1944–45 and its Gold Award for 1946–47.

Cole, who had developed a more unified style to match the consistency of Moore's playing, ultimately found his name attached to an evolving school of jazz that Moore might more justifiably have claimed. In a post–World War II economy no longer able to support big-band superstructures, the "combo" phased from anomaly to rule. Count Basie pared his organization to the basics. Others—Oscar Peterson, Art Tatum, Herman Chittison—followed suit.

Press recognition for the trio had peaked when the group returned to California, where its Hollywood reputation yet endured, in 1943. Prince entered the military the following year and was replaced by Johnny Miller, a comparably gifted bassist who wrought no change in the established style.

Cole had developed a certain hubris about his voice by 1946. Singing more and more to popular acclaim that had little to do with jazz tastes, he accepted increasing numbers of pop tunes for trio sessions, and Capitol began touting that sweet and husky voice to near exclusion of the trio's instrumental gifts. Cole complied with this head-office approach, his inaction on his partners' behalf (for he was the star, and alone entitled to make a contractual move) leading to dissent within the trio. One executive memo described the salaries and royalties of Moore and Miller as "extravagant." Mary Lee Hester reports that Moore had gone from a thirty-five-dollar-a-week club wage in 1942 to a fifty-seven-thousand-dollar-a-year salary by 1946.

The pressures cost Cole his trio. He abandoned the piano, returning to it only for a Capitol-hyped nostalgia session *sans* Moore and Miller in the 1950s, but recouped his loss of jazz identification with such pop breakthroughs as "Nature Boy," "Mona Lisa," and, much later, "Those Lazy, Hazy, Crazy Days of Summer." He also pursued a movie-industry singing career that encompassed the coups of *St. Louis Blues* (playing W. C. Handy) and *Cat Ballou* before his death in 1965. Moore and Miller sued Cole for breach of promise in 1947—a token gesture of defiance—but adjudication, predictably, favored Cole.

Moore rejoined his brother in Johnny Moore's Three Blazers during 1947—excepting a brief army hitch in 1944, his first time away from the Cole outfit since its beginning ten years earlier. He brought to this formative R&B band a gentle touch the idiom had lacked, and proved a direct influence upon the developing ensemble sounds of Charles Brown and Ray Charles, both of whom had revered the Cole Trio. Oscar Moore spent the 1950s as a session guitarist, then left music to become a bricklayer, settling at length in Sherman Oaks, California.

His reputation intact by grace of such stirring recorded works as a Cole Trio reading of the Rachmaninoff "Prelude in C♯ minor," "Lonesome Graveyard" with Art Tatum, and the early collaborations with Hampton, Moore resumed a modest performing career during the latter 1960s, dying October 8, 1981, in Las Vegas.

First-generation Moore pressings are available today only at a premium, and official reissues are scant indeed, though Capitol narrowed the gap in 1982 with two *Best of the Nat "King" Cole Trio* volumes. (These should not be confused with *After Midnight*, a Capitol perennial credited to Cole "and His Trio," but in fact a post-trio effort featuring guitarist John Collins and violinist Stuff Smith.) Many off-brand and budget-label reissues spotlighting Cole "and Trio" also contain an abundance of work by the guitarist.

Jazz Guitar and Western Swing

Michael H. Price

 *I believe that western swing, as the prototypical synthesis music, has an important place in America's musical history. Extremely popular nationwide for many years, it brought the jazz sound and jazz ways of thought to wide popular notice, much as Paul Whiteman had helped popularize jazz in the twenties. Yet it remains little known and often misunderstood.*

Like its early players, looking for new sounds, new territory, I came to western swing because it was an extension of string-band music. One of the first records I happened upon was a Milton Brown reissue, with Bob Dunn on steel. Soon I had a closet full of lap steel guitars and half a long shelf of western swing albums. That shelf abutted, on the left, a complete Oregon collection and, on the right, a hundred or so "traditional" jazz albums, everything from Joe Oliver to Sun Ra.

Just as western swing is outside the mainstream of what we generally call jazz, so the steel guitar is outside the usual definition of jazz guitar, or, for that matter, guitar in general. But steel guitar has a vital place in the history of American music, and its best players, from the pioneer Bob Dunn through Curley Chalker and Buddy Emmons to Paul Franklin today, have all been (at heart) jazzers.

Eldon Shamblin was a session player for CBS and a regular in standard jazz and swing bands before he joined Bob Wills. His first records with Wills were made in 1938—one year before Charlie Christian's with Goodman—and showed an already mature, personal style. Metronome recognized Shamblin's place in jazz tradition as early as 1941; almost forty years later Rolling Stone wrote that he played the world's best rhythm guitar.

Clearly western swing deserves its place in any study of jazz, and its guitarists, while always a breed apart, were and are central to the music, intimately bound to its origins and evolution.

The border between jazz and country is as thin and sensitive as the topmost string of a guitar. Pluck that string and watch it vibrate, and the blur yields a vivid metaphor of how insubstantial the barrier is.

Such a blurring more than fifty years ago in Texas produced the music known as western swing. This music created new roles for the guitar, a legitimate ancestor of fusion jazz, and the only instance in which the promotional term *progressive country* could truthfully apply.

Practically every element of western swing (a patronizing, merchandising label in itself) hails from some other tradition. Of its four generations of loyalists, some call it "hillbilly boogie," others "cowboy jazz"; either expresses its predominant elements of rural white and both rural and urban black musical influences. Had its early shapers, in fact, been ignorant of the blues, there could have been no western swing. Nor could the fusion have occurred without the cross-cultural mingling Texas experienced in the preceding century. The savvy rustics who first made this music laid a foundation (by instinct, not design) upon Texas fiddle breakdowns from their own heritage and upon blues remembered from childhoods spent in naturally integrated farming communities. Onto this trunk they grafted Cajun and Creole strains from Louisiana; polyrhythms from black and Indian traditions; music of celebration and sadness from Central Europeans and Mexicans; and, ultimately, the make-believe cowboy glamor of the motion-picture industry.

The assimilation was so thorough that western swing, at the hands of an accomplished bandleader like Bob Wills, Milton Brown, or Spade Cooley, cannot be seen as ersatz anything. It was from the start—or at least from its earliest documentation on record—its own music, something more than its parts, allowing a freedom of expression offered neither by traditional country music (which would have no part in improvisation or between-the-beats rhythm) nor by the structured jazz community (in which no southwestern bumpkin would be likely to feel welcome).

What this freedom continues to contribute to the evolution of guitar is of key concern. The guitar has a triple importance to western swing: in addition to traditional rhythm and lead functions on standard guitar, there is the wholly different steel guitar, essentially a solo instrument embodying the capabilities of a piano or a horn section.

Jimmy Wyble's crossover from the western swing of Bob Wills to mainstream jazz with Benny Goodman in the sixties is probably the best-known instance of jazz's acceptance of its bucolic cousin. But Wyble did not suddenly begin playing jazz upon joining the Goodman band; he had long before developed as a jazz guitarist while playing in the superficially countrified bands of Wills, Cooley, and Hank Penny. Much the same could be said for Penny, "Honest" Jess Williams, and the undeservedly obscure Herman Arnspiger and Weldon Gidley, all masters of compelling rhythm guitar; for other lead guitarists like the brilliant Eldon Shamblin, who preceded Wyble in the Wills Orchestra but never saw fit to develop a jazz-elite identity; for the lesser-known but no less gifted Durwood Brown, Benny Garcia, William Muryel "Zeke" Campbell, and Frankie Kinman, all of whom have exercised powerful influence; and for steel guitarists epitomized by Bob Dunn, Leon McAuliffe, Billy Briggs, and Joaquin Murphy, all distinctive stylists with considerable responsibility for the ways in which steel is played today.

"It *was* jazz we were playing," says Jess Williams, a Texas Panhandle native whose rhythmic skills and sheer strumming stamina account for much of the drive behind the early Sons of the West recordings. "We just couldn't call it that and get away with it—not with our audiences thinking it was honky-tonk!" Lured from retirement one weekend in 1979 to sit in on a country-rock dance-hall show in his hometown of Amarillo, Texas, Williams demonstrated conclusively the power of western-swing rhythm guitar, freeing the band's drummer from reliance upon the sock-and-ride cymbals for "padding" and relieving the keyboard and bass players of stylistic contrivances evolved to compensate for the absence of solid six-string backup.

Such reliance on the guitarist has always been the essence of western swing, which began not as a guitar showcase but as fiddle music with guitar accompaniment. The first swing-tempo application of guitar to traditional Texas fiddle material may be reasonably attributed to Bob Wills and Herman Arnspiger, who performed during the late twenties as the Wills Fiddle Band. A third party, all-around string artist Ocie Stockard, would join them on occasion to play for Saturday-night dances in a schoolhouse east of Fort Worth, Texas.

"It was our custom to play the old hoedowns, Texas fiddle breakdowns like 'Great Big Taters' and 'Texas Wagoner,' and an occasional yodel or a minstrel song or a blues, with the fiddle in the spotlight," Stockard recalls. "Our guitars would hold the rhythm, drummerlike, with me switching to my banjo or my own fiddle off and on for the sake of change, while Bob's fiddle would lead it off."

The "birth of western swing" is said to have taken place on such an occasion during the winter of 1929–30. No documentation of the event exists outside participants' memories, but accounts given separately by Wills and Stockard jibe. Both hold that a sit-in vocal performance of "The St. Louis Blues" by an unbidden visitor, Milton

Brown, provided the turning point by encouraging all the musicians to seek a broader audience. In this broadening of appeal and subsequent expansion of personnel, the guitar gained freedom to challenge the fiddle for prominence. Wills and Brown became partners, hired Milton's brother Durwood as lead guitarist, and assigned the all-important dance-beat responsibilities to second guitar and tenor banjo. For material, they looked increasingly to authentic blues, minstrel, and jazzband records.

Tales of personnel shifts and interband intrigues need not be recounted here, save to note that these were turbulent as well as productive times, with both Milton Brown and Bob Wills striving to make the hottest music they could with such instruments as their people knew. The early-thirties departure of the Brown brothers, along with Stockard, to form the Musical Brownies prompted a search for guitarists by Wills that finally led him to Eldon Shamblin and Leon McAuliffe, both hired by Wills after Milton Brown had augmented his brother's lead work with Bob Dunn's stinging steel guitar. Earlier yet, in a brilliant break with string-band tradition, Brown convinced the Fatha Hines–influenced pianist "Papa" Fred Calhoun to join.

Calhoun, still a stirring performer fifty years after his association with Brown, recalls the common prejudice that nearly kept him from connecting with the Musical Brownies:

"I said, 'Why, they're a *string* band, aren't they?' You see, I didn't want anything to do with a string band, that hillbilly stuff. I liked *horn* bands, Dixieland bands. That was all I cared to play with."

Coaxed by some radio-program associates to visit a Brownies' dance near Fort Worth, however, Calhoun soon learned that *string* and *swing* can have more in common than rhyme. He was sitting in before the night was done and became a member soon thereafter.

As guitar had earlier framed the fiddle, now piano supported guitar (and virtually all other leads) under the Brown formula. Wills, who by the mid-thirties had moved to Tulsa and added not only steel and piano but also horns and drums, ultimately pared his own organization to a similar lineup. If not for Brown's death in 1936, many observers feel, there would have been no such household name as Bob Wills.

Country-bred guitarists intent on stretching beyond their native genre have traditionally turned to blues. Blues had attracted such prominent country players as Jimmie Rodgers and Riley Puckett, who used it to create an early relative of western swing. This was but one in a sequence of breakthroughs that included the assertion of distinctive styles by Charlie Christian, T-Bone Walker, and western-swing soloist Durwood Brown—not to mention the European artist Django Reinhardt, whose imported discs had a profound impact on all American jazz, and western swing in particular. The technology enabling players to amplify their instruments, though primitive, also played an important part in the guitar's changing role.

As players' influences changed, then, so did their technology. A "fiddle band" guitar solo by the middle-thirties no longer had to emulate a country-blues guitarist; amplification permitted single lines like a horn's—even trombonelike chromatic swoops.

So it was that the electric steel guitar came into being. Close kin to Hawaiian steel, deep-blues bottleneck guitar, and Dobro, the first such device in western swing was built by Bob Dunn from a standard guitar, to which he attached a crude pickup made from the magnets in a radio headphone. Contrary to established styles, Dunn chose not to make chords but to indulge in headlong plunges down the strings with the slide while plucking in staccato bursts. Recorded Dunn performances—in particular "Some of These Days" with the Brownies and "Stompin' at the Honky-Tonk" with his own Vagabonds—are at once self-indulgent and generous, unnerving when first heard, exhilarating on replay. Dunn, who survived Brown but retired to teaching before he could take part in the industry western swing became, inspired several imitators who gradually developed their own styles.

Leon McAuliffe's earliest work with Wills's Tulsa band shows a strong Dunn influence, and he was among the earliest to become a distinctive steel stylist. His single-note leads (as on his famous "Steel Guitar Rag") lack the cerebral, free-form quality that was Dunn's stamp, but his ear for offbeat chords and harmonies made him a role model; his playing today remains consistent with the manner he established during the thirties.

Less celebrated but likely a greater steel innovator is Billy Briggs, who by the age of nineteen in 1938 was a veteran of the country swing-band scene. He had filled in on occasion for Dunn, from whom he learned about magnetic pickups, and thought to improve on the Dunn formula of manufacturing one's own instrument. Using a guitar neck as his foundation, Briggs built a platform-like console, adding a seventh string and a long-legged framework that enabled him to "front" a band by standing while playing. Briggs's invention helped inspire the design of a mass-marketed steel instrument by Leo Fender, who approached Briggs about testing the prototype of the Fender steel guitar. "When I've learned all there is on this one," Briggs supposedly told Fender, "then I'll tackle yours."

Briggs's style was a guitar equivalent of stride piano: the combination of admitted Dunn imitations for the lead line with lush, three-string chords in syncopation. With the Sons of the West, on Okeh and Decca, Briggs enjoyed a modest recording career. He had an enduring radio and dance-hall popularity in the Panhandle region of Texas and became briefly, in 1951, a star on the strength of his novelty tune "Chew Tobacco Rag," which also proved a hit for the Lucky Millinder Band.

One quiet influence among six-string electric guitarists is the rural West Texas-born jazz sophisticate Frankie Kinman, formerly a teaching associate of George Barnes and Johnny Smith and composer (with bandleader Ted Daffan) of the western swing standard "I've Got Five Dollars and It's Saturday Night." To Kinman, now in real estate, his discovery of amplification at age fifteen in 1937 was "a godsend . . . for so long, we [guitarists] had been relegated to the background, and now here was this gizmo that would let us shine. I think a guitarist— I know I do—gets more feeling out of the unamplified instrument, but the projection compensates for the loss of pure sound." Kinman's style, when occasionally he plays today with central Texas bands, features chords that change with practically each beat to form a solo figure—a far cry from the single-note stylings he once borrowed from Zeke Campbell (who in turn acknowledges mimicking them from Reinhardt).

Western swing, then, had one distinctive guitar sound as early as the later twenties: a rhythm mode embodying the bass line, chording, and percussive functions of the conventional band's rhythm section. It gained a second characteristic guitar style, a steel approach like no other, during the 1930s. Not until Jimmy Wyble's path crossed that of Bob Wills in 1942 in Los Angeles, however, would the music's lead guitar come into focus.

Wills, who lost the core of his Tulsa big band to the draft and other career breaks, had moved to Hollywood chiefly to retain his own southwestern following, vast numbers of his Oklahoma and Texas devotees having migrated to West Coast defense-plant work. Wyble, a Port Arthur, Texas, native whose guitar inspiration derived from Eddie Lang, Reinhardt, Dunn, and Christian, had come to the West Coast from Houston in the company of a band known as the Village Boys. He and fellow Village Boys guitarist Cameron Hill sat in one night with Wills's Texas Playboys—a rare instance of good timing, since Wills needed such a team to replace his band's eroding horn and string sections.

With the Wyble-Hill teaming, Wills coined the term *twin guitars*, and this became the idiom's third distinctive guitar sound: a lead style with the grace of a harmonized vocal solo and the thrust of a horn section. Heard to best advantage on the middle-forties Wills recordings of "Hang Your Head in Shame" and "Roly Poly," this duo style lent a sentimental shading to the more direct country music and advanced the sophisticated, arranged feeling western swing was developing. The lushness it suggested would reach fruition in Spade Cooley's full-scale orchestrations; Wills and company would remain essentially a string band with occasional horns for punctuation.

Wyble's association with Wills gave him his first contacts with popular and jazz guitarists such as Al Hendrickson and George Van Eps, but he remained in the country market, often to his disadvantage. A stint with Hank Penny failed when a backer insisted that Wyble's style was insufficiently pure for a country program; with the Cooley Orchestra he worked only anonymous studio dates. Wyble's gratitude to Wills, Penny, and Cooley for their appreciation of his cross-cultural endeavors remains strong, though.

The year 1953 marked a turning point for Wyble with release of his solo jazz collection *Diane*, which included accordion and clarinet and reflected Wyble's studio association with guitarist Laurindo Almeida. The album introduced Wyble to vibraphonist/bandleader Red Norvo, who by the late fifties had brought Wyble into the core of Benny Goodman's touring ensemble. The Norvo association lasted until 1964, when Wyble began a solo career. Recent years have been devoted to teaching and writing (his *The Art of Two-Line Improvisation* is an acknowledged classic) as he continued studio and orchestra-pit work. As a teacher today at age sixty-one in southern California, Wyble has come full circle, sought out as much for his firsthand knowledge of Bob Wills's music as for his mastery of jazz guitar. And like other inheritors and advancers of this country-cum-jazz heritage—Hank Garland and steelman Buddy Emmons come first to mind—Wyble is disinclined to discriminate between musics.

So, it would appear, are increasing numbers of jazz aficionados, many of whom did not know until very recently that anything like western swing existed. Provoked in great measure by the hysterical popularity of fundamental swingster Willie Nelson and the more reserved acceptance accorded modern-day bands like Asleep at the Wheel, a new wave of interest has created a promising market for western-swing recordings neglected since their making forty and fifty years ago. For old-timers who heard western swing as beer-joint habitués the first time around, the new interest is valid nostalgia. But they have reason to envy the music's new discoverers, who will find in it a dimension to jazz that no one—neither the early jazz press nor record-company moguls—seems to have noticed the first time around.

That dimension is not so much jazz transcendent as it is jazz triumphant: the free spirit of rhythmic and melodic imagination overriding all else, whatever the material. Whitney Balliet, the *New Yorker*'s insightful jazz commentator, defines jazz as "the sound of surprise" and so titled a collection of his essays. Predictably, he omitted western swing from his overview of jazz; but anyone who has been stung by a bolt of blue-steel lightning from Bob Dunn's guitar or calmed by a Jimmy Wyble/Cameron Hill passage in the midst of a raucous Playboys jump-tune knows that sound of surprise more intimately than words can tell.

Swing Guitar
The Acoustic Chordal Style

Richard Lieberson

When, fourteen years ago, this came in and I had a chance to read it, my first thought was that it's a major historical piece (as is also, I think, Lieberson's other piece here on jazz guitar duets). My second thought, crowding closely in upon the first, was how unfortunate it was that there was virtually no outlet for such articles.

I wrote then that guitar publications were heavily oriented toward rock, pop music, and young people (who seldom care for history of any sort), while jazz publications largely restricted themselves to currently popular musicians and forms.

The situation hasn't improved in fourteen years; if anything, it's worse. I can't imagine where an essay like "Swing Guitar: The Acoustic Chordal Style" might be published today. Nor can I easily imagine coming across a musician like Lieberson, able to research and write it.

In a country of so various and rich a musical heritage, this is unforgivable. "One of the great sadnesses of American culture," I noted in The Guitar Players, *"is certainly that it contrives to destroy its own past." Yet I also pointed out that in recent years many young musicians have dedicated themselves to retrieving what they could of our musical past by playing ragtime, Delta blues, Hawaiian and ethnic musics, and old jazz.*

The arts, which don't progress by accrual but by deviation and rebellion, are cyclic: we're forever intimately connected to all the music that precedes us. This is something that writers and visual artists rarely lose sight of, but something that many musicians, and most listeners, seem to have forgotten.

In the years before Charlie Christian turned the guitar world around with his amplified single-line choruses, the guitar's role in the jazz band was primarily that of a rhythm instrument. If you did get to hear an acoustic guitarist solo with a band, chances are that the player

The author wishes to extend his thanks to Howard Alden, Barry Feldman, Marty Grosz, Rod McDonald, Nick Perls, George Van Eps, and the staff of the Institute of Jazz Studies at Rutgers for information and access to rare recordings and sheet music.

would deliver his message in chords rather than by way of a single-string melody. An acoustic player was more likely to be heard if he harmonized his melody with two or three supporting voices. Carl Kress, George Van Eps, and Allan Reuss soloed almost exclusively in chords; Dick McDonough, Carmen Mastren, Bernard Addison, and Al Casey traveled both the chordal and single-string routes.

Recognized as top-of-the-line in their day, most of these guitarists are just names or completely unknown to the contemporary jazz and guitar audience. This is due largely to the paucity of guitar solos and band-accompanied guitar features recorded in the pre-Christian era. Eddie Lang and Django Reinhardt recorded extensively as soloists under their own names, and most of this material is currently available on reissue LPs; the chordal stylists were not nearly as prolific in their solo output. There are a handful of solo and duo sides from Kress and McDonough, but the finest playing of Mastren, Reuss, Casey, and others is scattered in eight, sixteen, and thirty-two bar solos throughout jazz records of the thirties and forties. Even the pioneering, phenomenal George Van Eps, on the jazz scene since the early thirties, didn't really get to have his say on record until 1949. Although many choice sides featuring acoustic chordal guitar are out-of-print, a good number of classic examples cited in this article have been anthologized and can be located by the determined discophile.

The jazz band of the twenties and early thirties employed a banjo rather than a guitar in its rhythm section, and practically all of the chordal guitarists cut their teeth on the four-string instrument. After hearing Eddie Lang's trailblazing work with Joe Venuti, Paul Whiteman, and others, plectrists en masse began to take up the fuller, mellower six-string guitar. In this transitional period a number of banjoists took to performing on the four-string tenor guitar, tuned like the tenor banjo (C–G–D–A, low to high) or like the top four strings of the standard guitar (D–G–B–E). Others achieved a warmer tone by fitting the banjo's bridge with a metal mute. George Van Eps recalls that at first bandleaders put up a lot of resistance to the guitar, often forcing aspiring Lang-ites to stick to the banjo.

Even after the guitar was firmly ensconced in the jazz band, solos were few, especially at dances and other live engagements. A guitar solo was practically inaudible in these situations, and bandleaders didn't like the drop in the rhythmic pulse as the guitarist approached the microphone to take his chorus. The swing-band guitarist was hired as a timekeeper, not as a lead man. The dying art of rhythm guitar is deserving of a separate study; suffice it to say here that Kress, Reuss et al. were *crème de la crème*, highly valued for their contributions to the rhythm section.

Van Eps, McDonough, and Mastren are among the many who specifically credit Lang with having inspired them to switch from banjo to guitar. Lang, however, was primarily a rhythm and single-string man; although he did play occasional chordal modulations and turnarounds, the guitar historian attempting to trace the roots of the chordal style must search elsewhere.

The right-hand technique of the Kress/McDonough/Van Eps school owes an obvious debt to the vigorous chordal strumming and tremolos of twenties banjo styles. One is hard-pressed, however, to find any chord-melody banjo solos that anticipate the chordal vocabulary and harmonic imagination displayed by these guitarists in the thirties. The wide intervals of the tenor banjo's tuning do not lend themselves to the tighter voicings facilitated by the guitar's setup, and this may have thrown a wet towel in the face of chordal experimentation. George Van Eps submits that a good deal of sophisticated banjo playing did take place "behind locked doors" but went unrecorded because it was considered to lack commercial potential. Five-string banjo virtuoso Fred Van Eps (George's father) performed Chopin for Segovia at a private gathering, but was pigeonholed as a ragtime player on record. The more adventuresome playing of other jazz-oriented banjoists was similarly not captured on wax.

Carl Kress

In tracing the evolution of the chordal jazz guitar style, it is not possible to zero in on one player and state categorically, "This is the guy who started it all." All available evidence indicates that Van Eps, Kress, and McDonough arrived at their early styles at roughly the same time. Of the three, Kress displays the most basic conception, utilizing block-chord melody only occasionally interrupted by connecting single-string notes.

Born in Newark in 1907, Kress served some time on the piano before he began to fool with a banjo-uke at the age of fifteen. "After a short time I joined a kids' band and my father bought a twelve-dollar banjo for me as a birthday present. I never took a lesson on it, but instinctively did not like the A string on the banjo, which had a marked bearing on my adopting the inverted tuning years ago," Kress told fellow plectrist Frank Victor in a 1933 *Metronome* interview.[1]

Kress made peace with the tenor banjo by raising the C string an octave and dropping the offending A string an octave. This "inverted tuning" referred to by Kress permits closer, hipper voicings than the standard tenor arrangement. In this unique configuration the second or D string becomes the highest-pitched string and usually carries the melody in a chordal passage. The fact that Kress adopted this eccentric system early on suggests that he never, even at the beginning, seriously explored single-string playing. An arrangement of strings that does not naturally progress from lower to higher pitches makes the execution of a simple diatonic scale a hunt-and-peck expedition; single-string improvisation and sight-reading seem beyond the pale.

By the late twenties Kress had carried his "inverted tuning" over to the four-string tenor guitar. On this instrument Kress cut sides with Paul Whiteman, Red Nichols, and Boyd Senter, among others. Pianist-arranger Roy Bargy brought Kress to a 1928 session where the Whiteman band was scheduled to record "San." Kress "fished out of a dilapidated box what looked to me to be a ukulele," recalled Whiteman. "I called Roy Bargy aside and told him we couldn't use a ukulele in our big band. Bargy only smiled. He knew how Kress played, and a few minutes later I realized too that this boy could make a four-string guitar sound like a harp."[2] This bright, harplike tone, combined with a unique rhythmic bounce that characterized Kress's playing throughout his career, is also displayed in the guitarist's brief solo spots on Red Nichols's "Nobody's Sweetheart" (1928) and Boyd Senter and His Senterpedes' "Wabash Blues" (1929).

Somewhere along the line Kress decided to go whole hog and made the big move, the switch to the six-string guitar. Maintaining the "inverted" banjo tuning on the top strings (but probably bringing the C string back to its original octave) Kress added two more strings, continuing the banjo's arrangement of fifths. The resulting setup (Bb–F–C–G–D–A, low to high) extended a diminished fifth below the range of the standard guitar's tuning, permitting full, lush chords and bass

1. Frank Victor, "Who's Who among Guitarists—Carl Kress," *Metronome*, October 1933, p. 45.

2. Marty Grosz and Lawrence Cohn, *The Guitarists* (booklet included with Time-Life record set STL J-12), p. 22.

lines particularly well suited to accompaniments and guitar duets. Kress continued to experiment with tuning throughout his career.

By the time of his 1933 *Metronome* interview Kress had established himself as an original guitarist with an immediately recognizable sound that contrasted refreshingly with that of the recently departed Eddie Lang, with whom Kress had recorded two duets.[3] Kress was raking in the bucks (much of it spent on cars) as a sideman for the Boswell Sisters, Joe Venuti, Paul Whiteman, and other artists of the day. The guitarist became part-owner of the Onyx Club, a staple of New York's legendary Fifty-second Street jazz scene.

Kress has a honey of a guitar solo on "I Wish I Were Twins," waxed with bass saxist/vibes ace Adrian Rollini in 1934. In his half-chorus Kress presents cleanly articulated melody in double-stops, triads, and four-part chords, played with a relaxed rhythmic feel somewhat less pungent but no less swinging than McDonough's. Kress makes frequent use of sliding block chords and the technique of "ghosting" (implying more than fully articulating) some chords in speedy passages.

Frank Victor told *Metronome* readers that Kress "practices Sagovia [sic] quite a bit."[4] It is difficult to pinpoint specifically what is meant by this, as it is hard to imagine Kress's unorthodox tuning lending itself to the classical repertoire. What the statement does indicate is that Kress was aware of the classic solo tradition and wished to take his own music beyond the confines of the jam session and the thirty-two-bar pop-song format.

Even the adventuresome duets Kress recorded with Dick Mc-Donough in 1934 and 1937 do not fully suggest the compositional talent, harmonic variety, and instrumental facility revealed in the series of unaccompanied guitar solos Kress recorded in 1938 and 1939. On the basis of the pieces, a good argument could be made for Kress as the greatest melodist of the thirties chordal guitar crew.

"Afterthoughts," Kress's first unaccompanied solo, is a moody, affecting three-part lament for the recently deceased McDonough, and employs some single-string melody without chordal support in places. "Sutton Mutton" and "Peg Leg Shuffle" both contain bouncy, jazz-derived themes that modulate to langorous, expressive rubato strains.

3. The Kress-Lang and Kress-McDonough duets form an important part of the thirties guitar story and have been covered separately in "The Jazz Guitar Duet: A Fifty-Year History."

4. Victor, *op. cit.*, p. 45.

In the course of these pieces Kress makes use of sustained chords with moving upper and sometimes lower voices, contrary movement, and triads containing seconds, not often heard in thirties swing guitar.

Further from the jazz idiom are Kress's "Love Song" and "Helena," which appeared as the flip sides of "Peg Leg Shuffle" and "Sutton Mutton." "Love Song" is characterized by chromaticism, arpeggiated chords, and the contrast of restful and tense themes, including one section probably played with the pick in conjunction with the fingers. All this points to Kress's having given some serious listening to classical guitar and classical (most likely impressionist) composers.

"Helena," named for Kress's wife, singer Helen Carroll, borrows from flamenco guitar and Latin rhythms. There's a somewhat *misterioso* quality to the piece's third, minor strain, a quality accentuated by the impressionistic harmonies Kress creates by superimposing a series of descending triads over his open F and C strings.

Some might argue that the Kress solos, even those clearly utilizing jazz harmony and syncopation, should not be considered jazz because they do not allow for improvisation. If this is so, the same must be said for stride piano chestnuts such as James P. Johnson's "Carolina Shout" and for Bix Beiderbecke's impressionistic piano compositions, which are usually performed with little or no variation from the printed sheets. If we agree that Kress's pieces are guitar literature of substance, however, there is little point in haggling over what genre they most easily conform to.

Throughout the forties and fifties Kress busied himself with recordings, radio, and TV work. In 1961 he formed a guitar duo with the late George Barnes, which continued until Kress's death from a heart attack in 1965.

Dick McDonough

With Lang's death in 1933, Kress's duo partner Dick McDonough became the leading contender for the crown of six-string king. McDonough mixed single-string melody (looser, less rhythmically stiff than Lang's) with distinctive chord solos and rhythm work, making him a versatile player much in demand by bandleaders and vocalists. While working with vocalist Smith Ballew, McDonough became aware of the art of accompaniment, which he began to include in his daily practice. (Listen to McDonough behind the Boswell Sisters on

"Crazy People" or with Cliff "Ukulele Ike" Edwards on "I Wanna Call You Sweet Mama" to catch the variety of his backup work.)

McDonough was born on Manhattan's Upper West Side in 1904. His father was engaged in the "cloak and suit business," earning him the handle "Joe McDonough, the Irish Jew." McDonough began playing mandolin and banjo as a teenager and had his own seven-piece band while attending Georgetown University in Washington, D.C. His folks were set on his becoming a lawyer, and he entered Columbia Law School while continuing to work weekend gigs with bandleader Dan Vorhees and others. During this period McDonough began to study the six-string guitar "seriously and legitimately" with a man named Foden (probably performer/teacher William Foden, who designed a guitar for Martin in the twenties). After several unsuccessful attempts, McDonough finally got to hear Eddie Lang perform at a private gathering. "It was a great inspiration for me," recalled McDonough. "I decided then and there that the six-string guitar was the only instrument for me, and buckled down to some real work."[5]

McDonough made a number of recordings on both banjo and tenor guitar before packing them up to gather dust in the back of the closet. He sticks to single-string melody in a number of 1927 solos with Red Nichols and Jack Pettis, although there is a suggestion of the later chordal style in a turnaround on Pettis's "Steppin' It Off." One can only speculate as to what McDonough played outside the studios, but his recorded work indicates that he didn't make extensive use of the chord-melody style before switching to the six-string guitar.

McDonough's guitar is heard to good advantage on a 1933 session cut with Joe Venuti and His Blue Six. The guitarist supplies intros, modulations, and solos, and has two very effective choruses on "In de Ruff." After a first chorus employing bluesy triads with bends, McDonough goes to town on a stop-time chorus with speedy sliding triads and double-stops, very much in the Kress vein.

Another gem is McDonough's solo on Mildred Bailey's 1935 recording of "When Day Is Done." Picking up the lead in the second half of the chorus, McDonough displays some of the melodic mobility he was to develop further in his remaining years. Rather than harmonize every note of his melody with a new chord, McDonough often sus-

5. Frank Victor, "Who's Who among Guitarists—Dick McDonough," *Metronome*, November 1933, p. 36.

tains the lower voices of a chord while employing his free fingers for melody work. This technique is heard along with open-string effects and a kind of double-stop shuffle frequently used by McDonough, in which he plays a rapid series of double-stops alternating with open strings. The solo concludes with an ascending chordal melody played against a descending harmonic progression—hip stuff for a thirties guitar player.

Some of McDonough's finest (and best known) playing on record was his work on the 1937 "Jam Session at Victor" session. The guitarist was in heavy company here, recording "Honeysuckle Rose" and "The Blues" with Bunny Berrigan, Fats Waller, Tommy Dorsey, and George Wettling. McDonough begins his "Honeysuckle Rose" chorus with a chordal paraphrase of the melody. He follows with a chordal figure high on the fingerboard and then launches into some fancy triplet double-stop work that showcases his right-hand technique. On the second "A" section he toys with the melody an octave lower before getting into some bent double-stops on the top strings. Wettling gets to show his stuff on the drums in the stop-time bridge, after which McDonough, on the last "A," creates rhythmic tension by playing a series of dotted-quarter notes against the 4/4 rhythm, setting up a three-against-four feel. Oscar Moore quoted from this solo on one of the Nat "King" Cole Trio's recordings of this tune, and George Barnes remembered it practically note for note after not having heard it for almost thirty-five years.

In 1934 McDonough waxed three guitar solos for swing maven John Hammond. After collecting dust in the vaults for over forty years, these test pressings began to pop up on guitar anthologies in the late seventies. The solos attest to a musicianship and technical facility beyond that displayed by McDonough on his band recordings or even in his remarkable duets with Kress. While McDonough appears not to have shared Kress's impressionist leanings, there is a good deal of harmonic playfulness to keep the listener on his toes. On the two originals as well as the one standard tune, McDonough chooses medium rather than brisk or flag-waving tempos. The relaxed pace allows for greater melodic mobility while sustaining several notes of a chord. One hears movement in the inside as well as the upper and lower voices. In a four-beat measure composed entirely of eighth notes, the guitarist may supply harmonic underpinning on only the first and third beats. This eighth-note-supported-by-chords style is generally associated with Van Eps and Allan Reuss, but the test

Django Reinhardt with Quintette of Hot Club of France. Courtesy, Duncan Schiedt

(above) George Van Eps. Courtesy, Duncan Schiedt

(top left) Eddie Lang with Bing Crosby, from "Big Broadcast of 1932."
Courtesy, Duncan Schiedt

(bottom left) Eddie Lang with orchestra, from Vitaphone Musical short.
Courtesy, Duncan Schiedt

Charlie Christian, recording session at Blue Note. Courtesy, Duncan Schiedt

Lonnie Johnson. Courtesy, Duncan Schiedt

Oscar Moore. Courtesy, Michael Price, from the T. Sumter Bruton III Collection

(top right) Bob Wills and the Texas Playboys. Courtesy, Michael H. Price Collection

(bottom right) Joe Pass. Courtesy, Michael H. Price Collection

(above) John Abercrombie. Photo by Richard Laird. Courtesy, ECM Records

(top left) Herb Ellis. Courtesy, Herb Ellis

(bottom left) Mike Stern. Courtesy, Atlantic Jazz

Ralph Towner. Courtesy of ECM Records

pressings reveal that McDonough was already moving in this direction by the mid-thirties.

Bassist Artie Bernstein supports McDonough on "Dick Bernstein Ramble," a catchy four-themed romp in D major containing several examples of ascending melody lines supported by descending lower voices. McDonough's unaccompanied exploration of Fats Waller's warhorse "Honeysuckle Rose" is also set in D, permitting use of open bass strings as the roots of the I, II, and V chords. Without a rhythm section to reign him in, McDonough is free to indulge his whims as to tempo and harmony, much as Waller did in solo renditions of the tune. After a wistful intro, McDonough plays both rubato and in tempo, making extensive use of passing chords and rhythmic tricks (such as a three-against-four feel).

Perhaps the most impressive of the McDonough test pressings is "Chasing a Buck," a minor-key original. McDonough sets up his opening theme with an introduction in which he pedals his open low E over E-minor, E diminished, and A-minor sixth chords played on the inside strings. After two minor themes he cuts loose with technical and harmonic fireworks in the major-key third strain, which sparkles with harmonic surprises. The chord-supported melody leaps from the lower to the treble strings; it is apparent that McDonough is attempting to break away from the oft-repeated garden-variety voicings that fall easily under the guitarist's hand.

Like Lang before him and Charlie Christian soon after, McDonough was cut down in his prime. He died in 1938, a victim of pneumonia brought on by alcoholic excess.

George Van Eps

It is difficult to convey to the uninitiated the awe that the work of George Van Eps inspires among guitarists. "He's the world's greatest guitar player," says Allan Reuss, and there are plenty of other players from the top ranks of guitardom who speak of Van Eps in tones of near reverence. To date no guitarist has even approximated Van Eps's chordal chops or gone nearly as far as Van Eps in investigating the guitar's "harmonic mechanisms"—fingering devices for achieving counterpoint, contrary motion, and complex voice leading. From his early recordings as a swing-band sideman to his later albums of seven-string guitar stylings, Van Eps has demonstrated an uncanny ability to utilize these devices while playing chord-supported melody.

Van Eps was born into a musical Plainfield, New Jersey, family in 1913. His father was the noted ragtime five-string virtuoso Fred Van Eps and his mother was an accomplished classical and ragtime pianist. In addition there were three older brothers, all musicians: tenor saxist John, trumpeter/arranger Fred, and pianist/arranger Bob. The young Van Eps taught himself banjo at the age of eleven, and was out playing jobs a year later.

Like scores of other banjoists, Van Eps caught the guitar bug when he heard Eddie Lang on a radio broadcast with the Roger Wolfe Kahn big band. After gigs with outfits fronted by vocalist Smith Ballew and saxist/bandleader Freddie Martin, Van Eps landed the guitar chair in the Benny Goodman band in 1934. This was followed by stints with Ray Noble (1935–1936, 1939–1941), after which Van Eps free-lanced and worked with Paul Weston's house bands at Columbia and Capitol. In the late fifties and early sixties Van Eps recorded a series of albums showcasing his fingerstyle seven-string guitar renditions of show tunes and standards. After periods of semiretirement and inactivity Van Eps is, as of this writing, hitting the club and concert circuit once again.

Van Eps is fond of telling inquisitive guitarists that he plays "lap piano"; indeed, the key to understanding the Van Eps style is to keep in mind that his concept is essentially a pianistic or orchestral one. The parallel movement of block chords utilized by Kress and later guitarists such as Wes Montgomery was too limited for Van Eps. "I like to think of it as a harmonic line rather than block chords, because block chords rule out the idea of any kind of continuity with contrapuntal effects," Van Eps told *Down Beat* in 1964.[6] Rather than thinking "I'm going to play this C-sixth voicing with the root on top and follow with that voicing of F-thirteenth with the thirteenth on top," the guitarist thinking in the Van Epsian mode sees each chord as the converging of multiple lines, the result of melodic voice-leading from the previous chord. "The chord names are in my subconscious, and I'm aware of them. But I'm more conscious of them as collections of lines that swim. They're going someplace."[7]

A pianist desirous of achieving these effects is blessed with two hands on the keyboard that can function independently; the left hand

6. John Tynan, "George Van Eps: A Master Guitarist's Reflections and Comments," *Down Beat*, July 16, 1964, p. 16.
7. Ted Greene, "George Van Eps," *Guitar Player*, August 1981, p. 81.

can sustain a chord while the right plays a melodic figure, or ascending and descending lines can be assigned to separate hands. An arranger with a band at his disposal can have one or several instruments state the melody while others play fills or provide harmonic background. Van Eps had the audacity to bring these techniques to the guitar's limited, one-hand-on-the-fretboard setup. Although he recalls that there was "a certain amount of give and take" between Lang, McDonough, and himself, Van Eps worked out his system without much input from other guitarists. Rather, the influence came from pianists (especially his brother Bob) and, one assumes, from arrangers.

The Van Eps system is the product of a disciplined, analytical mind able to break down musical problems into their mechanical components. The mechanical inclination is reflected in other aspects of Van Eps's life: he learned watchmaking from his grandfather, studied aeronautical engineering, and once built a seaplane in his garage. An ornery compulsion to achieve the impossible has extended beyond his musical career; the same man who systematically investigated labyrinthine fingering devices spent about eight years of his spare time researching and constructing the world's smallest (1/10" scale) fully operating steam locomotive.

In 1939 *The George Van Eps Guitar Method* appeared—a meticulously prepared presentation of major, minor, diminished, dominant, and augmented triads in all inversions on each set of three strings. Movement of upper, lower, and inside voices was demonstrated along with examples of contrary motion (middle voice sustaining, outer voices moving in opposite directions). Guitarists were admonished to practice the material in all keys. Forty-one years later, in 1980, the first of the three *Harmonic Mechanisms for Guitar* volumes was published.

This intimidating set extends the principles outlined in the 1939 book, emphasizing chromatics and "the mighty triad" while demonstrating harmonic ideas far beyond the scope of the slim earlier volume.

The methodical investigation of fingering outlined in these books has given Van Eps the ability to improvise chordally using the entire fingerboard—a discipline few single-line players have mastered to the extent Van Eps has in the chordal style. Legend has it that Van Eps would sometimes challenge a fellow musician to tune any one of his strings down by a half-step; Van Eps would then adjust his fingerings and continue to perform flawlessly.

Richard Lieberson   **99**

The guitar explosion of recent years has created a new audience for Van Eps's work, and reissues of his forties Jump material have helped make listeners aware of his innovations. Van Eps's earlier work as a thirties big-band and swing-combo sideman, however, is not that well known today and is deserving of attention both for its historical importance and for the finesse and wealth of ideas he displayed in this style.

In 1934 Van Eps participated in some marvelously arranged sides cut by Adrian Rollini and His Orchestra, a studio group that also included Jack Teagarden and Benny Goodman. These recordings, and Van Eps's two state-of-the-art solos, were cause for considerable discussion among musicians. On "Somebody Loves Me" Van Eps begins his solo with a crisp paraphrase of the melody stated in triads. The solo displays typical chromatic playfulness and concludes with two measures in four-part chords in which the top melody functions independently of the chromatically descending lower harmonic line.

Van Eps supplies the intro and an eight-measure bridge to "Sugar" from the same Rollini date. The guitarist kicks off the proceedings with two measures of chord-supported eighth notes, then connects with his next chord by means of a chromatically descending lower voice. Another measure of melody in the top voice is followed by a repeated melody note supported by descending lower voices. (This is all child's play compared to Van Eps's later output, but it was advanced stuff for the thirties and still sounds great today.) The piano lays out under the final bridge, allowing Van Eps to step out a bit harmonically without worrying about clashing with the keyboard. This device of the piano dropping out was often continued in the Goodman band under both Van Eps's and Reuss's solos.

On the Rollini solos Van Eps favored the top strings in order to avoid conflicts with the bass player. Van Eps recalls that he was sitting eight feet from the mike at this session and had to play "harder than hell"; he broke several strings, using a piano ivory(!) for a pick in an attempt to get more volume and cutting power.

On "Jamaica Shout," recorded in 1934 with Louis Prima and His New Orleans Gang, Van Eps is heard in a brief, vigorous, and percussive block-chord solo. Even those familiar with his work from this period will be hard pressed to identify Van Eps here.

Further examples of early Van Eps can be heard on his recordings with English bandleader Ray Noble's remarkable American band. In this aggregation Van Eps was part of a stellar lineup that included Bud Freeman, Charlie Spivak, Pee Wee Ervin, and Claude Thornhill. On a byzantine arrangement of "Bugle Call Rag" (1935) Van Eps delivers a hot, swinging solo with chromatic moves and dominant substitutions that Allan Reuss would later get a lot of mileage out of. Van Eps was often heard behind Al Bowly's vocals with the band, his pianistic concepts and inner-voice movement evident on "Yours Truly Is Truly Yours" (1936).

Although we're concentrating on solo work, mention must be made of Van Eps's masterful accompaniment on Noble's recording of "Dinah" (1935). From the first notes of the guitar introduction, which leaps from lower-string broken triads to top-string chords in a higher position, we are made aware of the extent to which Van Eps had gained command of the fingerboard and gone beyond rhythm-guitar conventions of the day. Unencumbered by a bass player, Van Eps's accompaniment on the opening chorus presents an updating of the Eddie Lang shuffle. He makes extensive use of arpeggiated and passing chords in unexpected places before swinging the band on the uptempo choruses.

Van Eps gives us a taste of things to come on a 1938 session recorded in Los Angeles and issued as *Bill Harty Presents George Van Eps Musicale*. The nine-piece band performs bright, involved arrangements laced with interludes in which Van Eps reveals the fruits of his wood-shedding. A folio of three Van Eps guitar solos published by Epiphone in 1939 (including "Squattin' at the Grotto" from the Los Angeles date) provides a great deal of insight into the fingering devices employed by Van Eps in this period.

If Van Eps had never played another note after 1938 he would still be guaranteed an exalted place in jazz-guitar history. Van Eps refers to his thirties work as being in "the banjo style" and confesses that he was never greatly enamored of playing in this fashion. Even at this early stage of the game, Van Eps says, he couldn't "go where he wanted" harmonically for fear of clashing with the bass and piano. A bass man might easily have taken offense if you asked him to lay out on your chorus, he adds. Van Eps's developing musical personality was not well served by the limited solo space, harmonic constraints, and souped-up tempos of the swing and Dixieland ensembles. "In harmony with moving voices, if the progressions are played too fast, the ear can't assimilate them," says Van Eps.[8]

In 1938, desirous of extending his instrument's range, Van Eps had Epiphone make him a guitar with a fingerboard that would accommodate an additional bass string tuned one octave below the standard A string. Van Eps is quick to point out that the seventh string is not used just for root movement or bass lines, but is an integral part of the tuning system. He views the seven-string guitar as including three separate tunings: the first to sixth, second to seventh, and first to seventh strings.

Van Eps got a chance to display his evolving harmonic concepts on a series of recordings for the Jump label. Three sessions recorded between 1944 and 1950 find Van Eps participating as part of LaVere's Chicago Loopers, a sort of thinking man's Dixie band with an impressive lineup that at times included Joe Venuti, Jack Teagarden, and Billy May. Van Eps is heard playing the seven-string both fingerstyle and with the pick in an advanced version of his "banjo style." After eight years spent studying the classic guitar repertoire, Van Eps came to favor fingerstyle for the added control it offers in bringing out a particular moving line in a chordal passage.

Van Eps is allotted quite a bit of solo space on the LaVere sides, and the slower tunes present a fine opportunity to digest his moving chordal lines. There are also some very impressive "banjo style" solos on uptempo tunes such as "Carolina in the Morning." Technical considerations aside, the emotional tone of Van Eps's solos is much cooler than what one would expect to hear on a Dixieland date, and this contributes to the unique ambience of the LaVere sessions. Listen to the languid guitar intro to "Lazy River" or the introspective opening bars of "Royal Reserve Blues" (how many "Dixie" players would voice a major seventh chord with the root and seventh next to each other?), or the dandy bridge on "A Monday Date." Even in the solos played with the pick, one does not feel that Van Eps is out to impress as a hot or hard-swinging player.

In 1946 and 1949 Van Eps waxed a series of Jump sides as part of a trio with tenor saxist Eddie Miller and pianist Stan Wrightsman. This intimate chamber jazz setting was well suited to Van Eps's harmonic temperament. The guitarist turns in some particularly warm solos on

8. Ibid., p. 81.

the ballads, nicely complementing the work of his teammates. His playing on the livelier tunes brings to mind the oft-stated comparison of Van Eps and pianist Art Tatum. The analogy is apt not only in light of their shared harmonic wizardry and technical virtuosity, but in the sense of the coming together of jazz past and present one gets when Van Eps combines the older right-hand-oriented banjo style with more modern harmonies, just as Tatum utilized stride while developing his own pianistic vocabulary.

The clearest picture of Van Eps's musical identity at this point is provided by the intense solos (backed by bass and drums) he cut for Jump in 1949. There's a harmonic feast here that will intrigue even the most highly educated ears. A moody exploration of "Tea for Two" is engrossing, and "Once in a While" is breathtakingly virtuosic. Most absorbing, however, are the originals "I Wrote It for Jo" and "Kay's Fantasy," named for Van Eps's wife and daughter. Repeated listening does not diminish the awe one experiences listening to these four performances. Practically every measure bursts with some remarkable harmonic, rhythmic, or melodic feature, all executed with impeccable technique.

The Van Eps solos have an introspective, austere quality (to me at least) not likely to go over in a big way with the moldy-fig crowd. This cool, cerebral ambience is heightened by the lack of interplay between Van Eps and the bass and drums, which provide no kicks, bombs, or sudden bursts of enthusiasm. A steady stream of notes and ideas leaves little breathing space for player or audience, and demands considerable concentration from the listener.

In marked contrast to the Jump solos are the recordings Van Eps made in 1951 as part of a quartet led by pianist Jess Stacy, a fellow Goodman alumnus. Stacy has always been a rollicking, rhythmic piano man, and Van Eps rose to the occasion with what may constitute his hardest-swinging playing on record, turning in soaring, melodically inventive solos in his "banjo style" on up-tempo standards such as "I Want to Be Happy" and "Back Home Again in Indiana." Plenty of guitarists would eagerly enter into contracts with Mephistopheles to be able to improvise single-line choruses at the speed Van Eps tosses off chord-supported melody here.

Van Eps's later albums are sufficiently removed from the swing idiom as to preclude them from extensive discussion here. On these recordings Van Eps performs on an electric seven-string instrument, lending his personal touch to everything from Cole Porter to the

Beatles. The backgrounds and arrangements on these LPs are decidedly more "middle-of-the-road" than jazz buffs are accustomed to, but also more accessible to the general listener than the Jump solos.

Ted Greene, a marvelous guitarist who has absorbed much from him, lists the characteristics of the late Van Eps style in an astute analysis of "Lover" and "The Blue Room" from *Soliloquy*, the last Van Eps album to date. Most of his comments apply to the earlier Jump material as well:

1. delaying the entrance of notes in the chords so as to create an almost conversational texture or fabric—sometimes bass notes speak first, sometimes the melody, and sometimes the whole chord;

2. attractive rhythmic conception, communicating a feeling of joy and general well-being;

3. tremendous right-hand agility, especially when executing rapid-fire arpeggios;

4. exciting reharmonizations and surprise chords—sometimes just adding a few welcome additions to a basic progression, sometimes creating an entirely new chord progression for the song;

5. clearly audible moving inner voices, often resulting in chromatic or semichromatic lines;

6. striking interludes with subtle variations on the main theme of the piece;

7. a feeling of continuity due to brilliant fills, which often employ the chromatic line but often in the soprano voice;

8. use of sustained bass tones together with two or three floating lines on top;

9. the opposite—sustained soprano tones with two or three lines moving about underneath;

10. a general improvisational feeling or quality;

11. intriguing tags and endings; and of course

12. that deep, rich seventh string, helping to create the full pianistic sound that George loves.[9]

9. Ibid., p. 80.

If jazz were a sporting event in which the musician who played the most harmony with the greatest chops was the winner, Van Eps would have claimed the guitar cup for the past fifty years. Fortunately, this is not the case, and we can still respond to Kress, McDonough, and the other chordal guitarists without feeling that they have been "outdone" by Van Eps.

Allan Reuss

While many jazz-band guitarists were intent on lifting the guitar out of the rhythm section and fighting for more solo space, Van Eps protégé Allan Reuss preferred to play time and "make everything else sound good." "I was forced to play solos," the now-retired Reuss said in a recent phone interview. Steve Jordan, a Reuss student who held the guitar chair in the Goodman band for a number of years, calls Reuss "the greatest rhythm section player there ever was, including everybody."[10]

His preference for timekeeping notwithstanding, Reuss's recorded solos with the Goodman, Teagarden, and Hampton bands, as well as his work with smaller units, identify him as one of the top chordsters in regard to ideas, tone, facility and swingmanship. Readers of *Down Beat* must have considered these qualities when they voted Reuss best guitarist of 1944.

Native New Yorker Reuss took up the banjo in 1927, took one lesson, then studied banjo and guitar on his own before commencing studies with Van Eps in 1933. When Van Eps couldn't make a Goodman broadcast because of a previous commitment with Ray Noble, Reuss was sent as a sub. Impressed, Goodman hired Reuss, which was fine with Van Eps, himself itching to join the Noble organization. After leaving Goodman in 1938 Reuss continued on the big-band route with Paul Whiteman, Jack Teagarden, Ted Weems, Jimmy Dorsey, and Harry James. He led his own trio in 1946, and recorded with a number of small groups as well as the big bands. Most of Reuss's later career was spent free-lancing in the Hollywood studios.

The Van Eps imprint is felt throughout Reuss's work. Setting his guitar up with "the heaviest strings I could find" and the action "as high as I could play it" (factors that contributed to his clarity

10. Steve Jordan, *Here Comes Mr. Jordan*, Fat Cat Records 119 (liner notes).

and cutting power), Reuss combined some of the maestro's harmonic wizardry with a more aggressive rhythmic drive, perhaps sacrificing some of Van Eps's complexity to the interest of swinging harder. Following Van Eps's example, Reuss mastered triads and voicings on all sets of strings, enabling him to play chord melody without dashing up and down the neck with the melody on only one or two strings.

A typical big-band Reuss solo might contain a chordal paraphrase of the tune's melody, chord-supported eighth-notes and triplets, harmonized blue notes, and chromatic playfulness *à la* Van Eps. Unlike guitarists of today's everybody-gets-to-do-his-thing age, Reuss usually had to speak his piece and be done in eight or sixteen bars. Every note counts in Reuss's deftly crafted solos, which are self-contained gems all the more valuable for the infrequency with which they appear. Reuss was also a whiz at constructing intros and cascading modulations that hopped around from key to key before settling down for the band or vocalist. Did Reuss ever work his solos out prior to recording? "They were all improvised," he says. The guitarist preferred to sit close to the bass man, who would have to keep his ears tuned for any harmonic curves thrown by Reuss.

During his tenure with the Goodman band Reuss turned in memorable guitar spots on "Rosetta," "Love Me or Leave Me," and "If I Could Be with You One Hour Tonight." Reuss had a whole chorus to himself on the latter tune, and many an aspiring guitarist attempted to copy it. While a member of the Goodman band Reuss also recorded with Teddy Wilson (nice intros on "Coquette" and "Here's Love in Your Eye") and Lionel Hampton (good stuff on "Judy" and "The Object of My Affection"). A half-chorus of hard-swinging, facile Reuss guitar appears on Hampton's "Rhythm, Rhythm."

Reuss left Goodman for the Whiteman band in 1938 and a year later moved on to work with the great trombonist and singer Jack Teagarden. With "Big T" Reuss got to blow an exciting sixteen bars on the Dixieland standard "Wolverine Blues." In much the same vein as the "Rhythm, Rhythm" solo, this half-chorus swings like the proverbial garden gate, showcasing Reuss's right-hand agility and melodic mobility in the chordal style.

In 1939, supported by the Teagarden band, Reuss recorded "Pickin' for Patsy," a full-length guitar feature. This multi-themed, constantly modulating piece did much to alert the public to Reuss's talent. It would be difficult to put in a claim for "Patsy" as a great moment in jazz or a profound piece of writing; nonetheless it contains some terrific guitar playing and deserves serious listening from anyone interested in thirties guitar.

Sometime in the late thirties or early forties Reuss appeared on an unusual recording of the standard "I Never Knew" with a group entitled Peck's Bad Boys. This all-string group, comprising steel guitarist Jimmy Smith, electric tenor guitarist Mike Widmer, bassist Leonard Corsale, and Reuss on acoustic guitar, creates a sound more evocative of the Texas/Oklahoma western swing bands than of the New York jazz scene. Fueled by Reuss's solid beat, Smith plays hot single-string melody that brings to mind pioneering steel ace Bob Dunn, and Widmer turns in a chorus with Django-like flourishes. There's also an exciting chorus from Reuss, who swings even harder than usual in this drumless, hornless combo. Unfortunately, neither Reuss nor Moe Asch, on whose label the recording appeared, are able to recall anything about the group or the session.

A more harmonically advanced, thoughtful, and Van Epsian Reuss appears on a number of mid-forties small-band dates. Either Reuss had been holding back this side of his playing in the constricting big-band environment or the changing harmonic climate of the forties inspired him to investigate new territory. On a fifties questionnaire circulated by critic Leonard Feather, Reuss cited as his best work to date his playing on "Minor Blues" (1946), recorded with Corky Corcoran's Collegiates. On this track Reuss sets up Willie Smith's lithe alto-sax chorus with a moody unaccompanied intro echoing Van Eps in its use of chromatics and moving inner and lower voices.

While a member of the Harry James band Reuss participated in several small-band dates led by tenor-sax giant Coleman Hawkins. The rhapsodic Hawk is heard at the peak of his powers on these sides, and Reuss's rhythm work is more easily discerned here than on the big-band recordings. The guitarist contributes a particularly memorable bridge to "Stuffy," a Hawkins original.

In 1946, when most guitarists had already abandoned the acoustic chordal style, Reuss waxed some of his most impressive solos with a quintet led by pianist Arnold Ross, a teammate from the James band. The Ross date offers a plentiful serving of Benny Carter's buoyant alto sax. Reuss's chorus on "Bye Bye Blues" is a technical dazzler that swings like crazy; there is exceptional guitar on "The Moon Is Low" and "I Don't Know Why" as well.

Today Reuss maintains a self-effacing attitude toward his solos, explaining that he never cut an album as a leader because he always viewed the guitar as primarily a rhythm instrument. It's a shame we don't have more extended playing on record from Reuss; his crisp, technically impressive, consistently swinging solos deserve greater acknowledgment by today's critics, guitar historians, and musicians.

Carmen Mastren

Another accomplished exponent of the chordal style was the late Carmen Mastren, winner of the 1937 *Down Beat* and 1939/1940 *Metronome* readers' polls. Mastren soaked up a good deal of the Kress/McDonough/Van Eps style, adding some original touches along the way. His marvelous rhythm work was much in demand by small combos (Wingy Manone, Joe Marsala), the big bands (Tommy Dorsey, Glenn Miller), and contractors for the New York radio/TV/studio scene. Mastren did not often get to stretch out on record, and consequently he is not particularly well known to the public although he enjoys a considerable reputation among musicians.

Born into a musical upstate New York family in 1913, Mastren took up violin, banjo, and finally guitar as a youngster. Arriving in the Big Apple in 1934, Mastren found most of the lucrative studio/radio guitar gigs wrapped up by Kress and McDonough, but landed a quartet job with trumpeter Wingy Manone, clarinetist Joe Marsala, and bassist Sid Weiss at Adrian Rollini's Tap Room. Two years later Mastren claimed the guitar chair in the Tommy Dorsey rhythm section, where he was occasionally heard in brief spots on such tunes as "There's Frost on the Moon" and "After I Say I'm Sorry."

Mastren was particularly proud of his work with the Sidney Bechet–Muggsy Spanier Big Four, which recorded eight titles in 1940. The guitarist and bassist Wellman Braud provide the only backing for the front-line horns, and Mastren solos without benefit of piano or drums. He rises to the demands of this tough assignment, swinging the group and contributing succinct chordal statements to several tunes. His chorus on "Sweet Sue" is a neat little swinger, with Bechet's clarinet providing a punchy obbligato. Mastren can be heard in a grittier, more down-home solo on the Delta Four's 1935 "Swingin' on that Famous Door."

In the seventies and until his death in 1981, Mastren played banjo and guitar with swing and Dixieland bands in New York clubs, occasionally taking the spotlight on a chord-style guitar feature.

Bernard Addison

A funkier, more gutbucket player than any discussed so far is guitar pioneer Bernard Addison (1905–). There were few guitarists for Addison to borrow from when he took up the instrument in his hometown of Annapolis, Maryland. Moving to New York in his early twenties, Addison traded licks with Eddie Lang ("I gave him a few lessons on the banjo, and he gave me a few on the guitar") and joined Kress and McDonough in Harlem jam sessions. Surrounded by these guitar heavies, Addison still chose to follow his own path stylistically.

In the course of his career Addison was privileged to work with Louis Armstrong, Jelly Roll Morton, Sidney Bechet, Fletcher Henderson, Art Tatum, and Stuff Smith—an impressive résumé, to say the least. Addison's intros and backup can also be heard on recordings by the Mills Brothers, whom he joined when John Mills, Jr., was stricken with tuberculosis.

Addison fought hard to elevate the guitar's status in the jazz band, sometimes breaking in on others' solos in frustration. "I couldn't resign myself to just beating that four. I had to cut loose," he said recently. And cut loose he did, with his personal brand of strong chord and single-line work.

Addison's *tour de force* is the 1935 "Toledo Shuffle." From the first notes of the unaccompanied guitar intro we know that Addison means business. When the band joins in, the guitarist launches into the theme with a blood-and-guts ferocity that makes the Van Epsians, with their delicate "harmonic mechanisms," seem almost effete. (Addison is a great admirer of Van Eps, whom he knew when the latter was active in the New York jazz scene.)

As of this writing, Addison continues to do some teaching out of his Long Island home.

Al Casey

One might have to wade through a couple of hours of Goodman sides to hear eight measures by Allan Reuss, or endure vocalists of questionable merit in order to catch a chorus by McDonough or Van Eps. But cue up some sides by Fats Waller and His Rhythm and it probably won't be long before you're treated to some bouncy chordal guitar courtesy of Al Casey. Due to Fats's immense popularity, Casey's name and playing are known to many who have no familiarity with any of the other players profiled here.

Born in Louisville, Kentucky, in 1915, Casey took up guitar as a youngster and listened to Eddie Lang, Carl Kress, and Django Reinhardt, among others. Casey was still in high school when he played his first jobs with Waller and only joined the band full time upon graduating in 1933. Up until the time of Waller's death in 1943, Casey was heard behind the pianist's vocals and in solos on tunes including "I Ain't Got Nobody," "You Look Good to Me," "Whose Honey Are You," and "Rump Steak Serenade."

Casey's work with Waller may owe something to the playing of Bernard Addison, for whom Casey has expressed admiration. In the Casey style, however, Addison's more rough-hewn qualities are tempered with an easygoing, relaxed sort of swing. While Casey did not possess the chordal vocabulary of Kress, McDonough, or Van Eps, it's difficult to imagine a more appropriate guitarist for the buoyant, we're-having-a-ball ambience of the Waller sessions.

In 1941 Waller featured Casey on "Buck Jumpin'," a riff-heavy romp over blues changes. In the introduction and throughout the piece Casey displays his fondness for certain rootless ninth and thirteenth forms on the top four strings, using these chords a minor third or a diminished fifth above the dominant chord stated by the rhythm section; this device is typical of Casey's chordal solos with Fats. Although he's playing an acoustic guitar here, his phrasing in the single-string passages suggests that Casey had already caught the Charlie Christian bug. Indeed, it was not long before Casey adopted the electric guitar as his main instrument and pretty much abandoned the chordal style because he felt it didn't come off well on amplified guitar.

After Waller's death Casey gigged and recorded with jazz luminaries including Coleman Hawkins, leading a trio of his own for a while. The rock years found him backing R&B sax ace King Curtis on solid-body electric guitar. After some lean years Casey is gigging around New York again with the Harlem Jazz and Blues Band.

In addition to the innovators and better-known players already discussed in this article, a number of other fine chordal guitarists were heard on jazz recordings of the thirties and forties. Frank Victor contributed some nice touches to the 1934 Joe Venuti Four sides; Art Ryerson is heard in memorable two-guitar passages with Tony

Gottuso and Dave Barbour in small Paul Whiteman groups (Bouncing Brass, Sax Soctette, Swing Wing); Gary McAdams played highly rhythmic chord solos with Louis Prima's New Orleans Gang; multi-instrumentalist/bandleader/entertainer Bobby Sherwood was featured on the impressive 1943 "Swingin' at the Semloh"; Goodman/Shaw/Norvo alumnus Dave Barbour turned in some nice acoustic guitar spots on the all-star 1943 Capitol Jazzmen date ("Clambake in B-Flat," "Casanova's Lament"); and Hy White came out front on a number of blues titles ("Blue Ink," "Red River Blues," "Blues Upstairs") with the late thirties/early forties Woody Herman band. Special mention must be made also of the dean of West Coast studio guitarists, George M. Smith, who recorded (and published) a number of marvelous guitar compositions in 1946, many of them in the chordal style.

In the seventies Bucky Pizzarelli paid his respects to the thirties chord style on recordings with Joe Venuti and with his daughter, with whom he recorded some of the Kress-McDonough duets. Bucky also recorded several of Kress's solo compositions, and his electric seven-string renditions of "Afterthoughts" and "Love Song" are the only currently available recordings of these pieces.

Probably the only currently performing guitarist working exclusively in the thirties acoustic chordal style is Marty Grosz. In an age when electronic effects boxes are *de rigueur*, Grosz (son of noted German caricaturist George Grosz) persists in cranking out four-to-the-bar rhythm and swinging chorded solos on a vintage acoustic archtop, noncutaway guitar. Echoes of Kress, Addison, and other thirties chordsters are heard in his snappy solos. Relocating to New York from Chicago in the seventies, Grosz contributed guitar, banjo, and Walleresque vocals to the Bob Wilber–Kenny Davern Soprano Summit, and explored the jazz-guitar duet repertoire with Wayne Wright. Grosz is heard to particularly good advantage on *Take Me to the Land of Jazz*, an LP where he shares the spotlight with pianist Dick Wellstood.

The appearance of Charlie Christian and his electric guitar on the scene in 1939 sounded the death knell for the acoustic chordal style. Up-and-coming players began to consider the Kress-McDonough style to be old hat and drew their inspiration from Christian and the melodic inventions of saxophonists such as Lester Young and Charlie Parker. A number of electric guitarists in years to come continued to exercise their chordal chops on up-tempo material (Barney Kessel, Wes Montgomery, and Howard Roberts come immediately to mind), but chordal playing more and more was reserved for ballads, with emphasis on harmony rather than rhythm. The harmonic language of the sixties and seventies, developed by such pianists as Bill Evans and Herbie Hancock, is spoken by a number of contemporary guitarists including Jim Hall, Ed Bickert, and Lenny Breau.

Guitarists partial to the rhythmic thirties chordal style have sometimes expressed the sentiment that single-string players are only imitating the saxophone, whereas the chordal artists played the *guitar* for all that it's worth, cashing in on the instrument's inherent potential. Even the greatest admirers of Kress, McDonough et al. must concede, however, that the harmonies and banjoistic rhythms of a thirties guitarist would be as out of place in the bop and post-bop environment as the left hand of a stride pianist. But while the older piano styles have been kept alive by veteran jazzmen and revivalists, the acoustic chordal style guitar is just a few steps from extinction today. It is encouraging, in this light, to find an occasional young guitarist, interest aroused by recent reissues, taking apart some long-forgotten gem by McDonough, Van Eps, or Reuss in an attempt to get a handle on this important chapter in the history of jazz guitar.

Middle Ground

Herb Ellis, Howard Roberts, Jim Hall, Kenny Burrell, Joe Pass, and Tal Farlow

James Sallis

Had I unlimited space and budget, each of these guitarists, and a dozen or two dozen others as well, would have his own major article. With such a sprawling landscape to cover, I've had to make many unhappy choices, and to settle, here, for these quick sketches. I apologize to the players, each a fine musician and deserving far better treatment. That they do not receive it may be the fullest measure of jazz guitar's fecundity.

There's a large "middle ground" of guitarists who have brought the Charlie Christian tradition forward to the more adventurous, eclectic playing of today. Certainly they built on that tradition, ever refining and expanding it, but they remain, at least historically, aligned with it. Included in this middle ground are Tal Farlow, Barney Kessel, Herb Ellis, Jim Hall, Howard Roberts, Kenny Burrell, and Joe Pass—the top names of jazz guitar.

Herb Ellis

Herb Ellis was born in McKinney, Texas, and began playing banjo at age seven, guitar about four years later. He attended North Texas State College (now North Texas State University and noted for its jazz program) as a music major, studying string bass since there was no guitar curriculum. It was here he first heard Charlie Christian—still, he says, his major influence by far—and met other students interested in jazz. One of these was future reed great Jimmy Giuffre. "He was already in jazz, and I became interested right away," Ellis remembers. "As soon as I heard it, I tried to switch the way I played."

Forced to leave school from lack of funds, Ellis auditioned for a traveling college band and got the job. He played with Glen Gray's Casa Loma Band for most of 1943, receiving enthusiastic mention in *Metronome* and *Down Beat*. Although he had cut some records with Glen Gray, his first recordings as a soloist were with the Jimmy Dorsey Band, among them "Perdido" and "J. D.'s Jump." "At that time," Ellis says, "you had to play mainly rhythm guitar. However, in Jimmy Dorsey's band I played a lot of solos and a lot of lines with the different sections, which was quite unusual at that time."

Ellis then spent four years traveling with the vocal and instrumental group Four Winds, finally, from 1953–58, joining bassist Ray Brown and pianist Oscar Peterson in one of the classic trios. (Barney Kessel had once been Peterson's guitarist.) He then toured with Ella Fitzgerald and in 1961 moved to Los Angeles, where he stayed busy with studio work for fifteen years, including a lengthy stint as guitarist on *The Merv Griffin Show*.

In the early seventies Ellis and Joe Pass formed a quartet, and in 1973 he joined Barney Kessel and Charlie Byrd as part of the Great Guitars, continuing duo work with Kessel or Pass.

"I'm a direct descendant of the Charlie Christian school," Ellis has said again and again. And something of the base these musicians all share is reflected in Ellis's comments on working with Joe Pass and with Barney Kessel.

Of Pass: "We could play two improvised lines at the same time, and it would come out as if someone had stayed up all night and written it out. It's uncanny—the involvement, the harmonization, the counterpoint—all kinds of stuff that we would get into."

And of Kessel: "It's unreal; we start out playing lines that are parallel or counter or crossing, and we'll wind up playing the same phrase almost."

Howard Roberts

At age seventeen Howard Roberts had a dream: he was watching Barney Kessel at a studio session, watching him through the glass so he couldn't hear him, but he could see his hands moving and hear the sounds those movements made. It was the culmination of a revelation for some time gathering: he was somehow plugged directly into music, and into guitar.

Roberts was born in Phoenix in 1929. He was sitting in at black jazz clubs by the time he was eleven, and working gigs at fifteen. Following a period of intensive study, he moved to Los Angeles in 1950 and lived hand-to-mouth while jamming with everyone he could. (He remembers wearing the same blue suit, held together with staples, continuously for a year.) One of the musicians he met in those jams was Barney Kessel. Kessel introduced him to Jack Marshall, who in turn took the young guitarist under his wing, introducing him to top players all over town. Soon Roberts was working with many of them on L.A. and Las Vegas gigs.

Finally, Roberts decided to settle back in Hollywood and devote his time to working the studios and perfecting his technique. He remained active in the studios until the early seventies, cutting more than five thousand numbers as a sideman and over twenty albums as featured artist, along with numerous TV and film soundtracks. Among these were early rock and roll sessions that Roberts has characterized as "grinding away on a G-major triad for three hours." He and Kessel were in fact among the first jazzmen to go into the studios during a time when such "commercial" playing was scorned.

In later years Roberts became progressively involved with teaching, at first giving seminars, then helping found the Guitar Institute of Technology and beginning his own publishing company, Playback. He protested the arbitrary labeling of music, believing *jazz* (Stan Kenton? John Coltrane?) to be a fairly useless term and recognizing that "fusion" is constantly at work throughout music. He said that his own playing, the way he really liked to play, fit into no convenient category, and that he thought of himself as an explorer or a hobbyist who "fools around putting pitches and notes together" to see what happens.

Jim Hall

"In the fifties," *Guitar Player* magazine once said, "Jim Hall took his Bachelor of Music degree from the Cleveland Institute of Music and set about becoming one of the greatest guitarists in modern jazz history."

Hall's first step was to move to Los Angeles, where he joined Chico Hamilton for a year, then Jimmy Giuffre for the next three. Critics compared the Giuffre trio (reeds, guitar, bass) to classical chamber-music groups. Hall also taught with Giuffre at the Lenox School of

Jazz, but felt finally the lure of New York, to which he moved in 1960. He worked there first with alto saxist Lee Konitz, then tenor great Sonny Rollins, eventually with trumpeter Art Farmer, all the time doing record dates with Konitz, Rollins, Paul Desmond, Quincy Jones, and Bill Evans. (Evans and he cut a fine duet album for United Artists, *Undercurrent*.)

Weary of road life by 1965, Hall eagerly assumed the chair left vacant on *The Merv Griffin Show* by Mundell Lowe's departure for the West Coast. He worked nightclub jobs with a quartet and in 1969 joined Kenny Burrell and Attila Zoller, under the auspices of the Newport Jazz Festival, for a tour of Japan, the three also participating in guitar workshops during the tour. A subsequent Oriental tour found Hall in the company of Barney Kessel and the Herbie Mann band.

A duo job with bassist Ron Carter at the New York club The Guitar in 1970 (then owned by Kenny Burrell) alerted Hall to the potentials of that pared-down combo and led to a duo album, *Alone Together*, on Milestone. Hall continued the duo concept with Jay Leonart when Carter went into studio work, then after seeing pianist Oscar Peterson play solo at the Newport festival became interested in the possibility of solo guitar. Hoping to combine something of the acoustic's delicacy and purity of sound with the amplified instrument's power, he commissioned a custom-built acoustic from luthier Jimmy D'Aquisto. Albums on Horizon spotlighted work on that guitar, and on electric, in solo, duo, and full combo settings.

Kenny Burrell

Kenny Burrell was born in Detroit in 1931, into a family in which everyone played music. His mother was a pianist, his father played guitar, banjo, and uke, and one brother is still active as a bassist in the Detroit area. Burrell's first love was tenor sax—that great sound Lester Young got, or Coleman Hawkins and Herschel Evans. Unable to afford such an instrument, Burrell began losing interest in music. But then he heard a radio broadcast of the Benny Goodman band, with Charlie Christian on guitar: Christian's lines, even the sound he got from his electric instrument, were like those of tenor sax. Burrell started playing again, and by 1951 he was well known around Detroit, sitting in at one point with Dizzy Gillespie, who passed the word on. Burrell received several offers to tour but decided to remain in college, receiving in 1955 his bachelor's in theory and composition.

After graduation he substituted for Herb Ellis, who was ill for a period, in the Oscar Peterson Trio, and thinks his love for Oscar Moore's playing was a factor in being chosen as sub. "That's probably one of the reasons Oscar Peterson hired me," he later told *Guitar Player* magazine, "because I understood that relationship from listening to Moore with Nat Cole's trio—how they worked in terms of voicing, spacing, and balancing sound."

Upon Ellis's return to the trio, Burrell moved to New York, where his reputation had preceded him, and began doing studio work— Kenny Clarke was an early booster—for Savoy and Prestige, and finally for Blue Note. *Introducing Kenny Burrell* (1956) led to a series of feature albums for Blue Note as he continued to free-lance other labels. There was no lack of studio work: these were the early days of rock and roll "and at the time there weren't many guitarists who could play blues as well as read."

Burrell continued to work the studios from 1957–63, in sessions ranging from one co-led with John Coltrane to backup work for the Shirelles. He was growing dissatisfied, though, with being always so busy and having little time left to concentrate on jazz, always his first love. Eventually he found his way into working Broadway shows and liked that pace far better; it allowed him time, he said, "to practice, to eat, to think." *Midnight Blue* resulted, did well, and made him a viable leader.

From 1963 to 1970 Burrell brought out albums on various labels, also working as featured sideman on albums by Illinois Jacquet and Hank Jones that brought him further attention. In 1965 he collaborated with Gil Evans on *Guitar Forms*, a double-album showcase of classical and electric guitar in solo, combo, and orchestral settings. This led to a series of orchestrated albums.

Burrell moved in 1970 to California, where he signed with Fantasy Records. He taught a self-created course on Duke Ellington at UCLA and gave annual seminars at friend Bill Harris's Washington, D.C., studio.

"There's no finer guitar player," George Benson says of Burrell, an opinion held by many others. "There may be somebody else who is as good, but you can't play *finer* guitar than Kenny Burrell."

Joe Pass

Feeling, immediacy, spontaneity: these are words that might easily occur to you as you listen to any of Joe Pass's one-take Pablo albums. Not surprisingly, the same words, or equivalent ideas, surface whenever Pass talks about his music.

"During thirty-eight years of playing," Jon Sievert wrote in *Guitar Player* magazine, "Pass has developed an improvisational style and technical virtuosity perhaps unrivaled in the instrument's history."

And in recent years Pass's primary line of development has been toward an innovative solo-guitar style. He has said that he believes this a natural direction for jazz guitarists. He tries to get on the stand or in the studio, he says, and just follow ideas where they take him: "It's then that I start finding new things, because it calls on everything I have inside me. That's when I get closest to playing music." (Ralph Towner and Paul McCandless of Oregon have spoken similarly of improvisation as "finding out what's *in there*, what's possible.")

In his book *Solo Jazz Guitar* Alan de Mause relates his confusion upon first hearing Joe Pass play solo—until he realized that Pass had changed the whole concept of what solo guitar was. "It took Joe to show us in the mid-seventies," De Mause writes, "what pianists such as Bud Powell in the 1940s showed traditionalists in the two-handed Art Tatum or Teddy Wilson school: melodic bebop lines could stand on their own, with chords used only as punctuation or as harmonizations of those same lines."

Joseph Anthony Jacobi Passalaqua was born in New Jersey but spent most of his early years in Johnstown, Pennsylvania. He got his first guitar, a seventeen-dollar Harmony, at age nine after seeing Gene Autry play one in a movie. He soon replaced this with a Martin, and his father began requiring him to practice at least six hours daily. "I'm doing this because I don't want you to have to be a steelworker or coalminer," his father told him, and the regimen stopped only when his father grew ill and was hospitalized.

Pass put the guitar away when his father left, but soon returned to it on his own and by 1949, age twenty, was on Fifty-second Street jamming with the likes of Charlie Parker, Dizzy Gillespie, Coleman Hawkins, and Art Tatum. A subsequent heroin addiction led to twelve lost years, five of them in a Texas prison. In 1960 Pass entered the Synanon drug rehabilitation program, and a few years later reentered jazz, playing club jobs and doing L.A. studio work, finally joining

George Shearing for a couple of years. In 1973 he signed with Norman Granz's Pablo label, his first album, *The Trio* (with Oscar Peterson and bassist Niels Pedersen), winning a Grammy. Granz gave Pass exactly the opportunity he needed to find out "what's in there, what's possible." Pass's playing developed new subtlety and control, new freedom and power, resulting in the first solo albums, *Virtuoso* and *Joe Pass at the Montreux Jazz Festival 1975*, and a new direction for jazz guitar. He recorded several more *Virtuoso* albums, dying in 1994 as this book was being revised.

Tal Farlow

A direct heir to Charlie Christian, Tal Farlow was later strongly influenced by Lester Young, Art Tatum, and Charlie Parker. He remains noted (along with his taste and steady swing) for the astounding speed he says he developed to keep up with Norvo and Mingus in the Red Norvo Trio. He also remains a nonreader, with an unorthodox, highly personal approach to technique and his (customized) instrument.

Farlow was born seventy-four years ago in Greensboro, North Carolina, and began playing mandolin and guitar while young. He eventually worked as a sign painter and one night while working at his bench heard a radio broadcast of the Benny Goodman band with Charlie Christian on guitar.

"I could already play the guitar a little bit," he says, "but the guitar was, in most cases, a part of a hillbilly band—you know, with three chords. Then Charlie Christian would come on like a sax, and it sort of made me think, 'Now, I've got an instrument here that can conceivably move out front.' I hadn't tried to play any single-string till then. I got those records and I learned to play those solos note for note."

Farlow worked with various groups, Buddy De Franco's among them, before signing with Norvo (Mingus was eventually replaced by bassist Red Mitchell) in 1950. Three years later he left to join Artie Shaw's Gramercy Five for a year, then rejoined Norvo—with whom he's recently been playing again—for another year or so. Then the Tal Farlow legend began.

Tal didn't care much for the city, and less for road life. What he liked most was being at home, and at ease—and his music. So he withdrew from the jazz scene to work again as a sign painter, playing local gigs alone or with a pickup group of friends, occasionally getting into a studio to record. Article after article in the jazz press announced Farlow's "return." They were all wrong. Or as bluesman Joe Callicott told a researcher who asked where he had been for so many years: "I ain't been nowhere. I ain't been lost. I been here all along."

Eventually Farlow did begin working again with Norvo and with his own trio, while recording for the fine jazz label Concord, which in fact arranged his reunion with Norvo.

A major fascination, of course, is that Tal Farlow pursued his music with little regard for public acclaim. In this he seems almost the image of American genius—self-directed, coming to its own in solitude, and traveling its own road. From Hawthorne and Ives to Pynchon and Harry Partch, such quirky individualism has been at the bedrock of much American art.

But, always, the music is the important thing, and it too often gets obscured by our interest in the artist as symbol of something other than the music flowing out of the world's *thingness* and disorder, through him, to us. Tal Farlow's refusal to let business and practical details bury his music testifies to that music's primary importance in his life.

Joe Pass

Wayne Enstice and Paul Rubin

Music is not something you make *so much as it is something you* find *within you. The excavation's not always easy, and sometimes you come up with old candy bars or Aunt Bertha's drawers alongside those moments of union, of oneness, you were rooting around for.*

Square on the line of succession from Charlie Christian and Wes Montgomery, thought and technique powerfully influenced by bop, Joe Pass probably had his greatest impact with his Virtuoso *recordings for the Pablo label, a landmark series of unaccompanied solo-guitar albums.*

As I've written earlier here, news of Joe Pass's death came as I was working on this manuscript. He was 65. He had released close to twenty albums under his own name and appeared on maybe fifty others, with people like Oscar Peterson, Count Basie, Duke Ellington, and Dizzy Gillespie.

Joe Pass had fought his way to the music within him, had fought for thirty or more years (as any artist must) to purify, refine, and renew it.

He won.

Joseph Anthony Jacobi Passalaqua, more commonly known as Joe Pass, is one of the most brilliant heirs to the jazz guitar lineage established by Django Reinhardt, Charlie Christian, and Wes Montgomery. Pass possesses a sonorous tone and impeccable technique, with a rhythmic and harmonic conception that is deeply rooted in the bop tradition. Although the vicissitudes of his profession, combined with personal crises, made Pass's ascendancy painfully slow, he has enjoyed international acclaim since the mid-seventies.

Born in 1929, Pass began performing for dances and weddings at the age of fourteen in his hometown of Johnstown, Pennsylvania. His exposure to bop in the late forties helped shape his musical direction, but Pass also became addicted to heroin along the way. That addiction consumed him for more than a decade, until he committed himself in 1960 to Synanon, a well-known drug rehabilitation facility based in Los Angeles. Pass spent three years at Synanon, emerging with renewed commitment to his music and a vision about a life free from drugs. In 1962 Dick Bock, owner of World Pacific Records and one of Synanon's sponsors, heard the little-known Pass play in a band composed of Synanon residents. He quickly arranged a recording for the group and launched Pass's career.[1]

Over the next year Pass did studio work accompanying World Pacific stablemates Gerald Wilson, Richard "Groove" Holmes, and Les McCann on a series of recordings. He stayed away from drugs during this critical period, erasing questions about his professional reliability, and he established credentials as a first-rate jazz soloist.

Pass's growing reputation within the inner circle of jazz was confirmed in the spring of 1963 when he won a *Down Beat* magazine poll as the best new voice on his instrument. On the heels of that award, World Pacific Records released *Catch Me!*, Pass's much-praised first album as a leader.[2]

During the next decade Pass played on numerous recording sessions; he also did television work and toured with George Shearing. In 1974 his fortunes rose dramatically, when jazz impresario Norman Granz signed Pass to his newly formed label, Pablo. Pass's first recording for Pablo, *Virtuoso*, was a stunning solo *tour de force* that proved how satisfying an unaccompanied single-line instrumental performance could be.[3] That recording earned him accolades from listeners and critics alike.

Since the unprecedented success of *Virtuoso* and the quality of its successors *(Virtuoso II–IV)*, Pass has been a prolific and consistently inspired recording artist.[4] He is in demand worldwide as a solo act and in the company of other jazz luminaries, such as vocalist Ella Fitzgerald, trombonist J. J. Johnson, and pianist Oscar Peterson. Joe Pass today is one of the giants of the jazz guitar.

Recorded 1980

PR: How did you get started in music, Joe?

JP: All I remember is that I was nine years old, and I asked for a guitar for my birthday, and I got one, an old Harmony guitar. I started playing for neighbors, Italian friends of my father's, and I learned the

1. *Sounds of Synanon*, World Pacific Jazz Records, 1962.
2. Joe Pass, *Catch Me!* World Pacific Jazz Records, 1964.
3. Joe Pass, *Virtuoso*, Pablo Records, 1974.
4. Joe Pass, *Virtuoso II*, *Virtuoso III*, and *Virruoso IV*, Pablo Records, 1977, 1978, and 1983.

chords from them. My introduction to the guitar, was, I think, I heard Gene Autry once in the movies. As a matter of fact, I saw the movie was advertised in the local papers to play tonight. It's called *Ride, Tenderfoot, Ride*. But no one in my family played any music, so I just asked for a guitar and got it. I learned what the local neighborhood players played, and then I studied with a friend of my father's for about a year. He played violin and saxophone, but he taught me to read music. Not really hard music, but just Nick Lucas books—simple guitar chords—and the rest is just playing.

PR: When did you start playing professionally?

JP: I started playing gigs when I was about thirteen or fourteen. I played weekends at local clubs and parties. My father had some friends that were in the music business. They were barbers by day and musicians by night [laughter]. I played with their group. It was called the Gentlemen of Rhythm. It was two guitars, a bass, a violin, and it was modeled after Django Reinhardt's Hot Club of France. Somehow I learned how to play melodies quick, so I played lead. I played all the pop tunes, "Stardust," all the tunes, and it was always a swing kind of group, and I played with this group around Johnstown, Pennsylvania. And I played with a group called Mason and His Madcaps, which was a blues-swing group. Then when I was about fourteen or fifteen I got involved with Tony Pastor's Orchestra, and I went on a tour of theaters with him. At that time they had theaters where they had a movie and a stage show on weekends. Bands toured all over the western part of Pennsylvania and in Ohio and Maryland and Jersey. I couldn't work any clubs, or if they went to the Hotel Pennsylvania in New York, I couldn't do that—I was too young.

Then I played with Johnny Long's Orchestra in the same fashion— sort of in a package. I would come out and play a few solos with the band, and that was that. And then most of the time I just played with a lot of jazz groups.

WE: There must have been quite a jazz scene back then in Pennsylvania?

JP: In Johnstown, there were a great many older musicians that played in big bands. Ray McKinley's band and Artie Shaw's band—and there were many musicians, maybe ten or fifteen guys, saxophone players, piano players. One piano player, Johnny Betoker, played with the Dorsey Band when it was at the height of its popularity. So there was a great deal of interest in jazz in Johnstown, and the gigs I played were like jam-session gigs. We listened very much to Jazz at the Philharmonic, which was very popular then. I played with this group—the violin player played like Stéphane Grappelli, and that's who we listened to. So right from the word go I was playing swing or jazz music—"Night and Day," "Lady Be Good"—and it just started like that. There's a tendency for players that are interested in jazz music to kind of get together, and Johnstown being a town that's not too big, we made sure that we got together on all the gigs. Every time musicians or bands would come through town—there was a great deal of bands going through town every week—Mel Hallett, Bob Chester, and bands you probably wouldn't have known about. Tony Pastor, Johnny Long, Duke Ellington, Count Basie—there'd be jam sessions, and that's where I really got my feet wet learning to play.

WE: At what point did you move away from Pennsylvania?

JP: I went to New York and played with Brew Moore, around 1948 or 1949. I played with a lot of jazz groups, but most of the time there wasn't a lot of work. Most of the time I was just sort of goofing around, just being around listening to everybody play on Fifty-second Street—Charlie Parker and those. I would go out on the road and tour with different little trios and quartets when I needed the money. Then I'd come back to the city and hang around. Then I went to New Orleans and did some playing there. There are lots of jazz players that have never made a national name for themselves, but they're known with the musicians. There was a long period of time where I didn't play. I got involved in personal problems, and I didn't really function as a working musician, fully. I spent so much time trying to get everything straightened out. It took me many years, about twelve years. So that would take me up to about 1960. Oh, I worked in Las Vegas for a while, and I played with various kinds of show groups; that was just working. But I always played jazz, always played gigs somewhere where I could play.

PR: Did you pay close attention to well-known guitarists as you were growing up and breaking into the business?

JP: The first guitarist I heard was Django Reinhardt. It was acoustic guitar. Charlie Christian played acoustic guitar. There was a little different concept there, I mean as far as an approach to rhythmic things. I would say that Django was more guitaristic, and Charlie Christian played more like a horn player, but I don't think there was any great deal of difference. The music was much the same. One played more notes than the other.

Then there were a lot of other guitarists during that time. There was Chuck Wayne, and Tal Farlow, and Jimmy Raney, but you see, I didn't listen to a lot of guitar players. I listened a little bit to Django and some to Charlie. I didn't have a record player, and you couldn't even get all the records in Johnstown. The stores wouldn't bring any of these records in. They brought in Perry Como [laughter]. Not that there's anything wrong with Perry Como, but we had a hard time getting a jazz record. But I heard some Charlie Parker records about 1950—maybe a little earlier. That's what really excited me, and that's the music I started to copy. I would copy horn players.

The first jazz record I heard, I would say, was Coleman Hawkins' "Body and Soul." That was the first thing that I really flipped over. I used to hang around a music store, and one of the clerks was really interested in jazz, so he would sneak in some of the orders—one or two copies—and we'd sit around and listen. There would always be a new record every week—Dizzy Gillespie; I remember Al Haig and Stan Getz. They were young players then.

My influence in my guitar playing came mainly from horn and piano players. In fact, I made a point of avoiding any guitaristic playing. There are certain things that are peculiar to the guitar that a lot of guitar players use—certain bending of notes, certain interval sounds, and rhythmic ways of playing that you could trace right through the history of electric jazz guitar—and I didn't do any of them. I played straight lines and horn-like lines, and I didn't play rhythm 4/4; I comped like a piano way back, so it has been only the last ten years that I started to listen to guitar players more. I don't listen to very many guitar players now. I still listen to horns or orchestras, but my influences were mainly from bebop players or swing—Lester Young, Don Byas, those kinds of players. I remember Barney Kessel a little bit on some records. One in particular was "Swedish Pastry," with a clarinet player. I used to listen to Artie Shaw and copy his things off of his big band—only his solos and things like that.

PR: What about the blues players? Did you check them out too?

JP: I never made a special point of listening to any blues guitar players. I knew about B. B. King a long time ago and some of the old blues players. I'll tell you one thing: we read about the great influences in music, and all these names mentioned have been known worldwide, but I think when you are first starting out as a musician you may hear some players like Charlie Parker or Django Reinhardt, but I think the big influences come from your immediate surroundings—the guys that you play with, who are never heard of. But they somehow have that feeling for playing, and you, as a new player, naturally join the local groups that are playing. And that's where your training ground and your musical thing starts to happen. Whatever town you are in. There were guitar players around—the Cashaw brothers, you never heard of them. One was a bass player, and one a guitar player. They played blues as good as any blues player around. I played with them. So I guess I can say the Cashaw brothers were instrumental in the blues for me.

WE: Joe, it's well known that you were addicted to heroin from about 1949 to 1960. Could you speak a bit about that time in your life?

JP: Well, offhand I'd say it was a waste of time. Many times I had opportunities to play. Johnny Smith, the guitar player, called me in New York and said to be in a certain place about a certain job. And of course, I was so busy doing the other thing that I never went. There were many opportunities I had that I missed because of not being responsible and being hung up. I don't think it did any good for my music. I found that the best music and the better things happened when I was sober, when I played clear-headed with all my faculties. If anything, drugs just set you back. I mean, it's an illusion. You think you are really doing a lot, but if you want to find out, you make a record under, and then listen to something when you're not, when you're straight, and listen to the difference.

WE: Dick Bock of World Pacific Records was kind of your savior in a musical sense, wasn't he?

JP: Well, Dick Bock came to Synanon and was sort of a sponsor of it and heard me play there. I played on Saturday nights for the guests— we had open house—and he said he would like me to make a record. We had a little group at that time playing, so we made a record. That was my introduction to records. I had made some records before; I made one with Tony Pastor and one with Dick Contino. But I never heard of them or saw them. I don't know where they are. Bock made the first record I was on in '62 or '63.[5]

My first record [after leaving Synanon], *Catch Me!* was my album. I had played several gigs with Clare Fischer and Ralph Peña, so when Dick Bock asked me who I would like to get—I mean, I only knew two guys [laughter]—so I said, "Clare Fischer and Ralph Peña." That's the

5. *Sounds of Synanon*, 1962.

way it works. Sometimes a record company will suggest to me, "I have a couple of players that are really good. Would you like to do a record with them?" Like they put me with Groove Holmes or Les McCann, or Gerald Wilson's big band.

WE: Even on those early records you have a distinctive identity, a distinctive sound.

JP: I think there's an identity to my playing that you could hear. Lots of guys, guitarists especially, would know. I can identify certain guitarists; certain others, I can't. I can confuse them with other players, but there are certain ones that I can tell you exactly who they are as soon as I hear them because it's their character, their identity, and I think I had that a long time ago.

It's just the way I play, my musical ideas or whatever, and I notice since I've been playing solo that there has been a certain style or a certain approach to the playing that has developed just from the sheer fact that I'd have to get out there and play. I was out there playing, and this was all going on subconsciously, like what do I do next to get from here to there.

None of it is worked out or practiced. I don't sit at home and say, "OK, I'm going to play this run or this chord, and then I'm going to do that." But actually, I do it by going out on the gig and doing it. And from that I've developed a kind of approach. I think what happens is when you play alone and you don't work things out, you're forced to develop some kind of style or approach just on the gig. Once you start that and you're doing it live, in person, for real, that stays with you. And it becomes part of your music vocabulary, your style, your way of playing. I notice certain things that I do on the guitar that weren't there three years ago. They developed just from actually doing the playing.

PR: When did your solo career actually start? And did you think you were taking a risk by walking out there onstage with just a guitar?

JP: When I play solo I get the feeling that I'm playing for an audience like they were sitting in my house and we were together and they asked me to play, which is the way I started playing solo guitar. I mean, I've been playing solo guitar for a long time. Every time I have guests at the house or I am visiting someone, it is always "Bring your guitar." They never say "Bring the drums and the bass" [laughter]. So I'm always sitting there, and then they say "Play," and I play for an hour. And they say, "Play this tune" and "Do you know this tune?" and somebody starts humming, and so I'm playing the guitar, and I've been doing that for years. And someone once said to me, "You ought to go out and play on the stage, you know, solo."

But I always felt like, no, people wouldn't dig it. They're going to say, "Well, jazz—where's the bass and where's the drums and where's the rhythm?" So I was always hesitant to do this, and occasionally in a club I'd play one or two tunes solo, and that would be it. Like waiting for the bass player to come away from the bar or something. Now that I'm doing it, I feel a little more comfortable about it, and the response has been nice. Nobody has said "It's not loud enough" or "There's not enough excitement." But I don't think I'm doing anything special.

PR: Your solo concerts feature a large variety of tunes. How do you decide what to perform?

JP: I try to pace my music—try to play what I feel but try to change tempos, changing keys I especially think is important. I like to communicate with them—I like the feeling. Sometimes you get a feeling that they're not with you, and then you have to make a change. I might play eight bars of a tune and just stop and go into another tune because I don't feel that it's what I want to play.

Maybe you start a tune, and you can't get into it, and you're trying to get into it, and you see it is not working. That's just the way it is. Usually when that happens, that's it. No matter how hard you try to get into it, you're doing what you can do with that song at that time, emotionally and mentally, and whatever—I don't like to use the word *creative*. So generally I take the tune out. I try exploring it a little bit, but I just finish it and try something else.

What happens when you're playing solo is it's different, because one night you go up and play tunes and they all work out and they all sound like they're brand-new, and you're really having a ball with them; and the next night you go and play some tunes—say maybe a couple of the same tunes—and they feel and sound like you've never played them before, and they're like the hardest thing in the world to play, and you are struggling from the time you start. Sometimes it's free and loose and easy and it's a lot of fun, and other times it's a lot of work.

It's hard to sustain your interest—not to sustain your interest, but for things to come off like you want them to. You'll be a note off here and there, and that's just enough to throw everything off. I mean, lots of times the audience can't tell, or many times they say that they liked it, and you didn't like it, but that may be the difference in what you are communicating.

And you never know what it's going to be like before you sit down and play. Many factors enter in, like the sound of the room. If the room that you're playing in doesn't sound in the spectrum of what you want to hear, that can make you play different. The acoustics of a place change. I found that if my seat is a little bit too high or a little low, it changes things. I should actually have a stool made or a seat made for myself and carry it around, but I'm too lazy.

I noticed one time when I was doing some concerts and when the stage people set up my amp on my right, I didn't snap to it. I was so nervous about doing a big concert. I was with Ella Fitzgerald and Oscar Peterson, and that was the big time, and I had run out there to play and the amp was on my right. I never play with my amp on my right, and I couldn't figure out what sounded so different, and I had a hard time playing. Well, after about four concerts I noticed that, being quick to notice things [laughter]. I said, "Wait a minute, this should be on my left," because that is the ear I listen out of.

So lots of little things change—the temperature, if it is warm or cold. Air conditioning blowing on the guitar affects the strings, makes them tight. I played half of a concert last night, and there was no air conditioning on, and everything was loose. Then they put on the air for the intermission, and they left it on, and I was onstage, and all of a sudden the strings got tight. But you can't say "Please turn the air conditioning off."

A lot of things affect the way you play—how you feel when you wake up. I like maybe not to take what I'm doing seriously. I don't like to feel like I am doing some really important thing, but sort of have fun, relieve the pressure of playing and allow ideas and things to come through without censoring things. I like to take chances when I play, too, that is, make mistakes or whatever.

WE: We've been talking a lot about your solo work. But you still enjoy working with other musicians, don't you?

JP: Yes. There comes a time when you feel like you want a rhythm section for a change, or you get the thought, "Joe, it'd be nice to have a bass and a drummer." Lots of times I play with Oscar [Peterson]— we play duo—and just the mere fact that there's another instrument playing and another person's ideas stimulating me and make you work and think. . . . Every once in a while I think about it.

Of course, I play sometimes in groups put together by Norman Granz for jazz festivals, and this would have bass and drums. Not a lot of it, but four or five times a year I'm playing for a week or so with a rhythm section—with horns, jam-session style—which is good, which is really different and stimulating. But mainly I've been doing solo. The next thing I've been doing is playing duo with Oscar, which is hard and demanding but exciting and challenging, because trying to keep up with him and be where he is, sometimes I have to play and dance at the same time [laughter].

PR: Signing on with Pablo Records was certainly a pivotal move in your career, to put it mildly.

JP: That label really is to me sort of the start of my career. Even though I made records before, and I had some kind of a little notoriety in *Down Beat* from other records. But I stayed in Los Angeles, and I have a family, and I started doing studio work, and I would always play jazz gigs around Los Angeles—Dante's, the Lighthouse—but I never left. I did a short tour with George Shearing, and then I came back because I had children. But I met Oscar Peterson through Herb Ellis and other musicians, and Oscar once said that he might start a trio up again with a guitar, and if he did would I be interested? I said yeah.

Norman Granz is his manager, and I'd forgotten all about Norman Granz and Jazz at the Philharmonic, and Oscar called me and asked me if I'd work three weeks in Chicago with him and Niels-Henning Ørsted Pedersen, the bass player from Denmark, and we went, and Norman Granz decided to start his record company, Pablo, in about 1973, I think. The first recording he made was a live recording of the trio with Oscar. So I met him, and he said he was starting a record company and would like to record me. I don't know if he said he'd record me or if I said, "Hey, record me!"

I did a record with Oscar and then one with Duke Ellington before he passed away, and that sort of snowballed, and I did one with Ella, but—I don't particularly like any records I make. You hear everything you should have done and your mistakes. I'm striving to make that perfect record, but the way with Norman is that the more you repeat a performance the more sterile it becomes. You may not make any mistakes, but you've lost all the spontaneity because you are so busy waiting for that spot where you goofed, and you do it, and you get it all right, and you are not taking any chances. The sound—it comes off not real, you know, at least that's what they say. And I kind of believe that too. Maybe I should change my ideas about not liking the things that I do. I think that maybe after a year or so, I may listen to something and say, "Well, it wasn't too bad." But that's the kind of attitude I have.

WE: One of our favorite records with you as a sideman is *Duke's Big 4*.[6]

JP: That was really one of the high points in my musical—I hate to use the word *career*, but now I have a career, because first of all I didn't know that Duke Ellington ever made any records with a small group or quartet. I always identified Duke and always heard his music with a band or orchestra or on solo piano, but later I found out that he had made some with Coltrane. So when I was called to do this by Mr. Granz I went down to the studio, and there was Duke Ellington sitting at the piano. I thought, "What's going to happen here?" There was Louis Bellson on drums, Ray Brown, and me. And that was the group.

The strange thing was that it was all a rhythm section, but Duke's playing piano, and I play electric guitar, which means I'm not *just* a rhythm player, it's understood. So that meant that it would be like me playing solos with Duke Ellington, you know. I was really kind of taken aback, careful, but he was really easy. He just sat down and started doodling on the piano—doodled out a little thing, and we started to play that. I mean, we didn't rehearse or anything. He just started playing "Sophisticated Lady," and then we just said, "OK, let's make a record. Let's do it," and that was it. No beginnings, no endings, and we did the whole album in three or four hours. I was really honored to be on a record with Duke Ellington. Man, that was a good start.

PR: We understand that you're not a big fan of some other guitarists of note, like Jimi Hendrix and John McLaughlin.

JP: First of all, I never heard a Jimi Hendrix record that I listened to thoroughly. I don't know what he did. I don't even know if he *was* a guitar player. He made a lot of noises, and he did a lot of things. I heard one or two tracks of his, and I couldn't tell if it was him or what was playing, because it was so loud. I never made a study of him.

And McLaughlin—I know for a fact that he was a jazz guitar player. I heard a record of his recently, from England, where he was playing a kind of bebop, and so he could play the guitar before he went into whatever he is doing now. He actually knew how to play the guitar.

6. Duke Ellington, *Duke's Big 4*, Pablo Records, 1973.

So the music he is into, I don't particularly listen to it, but I figure he knows what he is doing, because he can play. That's what my criteria is: if a guy knows how to sit down and play music like we all know it, and if he goes into some bag where he's going to play Indian music or spaced-out—I mean, if he knows what he's doing, and he's not shucking—I figure he's maybe trying to find something, so I think that's OK. But I think that the great many guitarists are overrated through the media.

PR: Rock players?

JP: Yes, rock players. I don't know how to say it, but a lot of them can't play. Put them down in a room and say, "OK, here's Joe the barber. Play something so that Joe the barber knows what you're playing. Take the amps and fuzz tones and wa-wa's away, and just play some music for me or my friends, and let's see if you can play some music." I think a lot of them wouldn't be able to play anything.

There's a lot of them—for instance, this thing came up—the *lead* guitarist. There's a lead guitarist, and there's another guy. The lead guitarist doesn't do anything but play lead [laughter]. That's his whole thing. Right? I think that's funny, myself. Why do they have to have a lead guitarist and another guy? The other guy knows three chords [laughter]. The lead guitarist knows—I hate to sound bad, because some of the music is good, and some of the players are good, but not the majority of them. They're all bending strings and using all the fuzz and wa-wa and Echoplex and everything. So if you could take all of these guys and put them in a room and each guy will take a chorus on the blues or something, you wouldn't know which one was which. They all sound the same.

WE: Are there any younger players who impress you?

JP: I never heard him, but I hear he's very good—Steve Khan. I like Larry Coryell—he's not too young—and there's Ralph Towner and John Abercrombie. Both of these guys are from Berklee [College of Music]. They are good players. Philip Catherine, I know him. He's a good player.

When you are talking about guitarists like that, you are talking about guys who can play the guitar in front already. So now what they're doing is trying maybe to find their identity, or a style, or an approach to playing what they like. And you must remember that these are guys of another generation, and they would no more go into the bebop thing or whatever is traditional jazz. They have to play from the point where they started just like I did.

For me to change now and say "OK, all these guys are doing this new thing, so I should jump right in there and do the new thing." Well, I listen to some of it and try to incorporate some of the sounds that strike me, and I put them in my music. But to deliberately go and say "I have to change all this and play different kinds of chords and different kinds of tunes because that's what's happening" is—I could do it if I practiced and studied, but it wouldn't be real for me. Because I am from a different time—music time. It doesn't mean that you are old or new; it just means that you do the music that you grew up in. That's your music.

So I like the players that know how to play. Regardless of what you are doing, though, you have to have the basic fundamental ability to play the instrument, and people like Catherine and Towner have that. I mean, they could play "Stardust," maybe in a little different way, but they do know what they're doing, and they know music. That is different.

WE: Among your guitar contemporaries, whose playing holds the most interest for you?

JP: Jim Hall, Barney Kessel, Pat Martino, and Kenny Burrell, too. Tal Farlow, naturally Christian, Wes, naturally. My favorite guitar player was Wes Montgomery. I feel that Wes was really a jazz guitar player regardless of what he did on the records. He just did everything the way he always did. They just sweetened the records. But I thought he was really *the* innovative, swinging jazz guitar player.

PR: Joe, are there musicians out there whom you'd like to work with?

JP: Gee, I never thought of that. I like to play with anybody who can play. It's always good to play with people that put demands on you. A good thing for a player to do is put yourself in situations where there's a lot of demands on you so that puts a challenge to you and brings out your abilities. I like to play in all kinds of different contexts.

One time I played in a rock context for two nights. I used the wa-wa and a big amplifier. These guys were pretty good, good blues-rock players, and I played with them just to see what it was like. I had the volume up, and I was right there. The only thing I got out of it was excitement, and it came from the sheer volume. It got so rhythmic, so heavy and loud that actually it'd lift you right off the floor. By the end of the night I was so tired I said, "I don't want to play in here."

The Fingerstyle Jazz Revolution

Howard Morgen

*In the early eighties, when the first version of this an-
thology was assembled, fingerstyle playing had gained
tremendous momentum.*

*The biggest push was from Laurindo Almeida and
South Americans like Bola Sete and Baden Powell, all
classically trained and jazz-inspired, though many years
before George Van Eps had already abandoned the plec-
trum for fingers in order (he said) to realize the guitar's real harmonic potential. The sixties folk revival also contributed to the growth of fingerstyle, as
the best folk players followed a natural progression from old-time and blues
fingerstyle playing into jazz.*

*For those interested in the technical side, good places to start are Alan
de Mause's several books for Mel Bay Publications (particularly* Solo Jazz
Guitar*), and Howard Morgen's own fine list of publications, including the
five-volume Howard Morgen Fingerstyle Jazz Series for* CPP/Belwin.

*Howard (who, like Van Eps, plays and champions the seven-string guitar)
has been the columnist on fingerstyle jazz for* Guitar Player *since 1988. He
wrote an earlier column for* Guitar World, *and his transcriptions appear
frequently in specialty magazines such as* Fingerstyle Guitar, Acoustic Guitar,
and Just Jazz Guitar. *Howard teaches at the Guitar Study Center of Manhattan's New School, in the Jazz Study Program at Long Island University,
and privately. Current projects include a book-and-tape compilation of jazz
treatments of Paul Simon songs to be distributed by Music Sales, Inc.*

*Were he not already so busy, Howard would have chosen to revise and
expand this piece. He originally included remarks on Emmett Chapman and
Britain's Big Jim Sullivan, but these were edited out of the piece when it was
originally published. Now, he says, he would want to include at least three
of the most popular, exciting fingerstyle players to emerge since then: Stanley
Jordan, Tuck Andress, and Jeff Linsky.*

One Friday evening I was playing in a club on Broadway, New York
City, when a guitarist named Ray Tico came in and asked me if he
could entertain during one of our breaks. Ray got up there all by
himself and proceeded to blow me away with something I'd never
seen or heard before. He played melody and chords to "How High

the Moon," accompanying himself with a walking bass line played with his thumb.

Now, I'd heard classical guitar many times, and also arrangements of popular standards played in a classical style. But I'd never heard anyone apply the thumb-and-finger techniques of the classical guitarist so logically and convincingly to a purely jazz conception. Ray was from South America, where classical techniques had long ago been applied to flamenco and other popular forms—so why not to American jazz?

That evening kept cropping up in my mind for a full year before I took the plunge into classical guitar, with the aim of combining its techniques with those I was already using. I was not alone. In fact, I was in pretty fine company. Charlie Byrd, a jazzman with country roots and a classical guitar student of Sophocles Pappas, was one of the first to popularize classical and jazz approaches, using a traditional nylon-string guitar in a trio setting. Another Pappas student, Bill Harris, emphasized the unaccompanied guitar with walking bass lines on the album *The Harris Touch*.

In playing fingerstyle, jazz guitarists altered the traditional classical hand positions and techniques. Chuck Wayne, a skilled jazzman who first came to prominence with the George Shearing Quintette, was one of the first to use a pick and three-finger technique. He thus retained the advantages of the flatpick for single-string improvisation while gaining the freedom to employ percussive, pianolike chord voicings and counterpoint.

Laurindo Almeida, a classical guitarist who played with the Stan Kenton Band in the late forties, added the fourth finger to the traditional thumb and three fingers to obtain chord voicings with greater color and tension. And former pick virtuoso George Van Eps, the daddy of all chord players and the inventor in 1939 of the seven-string jazz guitar, also began to use four fingers.

Concurrently with the melding of jazz with classical techniques, another set of influences came into the jazz field from an unlikely source—country music. Chet Atkins, who had started recording his thumbpick and three-finger style in 1947, mixed traditional country music with his interpretations of jazz and pop standards. He created a spirited yet easygoing style that attracted the attention of musicians in all fields.

Atkins, in turn, had been strongly influenced by the thumb-and-finger technique of country guitarist Merle Travis, who had brought the technique out of the coal-mining country of western Kentucky. Travis, too, had adapted his playing to noncountry standards. Both Atkins and Travis muffled the bass strings with the palm of the right hand as they played.

The sixties witnessed a surge in popularity and exposure for all kinds of music. Musical styles and techniques from many sources blended as never before. Players of pop, classical, folk, rock, latin, jazz, and country music were influenced by each other and experimented freely.

Jazz-inspired classical guitarists like Jorge Morel, Luis Bonfa, Bola Sete, and Baden Powell, all South Americans, incorporated jazz harmony and/or improvisation into their playing. Bonfa and Morel in particular emphasized the bass line supporting the chords and melody, and used altered hand positions to muffle the bass strings (in the style of Atkins and Travis) to produce a scratchy drum-brush effect.

The term fingerstyle came to mean any technique that enabled a player to produce melody, harmony, and rhythm (bass lines), to sound every note in a chord simultaneously, and to voice chords on widely separated strings. These techniques included use of the thumb and fingers, the thumbpick and fingers, flatpick and fingers, and tapping on the strings with the fingertips of both hands.

By the latter part of the sixties interest in fingerstyle had become widespread for two practical reasons. For one, improvements in equipment had made fingerstyle more feasible on all types of guitars—nylon-wound electric guitar strings, for example, and acoustic-guitar pickups that permitted acoustic or electric sounds made guitars more versatile. And the Gretsch Company's Van Eps Seven String Electric Guitar, with its bass range extending to A, was ideally suited for fingerstyle solo work or for providing accompaniment in a duo.

And secondly, economic conditions were beginning to cause club owners and restaurateurs to prefer solo performers or duos over larger musical groups. Guitarists were also hired for jobs that had once been the domain of cocktail pianists.

In 1969 a talented young guitarist from Winnipeg, Ontario, named Lenny Breau recorded two albums that eventually became among the most sought-after and influential jazz guitar albums ever produced, *Guitar Sounds from Lenny Breau* and *The Velvet Touch of Lenny Breau, Live.*

Breau evolved a unique piano-guitar style that combined Travis/ Atkins country picking and flamenco technique with the musical influences of Bill Evans's jazz piano voicings. He could thus "comp" rhythmically independent, beautifully voiced chords while improvising single-line jazz choruses. His albums also display his command of country, rock, classical, and flamenco idioms. His application of Atkins-inspired artificial harmonics to create the aural illusion of rapidly flowing harplike note "showers" is particularly interesting.

Throughout the seventies more guitarists adopted fingerstyle concepts. In 1970 Buddy Fite recorded three albums for Bell Records: *Buddy Fite!, Changes*, and *Buddy Fite and Friends*. Buddy played with a rhythmic piano style, employing sharp, biting, thickly textured chord structures to punctuate the melody and walking bass lines. Unfortunately, circumstances have contrived to keep Fite in Oregon, and his work is not widely known.

Other early seventies standouts were Earl Klugh, who played exciting contemporary lines on the classical guitar, and Bucky Pizzarelli's polished playing of the seven-string guitar in smart supper clubs around New York City.

In 1974, Norman Granz produced three albums that featured Joe Pass playing improvised fingerstyle jazz solos. These albums, along with Pass's exciting live performances, firmly placed the solo jazz guitar on a par with the jazz piano.

As the fingerstyle jazz revolution gathered momentum, fingerpickers in other fields came to the fore. Folk, country, and ragtime players like Leo Kottke, John Fahey, David Bromberg, Stefan Grossman, John Renbourn, Guy Van Duser, and Dave Van Ronk attained popularity. Jose Feliciano, Glen Campbell (pick and fingers), Jerry Reed, and James Taylor all reached star status through TV, recordings, and personal appearances. The fingerpicking movement blossomed.

Two popular contemporary players, Steve Howe and Ralph Towner, both well-trained musicians who are very much at home in rock, jazz, country, and classical music, sparked interest in both the jazz and classical guitar for a whole generation of young rock guitarists. Fingerstyle techniques spread through all branches of the guitar family.

The trend toward solo jazz guitar culminated in the late seventies with several widely varied albums. In 1977 former George Van Eps student Ted Greene made his debut album, *Ted Greene Solo Guitar*. Here Greene demonstrated a sophisticated harmonic sense, skillful use of voice leading, counterpoint, modern chord voicing, and Lenny Breau-inspired harmonics.

Howard Morgen   **137**

Jimmy Wyble went an entirely different route. He combined advanced harmonic and melodic concepts with counterpoint and improvisation on *Etudes*. And Frederic Hand, one of the new generation of concert guitarists, made an album that displayed both the classic repertoire and jazz, along with original compositions in both genres: *Frederic Hand Volume I*.

Using a very different format, studio and jazz musician Gene Bertoncini formed a duo with bassist Michael Moors. They successfully intertwined pieces from the classic repertoire with straight-ahead swinging jazz on *Bridges*.

In 1979 Egberto Gismonti, an exciting Brazilian jazz pianist and eight-string classical guitarist, played original Keith Jarrett–inspired piano compositions and contemporary guitar improvisations on *Solo*. The same year marked the much-awaited return of Lenny Breau with the release of three albums (some of which were originally recorded in 1977 and 1978): *The Legendary Lenny Breau, Now*; *Lenny Breau*; and *Five O'Clock Bells*.

Today the use of fingerstyle for contemporary chord voicing and contrapuntal playing is taken for granted by most jazz as well as pop players, especially the newer crop of fine jazz guitarists like Jack Williams, Mike Gari, Richard Boukas, and John Stowell, to name only a few.

And there are other signs of fingerstyle's popularity too. Several of the more recent publications for jazz guitar, such as Ted Greene's excellent chord books *Chord Chemistry* and *Modern Chord Progressions*, either assume or suggest that the books are to be played fingerstyle. In fact, many of the chord inversions in the Greene books, which were inspired by the electric pianolike voicings of great chord players like Ed Bickert and Lenny Breau, cannot be played without fingerstyle techniques. Fingerstyle has come of age.

Unforgettable Jazz Guitar

Jim Ferguson

Pick up a guitar and start playing jazz, and you're playing the music of Charlie Christian, Wes Montgomery, Django, Jim Hall—even people you've never heard. That's the way influence reaches down through generation after generation of creative work.

We're a lot more directly influenced, of course, by what we do hear. In this article originally published in JazzTimes, *Jim Ferguson asked a dozen top guitarists what single jazz-guitar recording had made the greatest impression on them, inviting them to pair a verbal dialog with the inevitable musical one.*

A jazz and classical guitarist, Jim Ferguson divides his time between performing, music journalism, arrangement and transcription, and teaching. He wrote the guitar-history entry and several bios for The New Grove Dictionary of Jazz. *For almost two decades he has contributed fine, perceptive pieces to magazines such as* Down Beat, JazzTimes, Guitar Player *and* Soundboard, *and he has annotated dozens of recordings, including Fantasy's* Wes Montgomery—The Complete Riverside Recordings, *for which he received a Grammy nomination.*

John Abercrombie

I've been really impressed with everything Jim Hall has done, but the album that had an amazingly strong impact was Sonny Rollins' *The Bridge* (RCA). The first tune, "Without a Song," especially changed my life and made me realize that there was more to playing guitar than playing guitar—there was playing music in the way Jim Hall accompanied and, of course, soloed. The initial rush of that tune was the way Sonny Rollins stated the melody while Jim added counter melodies and chords. When I first heard it, it was like a huge door had been flung open. Although I was very naive at the time, I immediately knew it was great. Up to that point, I had heard great guitarists like Tal Farlow and Barney Kessel who accompanied in block chords in a specific style, but Jim Hall all of a sudden seemed to say that there was a different way to play the guitar—one that was very anchored in tradition, but much more modern and fitting with the music around it.

Wes Montgomery's first Riverside record, *The Wes Montgomery Trio*, is also right up there. How he used his thumb to get such a fat, warm tone on " 'Round Midnight" was absolutely beautiful. I also love *Boss Guitar* (Riverside), which has an insane version of "Bésame Mucho" with so much melodic development. Recently, I noticed that he played little rhythmic games with melodies. I thought maybe I had invented that kind of thing because it was so advanced, but hearing Wes do it made me realize that nothing belongs to me. So anything Wes or Jim did changed my life and pointed the way to using the guitar as a real musical instrument.

Howard Alden

When I was 12 years old and just starting to improvise on the banjo, the single album that got me most interested in playing jazz guitar was *The Poll Winners* (Contemporary) with Shelly Manne, Ray Brown and Barney Kessel. I can't name a particular tune, because I listened to that album over and over to absorb the way the trio functioned and how Barney played chords and single notes and combined the two. Throughout, there's a beautiful continuity to the way his solos develop from chorus to chorus. When he punctuates with chords he almost becomes two people, playing a melodic line for a while and then accenting with a chord almost like a pianist's left hand or as if there were an orchestra behind him. Sometimes the chords are closely voiced and sometimes they are wide open. Right after that I was lucky to get exposed to tons of others, including Charlie Christian, Django Reinhardt, George Van Eps, Jim Hall and Kenny Burrell, but Barney's record was my biggest influence.

Charlie Byrd

Django Reinhardt's version of "Some of These Days" (original 78 issued on Vogue) had a great impact on me. I didn't even have a record player, so I used to take the record around to other people's houses to listen to it. It was the first virtuoso guitar playing I heard. I'd been playing for a long time when I first heard it, but I hadn't been playing anything like that! I still don't. Django's playing had such authority and made such a clear statement. It isn't that it's just technically precise, it's that his whole *intent* is precise.

I didn't get into fingerstyle by listening to any one piece. I became aware of classical guitar when I was living in New York. The first really good player I heard was Vincente Gomez, who played flamenco, original compositions and classical pieces. I also listened to Segovia and went to hear some of the players around New York like Rey de la Torre. Eventually I decided that I wanted to know something about it. I didn't know what was involved with trying to play both classical and jazz. If I had, I wouldn't have done it. I was young and foolish.

Larry Coryell

Yesterday I heard something on the radio that was incredible, but I have no idea who it was! I'm always hearing stuff that blows me away. But "D Natural Blues" (*The Incredible Jazz Guitar of Wes Montgomery*, Riverside) really got to me because it was one of the forms I could readily understand at the time; I was about 16 and couldn't improvise except to play a one or two-chorus break on a rock and roll song. Wes' playing was a brilliant improvisational tour de force, especially in terms of how it harmonically stretched the blues' limits. It made me try to take all of those phrases off the record. At the time I was also studying stuff by Johnny Smith, Tal Farlow, Barney Kessel and Les Paul, but "D Natural Blues" had an especially high level of improvisational creativity. Improvisation comes from *improve*, and Wes really improved the blues for me.

Sonny Sharrock

I've never been impressed by anything played on the guitar. The thing that started it for me was Miles Davis' "All Blues" (*Kind of Blue*, Columbia). When I first heard it I had been listening to jazz for about a year, and it seemed so dark and mysterious. Back then, you usually got introduced to jazz through something that was very popular, like Dave Brubeck. When I heard Miles, I hadn't started playing yet, but it made me want to be a part of this. Then I got into Coltrane's "Giant Steps" (*Giant Steps*, Atlantic) and all of his early classic quartet stuff. Then I moved on to Ornette Coleman, Cecil Taylor and Eric Dolphy. I was more into the newer cats, but I still like the Modern Jazz Quartet's melodicism. In other words, I like a mixture of the two sides, which is pretty much how it is now. There weren't any guitarists of that caliber then, and I don't hear anything like that now.

Scott Henderson

Several tunes made changes in my musical life. "What Is Hip?" (*Tower of Power*, Warner Bros.) brought funk into my jazz world, while the Mahavishnu Orchestra's "Birds of Fire" and "Celestial Terrestrial Commuters" (*Birds of Fire*, Columbia) brought jazz into my funk world and got me thinking that there were some other notes out there. Early on, the one tune that made the biggest impression was Led Zeppelin's "Whole Lotta Love" (*Led Zeppelin II*, Atlantic) with Jimmy Page. When I was a kid, that song somehow made it onto the radio and was the only one on the air at that time that had rock guitar. I just loved its sound and tone. It was so heavy. It made me want to play like that and made me do what I do now.

Peter Leitch

Three albums immediately come to mind: *Kenny Burrell* (Prestige), *The Incredible Jazz Guitar of Wes Montgomery* (Riverside) and René Thomas' *Guitar Groove* (Jazzland). René was particularly influential because he was the first guitarist I heard live; for a short while he lived in Montréal where I grew up. I also have to mention records that don't feature the guitar, like Sonny Rollins' *Saxophone Colossus* (Prestige) and John Coltrane's *Live at the Village Vanguard* (Impulse).

On all of the guitar records, the music is so strong and deep that it transcends the instrument; it doesn't matter what instrument those lines are played on. René swung hard and had beautiful tone. "Green Street Scene" has a particularly intense solo, while "Milestones" develops both rhythmically and linearly and still swings hard.

The Kenny Burrell record is from the '50s and has a great rhythm section: Tommy Flanagan, Douglas Watkins and Elvin Jones. "Don't Cry Baby" is a slow eight-bar blues with a wonderful rhythmic feel; "All of You" is a ballad on which he plays the first chorus rubato with chords. Wes Montgomery really comes out hitting on "Airegin." When I do workshops, I use his version of "Gone with the Wind" to illustrate how perfectly a solo can be built; he moves from single notes to octaves to block chords and then releases tension by going back to octaves but for very simple blues-based ideas almost like a big band shout chorus. Any instrumentalist could learn to build a solo by listening to that. When I first heard those, I was already fooling around with the guitar a little bit and had to find out what they were all about.

Lee Ritenour

Back in the late '60s, the first time I heard "Purple Haze" (*The Jimi Hendrix Experience*, Reprise) on the radio was a pretty amazing moment. Hendrix's sound was so incredible; it's still pretty powerful. It opened all the doors for a whole genre of guitar playing. I didn't become a big exponent of that style, but it certainly entered my life in a strong way during the fusion period that was coming together at the same time. I was a teenager in Southern California experiencing that avalanche of English players as well as groups like the Lovin' Spoonful and Canned Heat. When I heard Hendrix, I really got inspired to get out my solidbody. The Mahavishnu Orchestra's *Inner Mounting Flame* (Columbia) almost had the same impact on me— especially "Meeting of the Spirits," which was in 9/8. Then there were albums like Wes Montgomery's *Bumpin'* (Verve), Howard Roberts *Whatever's Fair* (Capitol), and *Duster* (RCA) with Gary Burton and Larry Coryell. Put those together and you have the sum total of my influences as a young guitarist.

John Scofield

No single record influenced me; there's too much good stuff out there. But when I started playing guitar, I had a Django Reinhardt album with "Somewhere Beyond the Sea" (*Djangology*, RCA), which was a ballad I had also heard Bobby Darin sing when I was real little. Hearing Django's version of a kind of pop song that I already knew didn't send me in any specific direction, but it represented the kind of jazz experience that was probably similar to what happened when people first heard Louis Armstrong and Coleman Hawkins play their stuff. Today, there isn't a connection between rock and jazz tunes. Not to put down rock, but it doesn't have those nice II-Vs to blow on. If a contemporary tune has vocals and II-Vs, it's considered to be old fashioned. I don't know if I consciously made the connection that you could take a familiar tune and use it to improvise on, but I know I like Django's version the best because he had such a beautiful, emotional, lyrical sound. Although I loved Django, I never became a follower, because it was an older style. After that, I started to pick up on Jim Hall, Wes Montgomery, Pat Martino and George Benson, so there really were a lot of records that affected me.

Tal Farlow

I suppose the one that made the biggest impression was "I've Found a New Baby" (original 78 issued on Columbia) with Charlie Christian and the Benny Goodman Sextet. I must have been about 18 and just getting an understanding of what jazz was all about. That record featured the very new sound of single-string electric guitar and was one of the better samples of how Charlie could construct a solo in such an excellent manner. Barney Kessel, Herb Ellis and a lot of others I've talked to were impressed with his playing, too. At the time, I was also trying to learn chord solos and stuff by Eddie Lang and Carl Kress. Back then, the sound of the electric guitar was new, and you can see the effect it's had on today's teenagers.

John Stowell

My favorite record is *Undercurrent* (United Artists) with Bill Evans and Jim Hall. It was recently reissued with an additional take of "My Funny Valentine," which gives you a chance to look at the creative process. Supposedly, the tune was used as a throwaway to set the levels, which is interesting because it's so marvelous. Essentially, Bill and Jim trade the melody with very little straight time. It's a great example of what Jim does because it contains all the different elements of his playing that I value so highly. It has compositional intent in the way he develops rhythmic motifs to create architectural structure in his solo. In the initial part of his solo, he takes a simple two-note motif and builds it conversationally with Bill in a way that is so interesting, musical and spontaneous. He puts that simple figure in different parts of the measure. Each time he pauses, Bill is there with a syncopation. At one point in one of Bill's solos, Jim turns his guitar down to where it's essentially acoustic and plays straight time, indicating that he was influenced by Freddie Green. It's an interesting twist because Bill essentially puts his left hand in his lap and solos with his right while Jim takes up the bulk of the accompaniment.

Jim emerged during a time when most of his peers were moved by the bebop vocabulary, but in one sense he took a step farther back and was influenced by swing players like Lester Young, Coleman Hawkins and Ben Webster. Somehow he combined that in a unique way with a more modern harmonic conception. It's a very personal voice. I seldom hear licks in his playing. Most of the time it sounds like pure melody. It's so compositional. With great solos, you can remove the backing and still hear memorable melodies and rhythms. Sometimes he plays an idea that is technically advanced, but he mostly uses technique as a tool, as opposed to something to bang the audience over the head with. He's grown over the years, but he was already very developed back in 1959 when the record was made.

Ralph Towner

Guitars are way down on the list of things that blew me away. Everything on *Sunday at the Village Vanguard* (Prestige) with Bill Evans, Scott LaFaro and Paul Motian influenced my playing more than any guitar record. It impressed me conceptually in terms of how to play with another person, the use of the bass, and harmony and melody.

As far as guitar playing goes, I would have to cite Julian Bream's *20th Century Guitar* (RCA), which has Benjamin Britten's "Nocturnal" and Frank Martin's "Quattre Pieces Breves." I don't know if it really blew me away that much, but his approach did make an impression. He made classical guitar sound not so much like a struggle. The most profound thing about the break Bream made from Segovia and Segovia-type guitarists was that his technique was so advanced that it released you from noticing a guitar was being played. In other words, you heard only the music. His phrasing was so legato that it was almost wind-like. When I first heard that album I played piano but hadn't really started with the guitar, and it represented my initial experience hearing a classical guitarist accomplish what I wanted to do. Electric guitar stuff hasn't had a huge influence on me, because it's such a drastically different instrument. I can't even imitate what electric guitarists do.

The Guitar

Joachim E. Berendt

Dizzy Gillespie once described jazz improvisation as "a gathering together of all the evidence you have of how to resolve going from here to here to here."

Any piece of music (like any poem or novel, or any painting) is in many ways an ongoing discourse with all that's gone before. Certainly on today's eclectic guitar scene there are almost as many ways to get from here *to* here *as there are guitarists hitching the ride.*

The essay below is from Joachim E. Berendt's The Jazz Book, *a marvelous one-volume (540-page) reference work first published in the '50s, profoundly revised and updated in 1992. Eminently readable and packed with information and insight, this piece is an ideal counterweight—a dialog or discourse, yes—to the Leonard Feather piece that opened* The Guitar in Jazz.

The history of the modern jazz guitar begins with Charlie Christian, who joined Benny Goodman in 1939, and began to play in the Minton circles shortly thereafter. He died in 1942. During his two years on the main jazz scene, he revolutionized guitar playing. To be sure, there were guitarists before him; along with the banjo, the guitar has a longer history than any other jazz instrument. But it almost seems as if there are two different guitars: as played before Charlie Christian and as played after.

Before Christian, the guitar was essentially an instrument of rhythm and harmonic accompaniment. The singers of folk blues, work songs, and blues ballads accompanied themselves on guitar or banjo. In the whole field of jazz prehistory—the field of the archaic, West African–influenced folk music of the southern slaves—the guitar (or banjo) was the most important and sometimes sole instrument. This was the beginning of the tradition that singers like Leadbelly and Big Bill Broonzy carried into our time, playing rich and long melodic lines that jazz guitarists per se discovered considerably later.

The surveyable history of the jazz guitar begins with Johnny St. Cyr and Lonnie Johnson. Both are from New Orleans. St. Cyr was an ensemble player, with the bands of King Oliver, Louis Armstrong, and Jelly Roll Morton in the twenties; while Johnson, almost from the start, concentrated on solo work. The contrast between the rhythmic chord style and the solo-type, single-note style that dominates the evolution of the guitar is emphasized from the very beginning in St. Cyr and Johnson.

The supreme representative of the rhythmic chord style of playing is Freddie Green, the most faithful of all Count Basie band members, from 1937 until the Count's death in 1984. (Green himself died three years later.) Indeed, what is meant by the concept "Basie" is in no small degree to Freddie Green's credit: the tremendous unity of the Basie rhythm sections. Nowhere else in jazz did rhythm become "sound" to the degree it did with Basie, and this sound, basically, is the sound of Freddie Green's guitar. He hardly ever plays solos or is featured, yet he is one of the most dependable guitarists in jazz history. Green is the only guitarist who surmounted the breach created by Charlie Christian as if there had been no breach at all. Green, by the way, has a very prosperous successor on today's rock, jazz-rock, funk, and soul scene: Cornell Dupree, who plays the kind of dependable rhythm guitar that Green has played for six decades in the Basie band. His playing, of course, is enriched by the many developments in the music since then.

Lonnie Johnson was the main influence on Eddie Lang, the most important Chicago-style guitarist, and he also made duet recordings with him. Lang came from an Italian background and reflects the tendency toward the *cantilena* and the *melos* of the Italian musical tradition noticeable in so many jazz musicians of Italian origin. The other important Chicago-style guitarist is Eddie Condon, more influenced by St. Cyr, purely a rhythm player and, until his death in 1973, the tireless guiding spirit of the Chicago-style scene in New York.

If you had heard everything played by these guitarists well into the second half of the thirties, and then had gone to Europe to hear Django Reinhardt, you would have understood the appeal that Django had. Django came from a gypsy family that had trekked through half of Europe and was mainly at home in Germany and Belgium (where he was born). Django's playing vibrates with the string feeling of his people—whether they play violin, like the Hungarian gypsies, or flamenco guitar, like the Spanish gypsies of Monte Sacre. All of this, combined with his great respect for Eddie Lang, came alive in Django Reinhardt's famed Quintet du Hot Club de France, consisting solely of stringed instruments: three guitars, violin, and bass. The melancholy strain of the ancient gypsy tradition lent a magic to Reinhardt's music; down through his last years (he died in 1953), he found his greatness in slow pieces. Often the very titles of his compositions capture the enchanted atmosphere of Django's music: "Douce Ambiance," "Mélodie au crépuscule," "Nuages," "Songs d'automne," "Daphne," "Féerie," "Parfum," "Finesse." In 1946, none other than Duke Ellington took Django Reinhardt on an American tour.

Django was the first European whose influence could be felt on the American scene, in countless guitarists. In fact, even a nonguitarist like pianist John Lewis named Django as a man who had influenced him through the climate of his music. Lewis named his composition "Django," one of the Modern Jazz Quartet's most successful pieces, in memory of Reinhardt. And even in the eighties, many guitarists showed allegiance to Reinhardt—in the United States, for instance, Earl Klugh, mandolin player David Grisman (see "Miscellaneous Instruments"), Larry Coryell; in Europe, French guitarist Christian Escoudé, Boulou Ferré, and Bireli Lagrene (all three from gypsy families), as well as the splendid and absolutely original Belgian guitar virtuoso Philip Catherine. It was above all Philip's sound that made Charles Mingus call him "Young Django."

The phenomenon of Django has often been cause for amazement. How was it possible for such a musician to emerge from the European world? In all probability, the only possible explanation—if one is not satisfied with the statement that Django simply was there—is sociological: European gypsies were in a social situation comparable to American blacks. Again and again, ethnic minority groups have been the sources of great jazz musicians: in the United States—besides blacks—Jews and Italians; and in the Europe of the thirties and forties, particularly Jews. Here too it once again becomes clear that authentic jazz, undictated by the music business, is a cry for freedom, whatever the racial environment and whatever the style.

Django's position as an outsider is somewhat related to that of Laurindo Almeida, a Brazilian musician of the rank of the great concert guitarists, such as Segovia or Gomez. Almeida employed the Spanish guitar tradition within jazz initially, in the late forties, as a member of Stan Kenton's band. The solos he played on some of Kenton's recordings emanate more warmth than almost anything else in the cold and glittering music of that phase of Kenton's development. Since the seventies, he has been one of the L.A.4, with altoist Bud Shank, bassist Ray Brown, and drummer Jeff Hamilton. They have been quite successful with their mixture of classical and Latin American music plus jazz.

Another guitarist who loves to mix different kinds of music is Charlie Byrd, who lives in Washington. He really is in command of everything that can be expressed on the guitar, from Bach to Brazilian bossa nova.

The connection of the Iberian baroque guitar tradition with the modern age (and also with a West African rhythmic feeling coming from the Yoruba tradition) was made even more convincing by the great guitarists of Brazil. The three best known are Baden Powell, Bola Sete, and Egberto Gismonti. Powell is the most original and rhythmically most dynamic of them. Sete, who has been living in the United States since 1960 and who played with Dizzy Gillespie, names Reinhardt and Segovia as his important influences. In the seventies, Gismonti appeared with Norwegian saxophonist Jan Garbarek and American bassist Charlie Haden. They played a kind of music that transcends style and geographical borders—world music in the best sense. As a writer, Gismonti has developed his own kind of chamber music, which intelligently combines classical and Latin American (especially Brazilian) music.

But back to Django Reinhardt (who also featured, in a totally different cultural environment but in a similar process of acculturation, many Ibero-Spanish elements). The melodic lines he initially played on unamplified guitar seemed almost to cry out for the technical and expressive possibilities of the electrically amplified guitar. Charlie Christian gave the electric guitar such renown that almost all guitarists switched from acoustic to amplified instruments at the turn of the thirties. Yet Christian was not the first to play amplified jazz guitar. First came George Barnes and Eddie Durham, the arranger, trombonist, and guitarist in the bands of Jimmie Lunceford and occasionally Count Basie. The earliest electric guitar solo we know of on record was played by Durham in Lunceford's 1935 version of "Hittin' the Bottle." In Basie's 1937 recording of "Time Out," the contrast between Freddie Green's rhythm acoustic guitar and Durham's solo electric guitar is charming. More recent guitarists as well—for example, Tal Farlow in the fifties, John McLaughlin in the seventies, or Pat Metheny in the eighties—have frequently made use of the possibilities for contrast between electric and acoustic guitar. As far as Durham and Barnes are concerned, however, they did not yet know how to exploit fully the potential of the electric guitar. They continued to play it as if it were the old acoustic instrument, only electrically amplified—as in the seventies many pianists initially approached the electric piano as if it were a grand, but with an electric sound. An outstanding musician was needed to recognize the new possibilities of the electric guitar. Charlie Christian was that man.

Christian is comparable to both Lester Young and Charlie Parker. Like Young, he belongs to the Swing era and to the pathbreakers; like Parker, he belongs to the creators of modern jazz.

Christian is the outstanding soloist on some recordings made privately at Minton's around 1941: "Charlie's Choice" and "Stomping at the Savoy." These records were later issued publicly and must be regarded as the first of all bebop records.

Christian charted new territory in terms of technique, harmony, and melody. Technically, he played his instrument with a virtuosity that seemed incredible to his contemporaries. The electric guitar in his hands became a "horn" comparable to the tenor sax of Lester Young. His playing has been described as "reed style"; he played with the expressiveness of a saxophone.

Harmonically, Christian was the first to base his improvisations not on the harmonies of the theme but on the passing chords that he placed between the basic harmonies.

Melodically, Christian smoothed out the tinny staccato that almost all guitarists prior to him had employed into interconnected lines that radiated some of the atmosphere of Lester Young's phrases. Not surprisingly, Christian had played tenor sax before becoming a guitarist.

Whoever comes after Charlie Christian has his roots in him. To begin with, there is the first generation of "post-Christian" guitarists: Tiny Grimes, Oscar Moore, Irving Ashby, Les Paul, Bill de Arango, Barney Kessel, and Chuck Wayne. The most important is Barney Kessel, who, as a member of the Oscar Peterson Trio and with his own groups, made many Swing-oriented recordings in the United States and in Europe. Strange how that which had seemed revolutionary in Christian appeared in Kessel, since the end of the fifties, conservative and not very daring. In the early fifties, Les Paul had an immense commercial success with recordings in which he overdubbed different sounds and tracks of electronically manipulated guitar voices. At the time, these techniques were put down in jazz circles as "extramusical trickery." Only from today's vantage point is it clear that—long before Jimi Hendrix and all the others about whom we will talk later—

Les Paul was the pathbreaker of modern electronic manipulation of sound. That is why, more than twenty years after his big successes, many young guitarists still refer back to him.

If Kessel could be designated the most rhythmically vital guitarist of the jazz of the fifties, Jimmy Raney is harmonically the most interesting and Johnny Smith the one with the most subtle sound. But before Raney and Smith comes Billy Bauer. He emerged from the Lennie Tristano school, and in the early fifties played the same abstract, long lines on the guitar that Warne Marsh played on tenor or Lee Konitz on alto. With Konitz, Bauer made duet recordings—just guitar and alto sax—among them, the slow, deeply felt "Rebecca"—one of the first duets in modern jazz that, even at that time, pointed toward the rich duo culture that evolved from the seventies. Jimmy Raney is also indebted to the Tristano school, but his melodies are more concrete and singable. Where Bauer played "dissonant" chords and pointed leaps in which the thresholds are barely exploited, Raney featured richly nuanced harmonies, whose interrelatedness seems rounded, logical, often almost inevitable. Johnny Smith unfolded these harmonies to the last note. A whole universe of satiated, late-romantic sounds evolved—the world of Debussy's *L'Après-midi d'un faune* brought into jazz; a fatigued, decadent faun who relaxes in the warm sun of late summer . . . or in "Moonlight in Vermont." The mood of this ballad has never been more subtly captured than by Johnny Smith.

All this comes together in Tal Farlow. Farlow initially stems from Raney, but with his big hands he had possibilities quite different from those of Raney, who only played single-finger style. After Tristano, and before Sonny Rollins, hardly any jazz musician swung such long, ceaseless, seemingly self-renewing lines above the bar lines of choruses, sequences, and bridges as Farlow. But these are not the abstract lines of Tristano; they are the concrete lines of early jazz classicism. It is regrettable that Farlow has withdrawn so much from the scene. Only George Wein, the jazz impresario, managed to lure him into occasional, albeit highly successful, appearances during the seventies. In the early eighties, he was reunited very successfully with Red Norvo, on records and in person.

Beyond the Bauer-Raney-Farlow constellation, yet inspired by it, stand the other guitarists of modern jazz: Jim Hall, Herb Ellis, Les Spann, Gabor Szabo, Grant Green, the early George Benson, Kenny Burrell, Larry Coryell, and finally the most significant, Wes Montgomery. Jim Hall—with his beautifully melodious, tuneful improvisations—gained renown, initially, through his work in the Chico Hamilton Quintet and in Jimmy Giuffre's trio; Herb Ellis, through his long cooperation with Oscar Peterson. Ellis often combines the stylistic elements of Christian with a shot of blues and country music (in which he has roots).

Jim Hall, when less and less was heard from the other great cool-jazz guitarists (Farlow, Raney, and Bauer), became a master of delicate, sensitive guitar improvisations that have long left behind the confines of cool jazz and, since the seventies, can be considered the truly ageless jazz guitar style. In this sense, Hall, who in the eighties made wonderful duo recordings with bassist Ron Carter, has become *the* timeless jazz guitarist par excellence.

Detroit-born Kenny Burrell could be designated *the* outstanding hard-bop guitarist, but he has grown in the most diverse directions, on electric as well as Spanish guitar. The steadiness of his improvisations is appreciated by many musicians. He has played with Dizzy Gillespie, Benny Goodman, Gil Evans, Astrud Gilberto, Stan Getz, and Jimmy Smith—which proves his versatility and openness.

The late San Francisco critic Ralph Gleason said that Wes Montgomery, who died in 1968, was "the best thing to happen to the guitar since Charlie Christian." Wes was one of three musical Montgomery brothers from Indianapolis (the others are pianist-vibraphonist Buddy and bassist Monk), who first became known in San Francisco. He combined a fascinating, at the same time almost inconceivable octave technique with hard and clear self-restraint, in statements in which the blues and the Charlie Christian tradition figured prominently— even when he moved into pop-jazz, as he did frequently during the last years of his life.

Wes Montgomery's development exemplifies the way in which so many jazz musicians become subject to the marketing process of the industry. His producer, Creed Taylor, produced him strictly from a market point of view, with string orchestras and commercial tunes. He did not even allow him to play the kind of music really near and dear to him on every third or fourth album, which would have been the least you could have expected, as critic Gary Giddins once remarked. In 1962, Wes said in a *Newsweek* interview, "I know the melody and you know the melody—so why should I turn around to lay the melody?" But only a few years later, he did nothing but play melody. Toward the end of his life, Wes said, "I'm always depressed by the result of my playing."

Wes Montgomery's legacy was carried on by many musicians, but especially so by two players who are diametrically opposed to each other: Pat Martino and George Benson, the latter in a commercial direction, the former in the opposite. Martino is one of the great outsiders on the contemporary guitar scene; he is one of the few players who have not only copied Wes Montgomery's octave technique but have made their own style out of it. George Benson, at first solidly within the great black guitar tradition, in the course of the seventies became the guitar superstar with recordings selling in the millions. Along with Herbie Hancock he was at that time the bestselling musician of modern jazz. Singer Betty Carter commented in a *Rolling Stone* interview, "It's like George Benson . . . the way he can play, why does he have to sound like Stevie Wonder to make money?" And Benson himself said, "I'm not there to educate an audience; I'm there to play for them." It is Benson's singing, of course, that made him so popular on records.

But we have advanced too far. In the meantime, a "guitar explosion," as the British *Melody Maker* called it, had taken place—a widening of the guitar scene by a factor of hundreds, if not thousands, within the span of a few years. Up to that point, the tenor sax had been the major instrument, now suddenly it was the guitar. Even psychologists have dealt with this phenomenon. Both instruments, they claim, are "gender symbols"—the tenor being a male symbol, the guitar, with its shape reminiscent of the human female figure, a female one.

Three musicians were the actual igniters of the sixties' guitar explosion, each in a different field of music: Wes Montgomery in jazz, B. B. King in blues, and Jimi Hendrix in rock.

B. B. King (more about him also in the section on the seventies) is the father of all guitar playing in rock and popular music of the sixties and seventies. He "rides" on the guitar sound: He lets it approach, jumps in the saddle and bears down on it, spurs it on and gives it free rein, bridles it again, dismounts, and jumps on the next horse: the next sound. It was King who fully realized the development that began with Charlie Christian: the guitar sound grew increasingly longer, was further and further abstracted from the instrument. Of course, this development began in fact before Christian: at the moment when first the banjo, then the guitar were used in African-American music. It leads straight from the metallic chirpings of the banjo in archaic jazz (so brief in duration one often could barely hear them), through Eddie Lang and Lonnie Johnson, who (still without electric potential) waged a constant battle against the brevity of their sounds, and via the saxophone style of Charlie Christian and the great cool guitarists of the fifties, to B. B. King—and from him, as we shall see, on to Jimi Hendrix. This development has a single goal: the continuous, determined elongation and the related individualization and malleability of the sound (which, however, as it became easier and easier to realize technically and electronically, finally began to lose its attraction). The aim of this development—the fact that one can do almost whatever one wants with the sound of the guitar, more so than with any other instrument—may have been the main reason for the immense progress and popularity of guitar playing in the sixties and seventies.

In the sixties and early seventies, B. B. King represented the apex of a development that points back to the history and prehistory of the blues. A particularly significant role in the transformation of the rural blues guitar into the "riding" guitar phrases of B. B. King was played by T-Bone Walker, who died in 1915. As we mentioned in the blues section, the South Side of Chicago has been a center of the blues tradition—with guitarists like Muddy Waters, Jimmy or "Fast Fingers" Dawkins, Buddy Guy, and Otis Rush. There is a white guitarist who stems from the Chicago school of guitar playing, influenced greatly by Muddy Waters, and who stands solidly in this tradition: Mike Bloomfield. About Otis Rush it is said that he carries on where B. B. King left off, playing the King style even harder and more charged with electric and emotional tension. Among the guitarists bridging the gap to rock are Albert King, Albert Collins, Jimmy Johnson, Luther Allison, Stevie Ray Vaughan, and, particularly successfully in the eighties, Robert Cray. Said Collins, "I wanted to play jazz. I wanted to sound like Kenny Burrell. . . . I've been known as a blues player, but I wanna be more than a 'rock-blues' guitarist." Cray epitomizes the new blues musician: a stylist who doesn't only play "down home" blues but is also a master of contemporary soul, funk, and rock, making clear their links with the source: the great legacy of black music.

The third great musician who, with Wes Montgomery and B. B. King, ignited the guitar explosion is Jimi Hendrix. Hendrix—born in 1947 as a "black Indian" in Seattle, Washington, died in 1970 in London as a world star—is surrounded by a halo of myths. Among instrumentalists, he was the real genius of the rock age of the sixties.

The exact cause of his death is still not entirely clear. An overdose of heroin, said the sensationalist press; suffocation in his own vomit was the coroner's verdict. "I don't know whether it was an accident, suicide, or murder," is what his friend, musician Noel Redding, said. And it is still unclear where all the money, certainly millions, that Jimi had earned with his music went.

Hendrix was the musical symbol of the counterculture of the sixties, comparable only to Bob Dylan. At the legendary Woodstock Festival, he shredded the American national anthem, but what he really meant was America itself. He ripped the anthem with machine guns, tore it to shreds with bomb explosions and the sound of children moaning.

Hendrix had strong links with jazz. Critic Bill Milkowski points out that at the end of his career the guitarist had grown weary of rock's simple forms and was devoting more attention to jazz. Hendrix jammed with Roland Kirk and later even with Tony Williams. He dreamed of a big band with vocal backing. Preparations were being made for working with Gil Evans when Hendrix unexpectedly died.

Hendrix has been dead for over twenty years, and there are half a hundred books about him. There are complicated analyses of his playing technique: his use of wah-wah pedals and whammy bars; how he used rings and bottle necks and occasionally even his teeth; how he played not only on his guitar but also "on" his amplifier, with switches and controls; how he retuned his instrument, fast as lightning, in the middle of a song, employing totally unusual tunings; the way he seemed to drum his guitar rather than pick it; the way he played with his own feedback, waiting for it and then answering it, returning it to the amplifier, as if asking questions that he then would try to reply to, which would lead to further questions. Often it seemed as if the feedback was his real partner, more so than the rhythm sections that never really satisfied him.

Jimi's actual accomplishment was to open the music to electronics. Electronics became his instrument, while the guitar served only as a control device. He was the first to explore the wide, unfathomable land of electronic sounds, the first to play "live electronics"—more than all of those who use this catch phrase today—and the first to transform electronics into music with the instinct of a genius, as if plucking the strings of an instrument made of waves, rays, and currents. Whatever can be called electronics in today's music—in jazz, jazz-rock, fusion, rock, and pop—comes from Jimi Hendrix. And that applies to guitarists as much as to electric piano and synthesizer players, and even to horn players who use electronics, as long as they employ them as more than a gimmick or a gag.

Jimi Hendrix spoke of his guitar as his lover. He got high just from playing it. But he also beat it, destroyed it, burned it—on stage. It was love and hate at the same time, a kind of sadism that was also masochism, as if someone were losing his mind, a lover who could neither give nor receive true love.

So these are the pillars of today's guitar playing: Wes Montgomery, B. B. King, and Jimi Hendrix. Many guitarists have built their structures on these pillars, but none as brilliantly as John McLaughlin. His range extends from folk blues and Django Reinhardt through the great guitarists of the fifties—in particular Tal Farlow—to the Indian sitar (see also the sections about jazz of the seventies, McLaughlin himself, and the combos of jazz).

McLaughlin has played the most diverse kinds of music—free jazz in Europe (with Gunter Hampel, for example), fusion with Miles Davis, highly electronicized music with his Mahavishnu Orchestra, Indian music with his group Shakti, solo guitar and duets with French guitarist Christian Escoudé. But whatever he plays cannot be thought of separate from his spirituality. "God," he said, "is the Master musician. I am His instrument."

McLaughlin's 1983 trio recordings with Al DiMeola and Spanish flamenco guitarist Paco de Lucia are an exhilarating feast of acoustic guitar playing, taken on the highly electronized fusion scene as a sign. Legions of "pure" acoustic guitar ensembles emulated the example set by this trio. Less successful was the reestablishment of the Mahavishnu Orchestra whose highly charged sounds seemed anachronistic in the eighties.

The guitar scene continues to explode. In order to get an even halfway correct picture, we can form the following groupings (remembering that they all blend into one another): rock, jazz-rock and fusion, folk jazz, free, free funk, no wave, cool, traditional, and neobop classicism.

Most directly rooted in Hendrix (and in the blues) are the rock players whom we can only mention summarily in this context: Eric Clapton, Duane Allman, Carlos Santana (who is influenced by Latin music and who has made recordings with McLaughlin), Jeff Beck, Adrian Belew, Robert Quine, Prince, and, perhaps the most individualistic rock guitarist of them all, Frank Zappa—to name only a very few.

In diametrical opposition stand those players who have transposed the tradition of the cool guitarists from the fifties to today's jazz. The most important of them, the one who was already active during those years, is Jim Hall, whom we discussed earlier. "The quiet American" is what *Melody Maker* called him when he appeared in London. And Hall himself has said, "Even though I never got to work with Lester Young, that's the sound I try to get from my guitar."

Other guitarists who deserve mention in this context are Hungarian-born Attila Zoller, Canadian Ed Bickert, and Americans Howard Roberts, Doug Raney (the son of Jimmy Raney, whose tradition Doug carries on), and Jack Wilkins. Zoller was initially indebted to the Lennie Tristano school. As the first among the guitarists, he transferred the long, singable melody lines he had learned back then into the freer realm of the new jazz, as in his collaborations with pianist Don Friedman. Zoller is a master of sensitive, romantic restraint, and it is hard to understand why a man of such talent is still known only to insiders. Bickert made recordings with Paul Desmond, the "poet of the alto saxophone," and Bickert's style is just as "poetic." Wilkins, perhaps the most talented of the younger guitarists of this direction, has become known through his work in trombonist Bob Brookmeyer's group.

Let's move on to the largest grouping, the jazz-rock and fusion guitarists. This grouping incorporates extreme positions: rock and blues on the one hand, cool and bebop on the other. This extensive group of jazz-rock guitarists falls into two almost diametrically opposed categories, with of course constantly fluctuating boundaries. On the one side the emphasis is on virtuoso playing with its sweeping gestures and expansive improvisations. That realm is predominantly shaped by older players who still phrase in the spirit of new departures and the striving for peak technical achievement that characterized early jazz-rock: musicians such as Joe Beck (who was chronologically the first), Larry Coryell, Eric Gale, Earl Klugh, Al DiMeola, Lee Ritenour, Allen Holdsworth from England, Holland's Jan Akkermann, and Finland's Jukka Tolonen. Younger masters have also pursued virtuosity in the eighties: most importantly Stanley Jordan, Kevin Eubanks, Robben Ford, Scott Henderson, Frank Gambale, Bireli Lagrene from France, and Germany's Michael Sagmeister.

Larry Coryell was already playing fusion music in the mid-sixties, when nobody even knew the term, in the Gary Burton Quartet and in the group Free Spirits. His major influences were Jimi Hendrix and John McLaughlin: "Jimi is the greatest musician who ever lived, as far as I'm concerned." But then he added, "I hate him, because he took everything away from me that was mine." And about John McLaughlin: "McLaughlin heard me in England, and I still hear some of my own style coming back at me. Then, when he came to the United States, I started listening to him. It's a two-way street." Coryell hails from Texas, which is his third major influence: "If you listen to me carefully, it must come through that I'm from Texas."

With keyboard player Richard Tee, drummer Steve Gadd, and the already mentioned Cornell Dupree on rhythm guitar, Eric Gale formed the successful group Stuff. At the outset of his career, Al DiMeola recorded a wonderful duet album, transcending all musical cultures, with the great Spanish flamenco guitarist Paco de Lucia; but he never subsequently fulfilled the promise of this duet. His brilliance, albeit very superficial, nevertheless continued to fascinate. Lee Ritenour probably is the busiest guitarist on the Los Angeles fusion scene. Allen Holdsworth, who emerged out of Soft Machine, has impressively transposed Coltrane's "sheets of sound" into jazz-rock guitar playing. With his IOU trio at the start of the eighties he made an important contribution toward a new, more economical concept of jazz-rock. Stanley Jordan revolutionized the technical aspect of guitar playing. As a street musician in New York his tapping technique attracted such attention that George Wein presented Jordan in the 1984 New York Jazz Festival. Since then Jordan's unaccompanied performances have been among the main attractions at all the big jazz festivals. Jordan doesn't pluck his guitar. He gets the strings to sound by tapping with the fingertips of both hands on the fingerboard just as if it were a piano keyboard. In fact Jordan says he developed this technique so as to attain the "orchestral" capacities of a pianist.

Jordan certainly wasn't the first person to develop "tapping" (also known as "hammering"). He was preceded by Jimmy Webster (who in addition wrote a guide to this way of playing), Eddie Van Halen, David Torn, and Adrian Belew. Those guitarists, however, used tapping merely as ornamentation and one playful method among many others, whereas Jordan is the first person to make this technique into the basis for his playing—with such rich polyphonic interweavings that you get the impression that two guitarists are playing here rather than one.

Critics have put Jordan on the same level as Wes Montgomery and Jimi Hendrix, but up to now Jordan has only revolutionized guitar playing technically, not stylistically. People also regret the thinness of his sound and the problems created by trying to integrate his polyphonic concept, so fascinating in solo appearances, into a group.

So much for the representatives of deliberately virtuosic jazz-rock playing. The other group of guitarists puts the emphasis on deliberately economical use of the guitar with less lavish, more concise phrasing, concentrating on what is essential. The early representatives of this way of playing included Larry Carlton, Steve Khan, Terje Rypdal from Norway, and German-born Volker Kriegel and Toto Blanke. But most of the stylists within this group come from the second and third jazz-rock generations, and their deliberately economical playing is a reaction to their precursors' overemphasis on virtuosity. Their number includes Pat Metheny, John Scofield, Hiram Bullock, Mike Stern, David Torn, and Japanese-born Kazumi Watanabe. Terje Rypdal paints pictures on his guitar, reminiscent of the fjords and dark mountain lakes of his Norwegian homeland. Hiram Bullock, first presented by David Sanborn and Gil Evans, plays a jazz-rock guitar full of droll humor and witty harmonic deviations. Steve Khan was also among the first fusion guitarists, but in the eighties he played purified jazz-rock that had shed all unnecessary pomp. His quartet with bassist Anthony Jackson, drummer Steve Jordan, and percussionist Manolo Badrena exerted an astonishing (and much too little remarked) reformist influence on the new jazz-rock. Mike Stern, who became known through Miles Davis, phrases flowing legato lines precisely on top of the beat, thereby gaining unusual drive and power. David Torn mixes Hendrix's wild, distorted sounds and Allen Holdsworth's complex harmonic sense, much influenced by ethnic music.

By far the most important musicians in this group are, however, Pat Metheny and John Scofield. Metheny is a magician of melody. He plays songlike, mellifluously sensitive, well-rounded lines, constantly renewing themselves from within and extending over a great dynamic range. His improvisations are founded on harplike, floating electric guitar sounds rich in harmonics—on his celebrated "Chorus sound," named after the device that duplicates the note being played at an octave's distance (as Wes Montgomery used to do "manually"). It's one of the most copied sounds of the eighties, but no one masters it so completely as Metheny. With other guitarists the Chorus sound is an effect; with Metheny it becomes an art. It is in his rare ability to make synthetic sounds seem "natural" that Metheny demonstrates

such sensitivity. Critics have found fault with the cloying character of his music and the rococolike ornateness of his arrangements,
much colored by Brazilian music (particularly through singer Milton
Nascimento). Even amid their tropical extravagance of weltschmerz,
kitsch, and sweetness Metheny's improvisations uphold that love of
clarity, homogeneity, and balance that have brought him a following
of millions. Of all the jazz-rock guitarists he is the most sophisticated
harmonically. His wealth of melody seems inexhaustible.

Pat Metheny was also the first person to play the guitar synthesizer
like an autonomous new instrument, beyond all sounds imitative of
keyboards and unlike his otherwise more ethereal playing: angular,
biting, penetratingly intense sounds. In "Endangered Species" (1986),
a recording from Ornette Coleman's album *Song X*, Metheny gained
an ecstatic element.

Metheny's playing of the guitar synthesizer fulfills the jazz guitarist's
dream of greater physical presence. The first step involved was the
changeover from banjo to guitar. Then came Charlie Christian's use
of the electric guitar, and next Hendrix's elongation of guitar sound.
And now with Pat Metheny the instrument (but only on the guitar
synthesizer) attains a new, augmented dimension of tonal penetra-
tion that actually achieves (rather than merely strives for) a hornlike
impact. Other musicians playing the guitar synthesizer include John
McLaughlin, John Abercrombie, Bill Frisell, and Harry Pepl from Aus-
tria. The extent to which Metheny's improvisations uphold both jazz
tradition (bebop, Jim Hall, and Wes Montgomery) and the country
music of his home state Missouri became clear when he recorded—
together with tenorists Dewey Redman and Mike Brecker, bassist
Charlie Haden, and drummer Jack DeJohnette—the *80/81* double
album, one of the most beautiful eighties jazz recordings.

John Scofield, who became known through playing with Billy Cobham and Miles Davis, transmits a strong feeling for bebop into the
jazz-rock context. He unites the legato feeling of Jim Hall and Wes
Montgomery with B. B. King's biting blues and funkiness. Scofield,
who also presented himself as a splendid neobop stylist, phrases jazz-
rock with a warmth and ardor that helped move this often cool realm,
dazzling with technical skills, toward an unanticipated revival, with
soulful, inventive improvisations. In the three years when he played
with Miles Davis he wrote a great deal of creative music for the
trumpeter. Scofield was as important for the "funky Miles" as Wayne
Shorter had been for his compositions in the sixties.

Scofield's wealth of unusual intervallic leaps and original runs influenced numerous eighties guitarists including Leni Stern, Mitch Watkins, French-born Marc Ducret, and John Schröder from Germany.

In some ways folk-jazz guitarists are related to jazz-rock players. That becomes particularly apparent in the music of Steve Tibbetts from Minneapolis. His magical sound paintings range from highly electronic, distorted, rocklike guitar sounds to the meditative acoustic tones of ethnic music (mainly Indian and Japanese). Independently of Hendrix he developed his own way of playing with extreme feedback. Considering how deeply rooted the guitar is in the ethnic music of many cultures, the existence of these folk-jazz guitarists is not surprising. Apart from Steve Tibbetts they include such different musicians as Alex de Grassi, William Ackerman, Leo Kottke, Ry Cooder, John Fahey, and Michael Hedges. Hedges plays a steel-string guitar and particularly relishes harplike, "open" string sounds full of a percussive quality.

Proceeding to the free guitarists, the first musician to play free-jazz guitar in the sixties was Sonny Sharrock, who played with Pharoah Sanders, Don Cherry, and the punk jazz group Last Exit. He was followed by Michael Gregory Jackson, James Emery, Eugene Chadbourne, Briton Derek Bailey, and Germans Hans Reichel, Uwe Kropinski, and Helmut "Joe" Sachse. Probably the most radical of these free players is Bailey; working on his instrument in all imaginable ways, he is one of the most original players on the European free-jazz scene.

James Blood Ulmer, who made his name in Ornette Coleman groups, has been more successful than anyone else in making the transition from free jazz to free funk. His concise, refractory, deliberately spluttering lines build a bridge from free jazz to funk, concretizing the former and musicalizing the latter. Ulmer's motto: "Jazz is the teacher: funk is the preacher."

Among the other important free-funk guitarists are Kelvyn Bell with his striking emphasis on "wiping" phrasing, Jean-Paul Bourelly who transposes Hendrix's sound into the unruly language of free funk, Bern Nix, Charles Ellerbee, and Vernon Reid.

Particularly original new sounds in the eighties came from the no wave guitarists, the players who most consistently pursued the demolition of stylistic categories in postmodern jazz. Although their origins are in free jazz, they transcend that by making numerous other fragments collide in their playing: punk and ethnic music, avant-garde and rock. minimal music and folk. Among the interesting guitarists here are Arto Lindsay, Henry Kaiser, Fred Frith, Elliott Sharp, Rhys Chatam, Franco-Canadian René Lussier, and German Caspar Brötzmann. Arto Lindsay makes the guitar sound like "a collapsing twenty-story glasshouse." He shaped such splintering, crashing, somber sounds when working with the Golden Palominos and alto saxophonist John Zorn; but Lindsay also commands the supple melodiousness of the music of Brazil where he grew up. In Henry Kaiser's playing the guitar is transformed (with assistance from computers, MIDI, rhythm machines, and other digital aids) into a "crazy" turbulent orchestra. There Kaiser batters and bends extremely disparate musical styles—Korean music and Delta Blues, Vietnamese traditions and punk, Captain Beefheart and Ali Akbar Khan—in such original fashion that these apparent extremes gain a degree of relationship. Fred Frith played no wave with the group Henry Cow as early as 1968 when that term didn't yet exist. He's an expert in collages, contrasting a broad spectrum of unfamiliar guitar sounds. René Lussier plays imaginary folklore full of droll humor. His lines often meticulously follow the course of linguistic patterns. Hence the vocal quality of his playing.

Diametrically opposed to the free and no wave players, to use another pair of contrasts, are the guitarists who remained connected with the Swing tradition. Among them are George Barnes (who died in 1977) and Bucky Pizzarelli, who formed a wonderful guitar duet; Cal Collins; Chris Flory; and the best known of them, Joe Pass. In the early seventies, Barnes co-led a quartet with Ruby Braff, in whose stylistic mold both he and Pizzarelli belong. Pass made recordings with many of the important jazz people of Norman Granz's Pablo label, among them Ella Fitzgerald and Oscar Peterson. He is a master of ballad playing as well as of swinging jam sessions. Like tenor man Scott Hamilton and trumpeter Warren Vaché, Collins is part of the new Swing movement that has been crystallizing since the end of the seventies.

Finally, the contemporary mainstream—which extends from bebop by way of Coltrane to classicism, where the all-dominant influence of Wes Montgomery lies—developed further within a large number of individual styles. John Scofield, Emily Remler, Bruce Forman, Joe Diorio, Joshua Breakstone, Peter Leitch, Henry Johnson, Rory Stuart, and others are among those who are a part of this mainstream. The best known is the already-mentioned Scofield whose trio—together with Steve Swallow (electric bass) and Adam Nussbaum (drums)—set standards for guitar groups in eighties jazz classicism, with its angular rock-and blues-imbued neobop improvisations integrated to an extent never previously experienced in such guitar trios.

Last of all, however, three particularly individual musicians, who don't fit into any of the leading groups, must be mentioned: John Abercrombie, Ralph Towner, and Bill Frisell. Since the mid-seventies Abercrombie has developed into a poet of contemporary guitar playing. He phrases sensitive, airy lines full of a chamber-music-like quality. His trio—with Marc Johnson (bass) and Peter Erskine (drums)—also attracted great attention in the eighties, illuminating the great timeless classics of American popular music in the spirit of the Bill Evans Trio. On the guitar synthesizer he plays massive, penetrating blocks of sound, which constitute a powerful contrast to the fragility of his actual guitar lines.

Ralph Towner, leader of the group Oregon, began as a pianist and still plays the instrument. His guitar style is molded by this piano element. Towner studied in Vienna, and he admits to not being quite sure which side he is more indebted to: European music—in particular music from Vienna, that is, Viennese classicism, romanticism, and avant-garde (Schönberg, Webern, etc.)—or jazz. "I wasn't on the jazz scene until I got a classically oriented technique on the guitar. . . . I do find acoustic instruments more sympathetic than electric instruments. . . . I treat the guitar quite often like a piano trio. If I'm playing alone, it's almost like a one-man band approach," he said.

In eighties postmodern jazz Bill Frisell is the guitarist with the greatest range: from Eberhard Weber's aestheticism to the free funk of the Power Tools trio, from the Bass Desires quartet's contemporary mainstream to John Zorn's noise music. No other guitarist negates the harsh percussive moment that occurs when striking a string so completely as Bill Frisell. His lines seem to come out of nothingness and to vanish back there again—floating sounds becoming louder and softer, a pearly chain of mellow legato notes sliding like wax dripping from a candle. Frisell played the clarinet before moving to guitar. Characteristically, it is the warm, wafting sounds of woodwind that made an unmistakable mark on his original style. Frisell "breathes life" into the jazz guitar. His lines combine elements of Jim Hall, Jimi Hendrix, and the pedal-steel guitarists of country music he heard in his home state of Colorado, creating one of the most original guitar styles in postmodern jazz.

The guitar has come a long way—from the African banjo to the instrument of John McLaughlin and Bill Frisell, from folk blues to the guitar synthesizer. Like the flute, the guitar is an archetypical instrument. The Greek god Pan, the Indian god Shiva, and Aztec gods have blown on flutes; angels and Apsaras (the female heavenly beings of Hindu mythology) have played guitars.

Six String Rapport

Jim Hall and Mike Stern

Bill Milkowski

 *Again and again I've insisted that music is, essentially, an ongoing dialog.*

Wes Montgomery, the first jazz guitarist to achieve wide popular success, and a guitarist square on the line of succession that began with Charlie Christian, died in 1968. In that same year Miles Davis used guitar for the first time on the cut "Paraphernalia" from Miles in the Sky; *George Benson, thought by many to be Montgomery's natural successor, was the guitarist. The following year Davis returned to the studio to cut* In a Silent Way *and* Bitches' Brew. *With him was John McLaughlin.*

Incorporating the improvisatory skills of the jazz musician with contemporary rock rhythms and electronic sounds, Davis brought a music rooted in jazz, for the first time, to rock audiences. Soon he was selling out rock halls like the Fillmores, and jazz (or jazz-rock, or fusion) was enjoying its greatest popularity since the swing era.

Jim Hall is one of the true giants of mainstream jazz guitar, one of the line of guitar players originating with Christian, flowing through Wes. Mike Stern came to prominence as one of Miles Davis's later guitarists, a young man who grew up idolizing Eric Clapton and Jimi Hendrix and playing Fender guitars.

Here, then, is a dialog in the truest sense: two men, separated by a generation and by musical background, coming together to talk about guitars and about the music that unites them (and which has the power to unite us all) in strangely timeless ways.

They are a generation apart. One grew up in the Midwest with heroes named Charlie Christian, Django Reinhardt and George Van Eps; the other came from Boston and as a kid idolized the likes of Eric Clapton, Jeff Beck and Jimi Hendrix. The elder statesman personifies a kind of walking-on-eggshells elegance while the younger plectorist can rip the back of your head off with his vicious blues-rock chops of doom.

Seemingly on opposite ends of the spectrum, and yet Jim Hall and Mike Stern have more in common than even they realized. Though the two guitarists had met briefly backstage at various jazz festivals over the past ten years, it was the occasion of this *JazzTimes* interview that brought them together for the first time to talk about their true love, the guitar. The following freewheeling conversation took place in the West Village apartment of Jim and Jane Hall.

BM: I understand that the two of you got together last week to get better acquainted before this interview, and you played some duets.

JH: Right, we played stuff like "Autumn Leaves," "Stella by Starlight."

BM: So you instantly had this common language.

JH: Yeah, it's very touching to me. I've played with guys in little towns in Italy where I couldn't get through a sentence with them, but they could play "Stella" and "Autumn Leaves."

MS: It's true. Knowing standards really is like having a common language. And for me, starting out as a rock player, it's a language that I had to learn. I remember hearing this stuff growing up. My mom used to play jazz records around the house and I wanted to get into that. I just loved the melodies and the feel. I don't know where that came from, I was just into it . . . that and, like, the Rolling Stones. It was kind of a weird combination but I was definitely into it. The trouble was, I couldn't play along with the records so I had to study a little bit more and learn how to approach that stuff. It was a little more complex harmonically. And the more I got into it, the more I loved it. I started really digging those tunes.

JH: Recently it really struck me that now there's a whole body of what has become standards that I don't even know. For instance, I don't know the Joe Henderson tunes that all my students play.

MS: Joe's got some tunes that he's been playing over and over again, like "Recorda Me" and "Inner Urge." They've all become new standards.

JH: Like the Wayne Shorter things. I've played with Wayne (*Power of Three*, Blue Note) but I don't really know his stuff. And the kids today go from "Stella by Starlight" to . . .

BM: "Footprints."

JH: Exactly, and it's all standards to them. But I sort of do what you described Joe Henderson doing. As a leader, I usually play maybe the same fifteen or twenty tunes for about two years and then I gradually add stuff. Mike, I just heard your *Standards (and Other Songs)* [Atlantic] yesterday. It's great, but I really loved hearing your new album [*Is What It Is*—Atlantic]. I love your writing, I must say. I like the standard album very much but I've heard standards before and I never heard your tunes. I've got a couple of tunes in that direction of your new album.

MS: Well, I think I probably copped them from you. I think one of your tunes that was really influential to me was "Careful," a diminished blues with a great line.

JH: I wrote that when I was with Jimmy Giuffre. It was supposed to be kind of like a swinging Monk tune and gradually it evolved into this kind of Greek blues with eighth notes.

MS: It's killin'.

JH: Well, I loved your writing. The harmonic content on your two ballads, "L Bird" and "Source" (from *Standards*), is gorgeous. And I really liked that tune "Swunk" on your new album. It's like juggling and trying not to drop things. It's got surprise and it kept my interest, and it was swinging too.

MS: That is what's really great about Jim. He's got that open-mindedness, which I hope I always have. It's so amazing to me . . . Miles was very open to stuff, Jim is open to stuff and Joe Henderson, who I've worked with lately, is also a very open-minded cat. We were talking about guitar players and I mentioned Stevie Ray Vaughan and Joe said, "Stevie Ray, man, is a mother-fucker!"

BM: And he once told me, "You wouldn't guess it, but I love James Brown."

MS: Yeah, and it doesn't seem to be any coincidence that we're talking about three giants . . . Joe, Miles and Jim. Guys that are open-minded.

JH: Well, to me it all has to do with self-expression. It's not just about staying in one period of music. And it isn't that you want to throw your values out the window. I do have certain values. As a matter of fact, I've walked out on players sometimes but usually it's guys that . . . I have a little problem with the born-again bebop thing that seems really regressive and kind of the opposite of what we're talking about.

MS: You know, I don't mind if someone says, "Whatever you're doing is cool, but this is where I want to stay . . . I just appreciate bebop." But there's certain people that are putting down the other stuff. I can't see where that's in any way really helpful. I mean, if you don't like it . . . don't buy a ticket, don't buy the CD. Why put the other stuff down?

JH: It probably comes out of fear in a way. I knew some really giant players who were kind of like that. I won't even say who . . . they're gone anyway. But I'm talking about great players who were, for instance, confused and bugged by Ornette Coleman. Threatened, I guess.

BM: I think Hendrix had that effect on a lot of people. He came along and kind of usurped their scene, obliterated their whole vocabulary.

JH: Well, maybe it's good that I seriously never feel like I've learned the guitar. There's nothing to obliterate there, so I might as well keep at it. In fact, I've been practicing today trying to get alternate picking together . . . after hearing this guy (Stern) with those chops.

MS: Part of the thing of the standards, for me, is just exploring many different kinds of musical styles within some kind of realistic parameters. Because I'm not one that can spread himself too thin and stay with each style as deeply as I wanna get into it.

JH: Yeah, I also am not able to spread myself too thin. For instance, I love Brazilian music but I can't play it at all. I'm a real gringo. Just the feeling . . . to me it's so subtle, what the real Brazilian guys do.

MS: I knew this cat from Berklee who was from Brazil and he was trying to show me the real way to comp with the fingers and everything. I can't get that stuff, man.

JH: I can't either. I was there in 1960 with Ella Fitzgerald. The bossa nova was just coming in and we used to go around and hear a lot of groups down there. I'd watch and get a handle on what everybody was doing, and just when I thought I had it, they'd move it all around. The phrasing, the note placement, the time feel . . . it's something you absorb just from living down there.

BM: It's like Louis Armstrong said, "If you have to ask, you'll never know."

JH: Well, I'm gonna ask anyway, I don't care. But I think what helped me was . . . and this sounds like a contradiction . . . having gone through music school helped to broaden me because I heard so much music. For instance, I didn't even know about Mozart. I came from sort of a hillbilly background and then it was jazz, Charlie Christian. And then I heard Hindemith and thought that was great because it reminded me of Stan Kenton's band. But I still thought Mozart was silly stuff. Then I got into school and now I think Mozart is a miracle. But I also heard Gregorian chant and 12-tone music and the beginnings of electronic music, and I think that all helped to give me a feeling about music as not just Charlie Parker or Charlie Christian or John Coltrane or something, but that it was something much bigger than any one individual.

BM: Jim, what kind of music did you hear in your home growing up?

JH: The first music that I remember was my uncle Ed, who used to sing "Wabash Cannonball" a lot. He played the guitar and was always drunk and had ladies around him all the time and I thought, "That looks pretty good." So I started taking guitar lessons and got into a little group in school. The guy who led our group was a clarinet player and I still remember the scene . . . we went to this record store to hear a Benny Goodman record. I was 13, I guess. And hearing Charlie Christian just turned my life around. And there were also some excellent players around town . . . Benny Bailey was around and Eugene Heard, who was a drummer with Erroll Garner for a while. Tadd Dameron was from Cleveland. So I did hear some good stuff early on. And by the time I was in my teens, that's what I was doing. But as a kid, I really didn't hear much jazz around the house. My mom kind of hated jazz. I think it was too sexy for her. So I'd wait until she went to work before I'd play these records I had hidden away.

BM: Midwesterners are notoriously intimidated by sexuality.

JH: You're telling me . . . and I'm one of 'em. But anyway, I got to hear a lot of different music growing up. There were some great gypsy orchestras. There was a large Hungarian population in Cleveland and they had all these great orchestras . . . two violins, one playing rhythm and the other guy playing melody. Real Hungarian folk stuff with great bass lines.

BM: Jim, do you have any vivid memories of your first time in New York?

JH: Yeah, the first time I came to New York with Chico Hamilton, we played opposite Max Roach with Sonny Rollins, Clifford Brown, Richie Powell and George Morrow. In some ways, I think I was too naive to be petrified. And one time Richie brought his brother by. I'm up there playing and I look out and there's Bud Powell in the audience. That was pretty heavy. It's good to be naive sometimes. In fact, I didn't even know how great Sonny was when I went to work with him until after the first rehearsal. Then my jaw dropped. I did a concert with him two years ago in Carnegie Hall. I hadn't played with him in 20 years and the same thing happened. As soon as he started playing, my jaw dropped. You're watching the guy playing and you still don't believe it.

BM: How as artists do you continue to challenge yourselves?

MS: One way, for me, was to check out this other kind of music (standards) rather than what I was initially into, which was more rock stuff and more straightahead blues stuff. Another way more recently is to try and write more. And that comes out of a combination of different elements. It's not necessarily a label; I don't much like labels anyway. You know, once you listen to it, it is what it is. But I think writing is really the main way I push myself today.

It's actually a more revealing act to put your own stuff across as opposed to relying on the safety net of standards.

MS: Well, playing standards wasn't so easy for me. Doing any of this always has some element of risk, and I'm always scared. And to think, "I wonder if so and so is going to like this" . . . that always goes through my mind and I have to tell myself, "Just do the best you can and be honest with it and play from the heart." So I put some time into it and put some effort into it and after that, who cares what anyone thinks? There's nothing more I can do than that. But that's a big part of the work involved for me is getting over that fear. 'Cause I have that big time.

BM: A lot of great artists have had to conquer fears. Laurence Olivier talked about being scared right up to the moment he walked on stage.

JH: Well, that's a good feeling, in a way, because having fear probably means you care then too. It's not exactly fear but it's some kind of thought that runs through your head . . . .

MS: Sometimes it's fear . . . no question about it. And I have to push past it. When I was in Boston and was about to play my first gig playing standards, I really couldn't even get it happening. It was a very conscious thing. I was still trying to make the changes and was naturally pretty scared. And it was Pat Metheny who helped me get through it. I was studying with him at the time and he was always very supportive. I was hitting all the wrong notes and he'd keep encouraging me. I remember being scared about this first gig in some dumpy little place in Boston and he said, "Just do it. You gotta push past it." Mick Goodrick also helped me a lot. It was like the best lesson I think I've ever had. It seems to be a little bit easier nowadays but as soon as I'm at a certain point with every record, I get panic-stricken and I have to get past it. But the *Standards* project was actually less so because the whole thing went down so fast. It was live, no overdubs. The other ones you have to tinker with some more . . . a few more overdubs so you can agonize more about it. But Steve Khan had the best advice: "Whatever record you're doing, just try to make it as fast as possible, and don't look back."

BM: It's easy to get lost in second-guessing in the studio.

MS: Definitely. That can paralyze me. You can really take the spontaneity out of a session if you get too obsessed with cleaning up the mistakes and making things just right. So you sometimes have to know when to let go. It's tricky.

JH: Yeah, just to let it go and forgive yourself.

BM: Jim, you probably had to address these questions on your solo project, *Dedications and Inspirations*.

JH: Well, I never thought I would do a solo album partly because, frankly, I find solo guitar boring after about ten minutes . . . even really good classical players. And again, my wife was really supportive and the company (Telarc) liked the idea. I thought about it for a long time and at first I wasn't going to do any overdubs because to me overdubbing has some kind of killing effect on music. I can almost tell when things are overdubbed. And when I've overdubbed on top of rhythm sections, like on some of the CTI things I've done, it can get very disorienting because I'm so used to reacting to live musicians. So for this solo project I figured I'd write a bunch of music and try to make it interesting to myself. But I was really concerned. I got really depressed right before I did it and I scuffled with that for three days. I did a concert with Pete Bernstein . . . two guitars . . . the night before. And Pete plays so great. In a way, that was a drag too because he sounded great and I was still depressed. But I got through it.

MS: For me, the more I know, the harder it is to get the analytical part out of the way. You gotta just listen from the heart. It's hard to assess music because I feel differently about it from day to day, from hour to hour. There's times when I wanna hear Trane and there's times when I wanna hear the Beatles, and with equal love for them. They're maybe coming from a very different place but it feels like the energy level is the same . . . the way I get off on it is the same. And sometimes it can be intellectually the dumbest stuff in the world and I might like that the best. And what am I gonna do, argue with my heart? If somebody's playing their heart out, who cares what key they're in.

JH: Either it reaches you or it doesn't. I was in Athens once with Ron Carter, and we were taken to this supper club and they were playing this kind of commercial Greek music, but it was this really complicated stuff and the people would clap with it at the end of phrases. And that really reached me. In Spain I heard some flamenco music where the people would clap along with it . . . I don't mean applauding, I mean getting involved in it. Really complicated rhythms that everybody instinctively knew.

BM: Mike, you mentioned Hendrix as a big influence. Did you ever get a chance to see him play?

MS: Yeah, I saw him at the Baltimore Civic Center. It was so great. I mean, he had such a loose way of playing. Just time-wise, he was singing with his guitar.

JH: I love B. B. King that way too. As a matter of fact, I would rather hear B. B. play about four notes than hear most guys play all night. He just really reaches me.

MS: He nails it. But Jimi . . . that was some other stuff. That knocked me out, totally. I remember listening to that first album forever. And the thing is, you still hear that stuff on the radio today and it's still totally current to my ears. Kind of timeless . . . amazingly hip.

BM: And now people have been reinvestigating his composerly side and checking out his whole harmonic approach.

MS: That's funny because you know he wasn't thinking like that when he was doing it. It's like Miles. When I joined the band I thought we'd be talking about Stockhausen and all these heavy intellectual cats. But he was just so straight ahead. He'd say things like, "Play the black keys . . . now play the white keys." I mean, it wasn't exactly like Einstein, you know what I mean? And he used to say, "That's all it is. We're just gonna do this and that's all it is." And I'm sure that's the way he approached "So What" or something like that. "That's all, just play it." You know, it's simple. And it's killing.

JH: Yeah, E=MC^{hip}.

BM: Jack DeJohnette once told me that he'd ride around in Miles' Ferrari listening to Buddy Miles tapes. Miles wouldn't say anything the whole time. Then after the drive, he'd say, "So, you understand?"

MS: He did that with me but it was with flamenco guitar. He'd say, "I want you to play like that, but *your* way." Meaning, don't get an acoustic guitar, play with a Stratocaster but with that flamenco attitude, which is all he was ever really concerned about anyway. He had a feeling for real earthy music. It was never too intellectual with him, from my experience. He'd just check things out for the feeling. I really love the fact that Miles would just take a little bit of something . . . maybe just the attitude or a kind of a feel . . . instead of getting deep into the thing. It would just have a kind of color of that thing. And he'd combine it with some other stuff and make great music with it.

JH: Miles is really the guy that I have to respect in so many ways . . . him and Duke Ellington. I never knew Miles well, I never played with him. But for his genius at picking musicians to be around and then trusting them . . . like Mike said, "Just do it your way." That's what Duke did. He picked these guys and then just trusted them to do something with his music. I was around Duke Ellington a little bit. I'm sure he was a very intellectual guy, but he was also very direct. Buddy Collette once told me about when he was in the studio with Duke working on the *Anatomy of a Murder* soundtrack. They had all this music spread out in the studio. It was hard as hell and everybody was complaining, and Jimmy Hamilton says, "I can't play this." Duke comes over and says, "Just do what you can." And Buddy said when the downbeat started, what came out wasn't what Duke meant exactly but it was great anyway. Miles and Duke were kind of the same in that regard.

MS: Miles used to talk to me before the shows. He'd say, "I know you're nervous. So am I, but fuck it." He'd talk about the anxiety.

JH: That was very nice of him.

BM: Jim, can you talk about Bill Evans?

JH: I knew Bill when he was working with Tony Scott in the quartet with Paul Motian and Les Grinage. They were playing in Chicago and I was there with Chico Hamilton. At the time, Bill was playing somewhere between Bud Powell and Lennie Tristano. He wasn't quite focused yet. He was playing Bud Powell stuff but maybe more across the barline. Anyway, I knew Bill for a long time. Chico's band worked opposite Miles a lot so I saw the impact he had on that group and vice versa. And as Bill started working more as a leader, he really started to coalesce his ideas. What I heard from Bill and felt and which really influenced me was first of all his harmonic sense but secondly what he did within a phrase with dynamics. In those days, most of the guys . . . jazz had sort of gotten like boxing. It was all bebop and pretty heavy stuff. And Bill seemed like he was not afraid to bring another, almost effeminate dimension, if you can put it that way, to jazz. That didn't scare him at all. He could use that foot pedal and make it seem like Debussy or Ravel or something. So to me, he brought a different dimension, certainly to piano playing, than what had been there before. I'm not denying what Tatum did, but Bill . . . .

MS: Definitely. Him and, of course, Miles had that same quality . . . so vulnerable, so lyrical. It still had guts but it had that more effeminate, lyrical approach.

JH: Miles could play silence better than most guys can play notes. And I got real mad at some of his detractors who put him down for his electric phase, talking about how you could tell when he went down the drain by the way he was dressing and stuff. I got furious at that. They got some nerve. I feel like in jazz we're all in the same family and that was like attacking someone in my family.

MS: Plus, Miles was so into that electric stuff. People said, "Oh, he's just selling out." Meanwhile, he was offered a lot more money to play acoustic and he was shlepping the synthesizers all over the place. And I'll tell you, man, that's a lot of bread to take that shit on the road. But he was serious about it, I know he was. He used to listen to tapes of our gigs all the time. Sometimes I'd think "Gee, I wish he'd play the other stuff too," just because I love that aspect of his music. But it seemed like he was so into what he was doing at the time that he'd never go back.

JH: Oh, he's a real artist. You wouldn't tell Picasso, "You gotta keep doing that Blue Period stuff. They were selling good . . . make some more."

MS: Jim, I gotta ask you about those duet records you did with Bill (*Undercurrent*, United Artists, and *Intermodulation*, Verve). When I first got into jazz, those were the ones I just absolutely loved. I was just wondering how you guys approached that.

JH: They were definitely Bill's dates. I mean, he was in charge.

MS: What about "My Funny Valentine" (on *Undercurrent*). Was that just 'go for it'?

JH: Yeah, we just did that. And in fact, there's a CD out with another version of "My Funny Valentine," which was slower and kind of funky. The producer wanted all ballads on the date. We did "I Hear a Rhapsody" real slow because most guys were playing it uptempo and we did "My Funny Valentine" real fast because everybody played it like a ballad. For quite a while after Bill died, I couldn't listen to those things. It was tough. But as I listen now I can hear, especially on "Funny Valentine," I can hear him bailing me out time after time. 'Cause I was scuffling trying to get into that solo with no rhythm section. And he's just sort of laying back, and you'll hear me pause and hear him sort of take me by the hand and lead me into the next phrase. He was such a great accompanist and real easy to play with. "Turn Out the Stars" on the second album (*Intermodulation*) . . . that's a tough tune. It's a beautiful tune. It sort of goes from the beginning and when you get to the end of it leads right back to the beginning perfectly. But we didn't really rehearse for those sessions. I think I went up to his apartment once. That was it.

MS: I just get a sense of . . . the influence I hear or the real common denominator between the two of you besides just the feeling . . . just two amazingly soulful players . . . there's that clarity of that kind of a compositional approach to the solo. Is that something you were influenced by in his playing?

JH: Some of it probably came from music school because I did a lot of writing there where I'd think about taking a little bit of material and stretching it through a piece. And it became, and still is, a fun thing for me to do . . . like building a model airplane and seeing if it'll fly. So I was kind of aware of that. And also I have this problem with clichés. I don't know what it is, it's almost an obsession. So for me, taking a short idea and stretching it out is one way for me to avoid clichés.

BM: How did you and Bill Evans avoid getting in each other's way on those duet sessions?

JH: Well, Bill just had so much common sense and musical sense. There's long stretches on "Funny Valentine," for instance, where he doesn't use his left hand at all because he just knew that I had that part . . . if not covered, at least I was playing down there. I think he just sort of sensed it. I'm sure we talked about it a bit. He liked the way I played rhythm guitar and when I was doing that he would just play with his right hand. Obviously he had such a strong sense of texture about what would clutter it up and what would keep it clear. I think I was working with Sonny Rollins when we did the first one, but before that I had been with Jimmy Giuffre . . . and for a while it had been just a trio with Bob Brookmeyer and Jimmy, so I was playing rhythm all the time. But I guess we didn't talk about it too much.

MS: And it seems like the time feel is definitely there between the two of you. You were breaking up the time a lot, especially on "My Funny Valentine." That's hard about a duo . . . the first thing that's got to be comfortable, I think, is the time feel more than anything. That's why when you add a drummer, he's the cat you gotta deal with first. He controls the dynamics, to a certain degree. Do you talk to the drummers much, about the attitude of the tune or whatever?

JH: Yeah, but that's backfired a few times. Depending on the person, the more you talk the worse it gets.

MS: That's true too. I've had that experience where somebody says precisely what they need from me and I get too self-conscious to play. But the time seems so crucial. And between you and Bill, it was just magic.

BM: It's that whole element of trust.

JH: Yeah, I really think that's a key word . . . trusting each other.

MS: Did you ever hook up with Wes?

JH: I knew him, yeah. He was great and had a terrific sense of humor. He was at the old Half Note on Hudson with Mel Rhyne and I was in listening to him. Wes had just ordered his dinner and it was time to play so he asked me to sit in for him. I didn't even have a guitar pick so like a dummy I played two or three tunes with my thumb. And then I made this joke once . . . he would always come to hear me when I was with Sonny Rollins. And one time I went to see him in San Francisco, we were hanging out, sort of taking taxis around San Francisco, getting something to eat. So I made a joke about it. I said, "Yeah, I was trying to catch his thumb in the taxi door," and somehow that's gotten repeated and it's starting to sound serious. But we were great friends. I asked him one time about practicing and he says, "No, I never practice. I open the case once in a while and throw in a piece of meat."

MS: I like that image.

JH: But you know he practiced a lot. And Wes told me he had a bunch of different jobs back home in Indiana because he was taking care of his family for a long time. He had been a lifeguard and some other things. And I asked him, "Well, what do you do if someone gets in trouble out there in the water." And he said, "Look the other way . . . they'll get out."

BM: Somehow I can't picture Wes floating too good.

JH: Me neither.

BM: What other guitarists do you admire, Jim?

JH: There are a lot of guitarists around who can do things that I can't do, like Mike. I loved Jimmy Raney's playing and Tal Farlow's playing and Billy Bean's playing and Chuck Wayne's playing. Chuck can play classical guitar, he can pick as fast as anything I've ever heard, he can play with pick and fingers, he can harmonize any tune, he can do anything. Really an astounding player. I sat next to him in a big band . . . it was on the Merv Griffin show, a pretty grim job. We had two guitars for some reason and I learned so much from Chuck about the guitar just by sitting next to him. I can't do it myself, but I noticed that he could do it. I also recently saw George Benson sit in with Lou Donaldson and, man, my life flashed before me. But I can't do what they do.

MS: Sometimes finding your own voice is defined as much by what you can't do as what you can do. You have to let whatever your voice or signature is . . . just let it be instead of trying to shape it too much. Because for a while I was trying to sound like other people. I was definitely trying to sound like Jim.

JH: And I was trying to sound different from Jim.

MS: It's funny, because at the same time you wanna push yourself to try different things but it's a tricky thing . . . you gotta let go to just let your signature be there.

BM: When you speak about your signature, what things play into that?

MS: Choice of notes, how many you might play, how few, and where you put it in the time. Also your tone is definitely part of your signature, the dynamics, the feeling. It's all a combination of all that.

JH: For me it's also involved with how I plan a set of music as a bandleader . . . what tunes I want to play. For instance, I still love playing "Body and Soul." There's a couple standards that I just love, but at the same time I love playing some "out" things and some kind of funkier things, more in the direction of what Mike does. Maybe some other leaders would have it more kind of all the same, but there's a lot of things that I like in music, so I try to present that in a set. And maybe even do a calypso . . . I can't really play it authentically but I just love the feeling of it. For me, that's part of my signature.

BM: Can effects get in the way of developing a voice?

MS: You gotta be careful of that stuff. Effects has kind of a life of its own, it's an independent part of the sound. So you gotta choose it carefully. And there's a lot of stuff out there and it can detract from the warmth of the sound, but sometimes some stuff enhances it. Most importantly, it's whatever makes you feel comfortable. Like if the amp isn't set right and it sounds gritty or there's too much pick noise, that drives me crazy. Of course, some people want more of that. Miles used to tell me, "Yeah, play real caustic." Whatever your sound is in your head, if whatever effects you're using helps you get it and makes you feel comfortable, that's cool.

JH: If I ever feel like I need an excuse for using an effect, I think of Duke Ellington. I mean, he used mutes and wah wah trombones . . . that's where the term came from, I guess. Actually Larry Goldings told me about this (Digitech) Whammy pedal. I was trying to get minor seconds like Don Pullen does so magnificently on his tune "Jana's Delight," and that's really hard to do on guitar. So finally Larry said, "You know, you can get an effects pedal that will probably do most of that for you." So I bought this thing and set it for thirds and that's kind of how I got into it. Bob Brookmeyer wrote a piece in the early '80s . . . we did it with the Stockholm Radio Orchestra . . . for orchestra and guitar. And he had me using a wah wah pedal and distortion pedal and chorus pedal. I loved the chorus, so I kept that and continue to use it. But in general, I find that if you can use them as tools and for orchestration and not think that they're gonna make you a zippier player, that can really be helpful. It can enhance a certain mood, it can throw my brain into a different frame of mind and different ideas come out from what would come out if I played it on acoustic guitar. I love acoustic guitar and I like to play softly, but soft can get boring as hell. So I like to have some kind of range of dynamics where I get pretty loud, just to keep it interesting. I have a low giggle threshold and a low boredom threshold.

BM: What was your experience with Ornette Coleman like?

JH: I've always loved Ornette's playing and his music. I never thought I could play with him. I never considered that. But then he asked me to play on something that he did for a woodwind group . . . I don't know if it ever came out. It was for Columbia. He wrote this thing . . . he didn't even transpose any of the parts. He just wrote out the parts . . . had Cedar Walton and Billy Higgins and Charlie Haden and me. Cedar and me were sort of like the straight men in the group. But I love Ornette. I love his writing. To me, he's got so many components to his music. He's got humor, pathos, chops, blues feeling, he's got everything. I got a kick out of being around him. Paul Desmond liked Ornette a lot. Paul was also very open-minded about music.

BM: Is there anything about Mike's playing or his concept that you want to ask him about?

JH: Yeah, I wanna get some of your tunes. Ideally, I would like to transcribe them myself. I really loved "L Bird." Harmonically I think they're gorgeous. And "Lost Time" had a great bass line. Did you write that?

MS: Yeah, that's kind of how I approach stuff for the trio . . . trying to have a really strong bass line and strong melody line and hopefully that's enough harmony . . . and not have to fill too much with chords. It's a little restrictive but for trio you gotta have that.

JH: You know Bill Finnegan, from Sauter-Finnegan? He's one of my best friends, and he said if he started writing now he would try to write mostly three lines. And he wrote for these giant things, Glenn Miller's band and Tommy Dorsey's band. But it's pretty much what you said, it can boil down to three good lines.

MS: Well, I'm flattered.

Ralph Towner

A Chorus of Inner Voices

Charles Mitchell

 *Guitarists generally, perhaps jazz guitarists particularly, tend to be mavericks. Yet oddly enough, the guitarist who is most squarely in a tradition may be the hardest to characterize. With a technique honed by many years of classical study here and abroad, Ralph Towner plays highly original, jazz-informed music on classical and twelve-string guitars. He also composes prolifically, plays trumpet, French horn, and piano, and was a founding member of the landmark improvisational ensemble Oregon.*

Towner is among the most intriguing guitarists, and among the most unusual jazzmen, to have emerged in recent years. Oregon has proved a major influence on contemporary acoustic, jazz, and improvisational groups. This article in turn, both for its thoughtful discussion of playing guitar in solo and in ensemble settings, and for its insights on improvisational music, is one of the finest pieces I've seen. A fitting end, then, for this multivoiced book on guitar, on jazz, and on improvised, traditional, Afro-American, American-European music.

The sound is elemental, formed of metal and wood—a guitar sound, not the white-hot electronic synapse-screams one is accustomed to within the realm of contemporary improvised music. The playing is jagged, deliberately voiced, with rushing lines linking together harshly plucked, semichordal string groupings. Yet there is a coherent, stable rhythmic sense implied.

Ralph Towner's playing on the opening section of Wayne Shorter's "The Moors" (from Weather Report's *I Sing the Body Electric*) cast him briefly into the spotlight on one of the most important fusion music sessions. Listeners were set on edge for further development of the acoustic direction implied by Towner's captivating acoustic twelve-string textures. The cults had been forewarned, as usual, by Ralph's work with the Paul Winter Consort, represented on disc by *Road*, one of those albums that turns up) in quite a few record collections where you'd least expect it. After the Weather Report album, there was another from Winter's Consort in late 1972, and shortly after that, the nucleus of the Winter band broke off, calling itself Oregon and releasing the first of several collections of finely crafted acoustic music.

Along with his three partners in Oregon, as well as Keith Jarrett, Jan Garbarek, and McCoy Tyner, Ralph Towner is one of the main reasons why we're again looking at acoustic possibilities in the area of contemporary improvised music. This is not so much a reaction to recent electric onslaughts; it's more of an unfolding of further opportunities, ways of being in sound. Return to Forever and Mahavishnu both included acoustic segments in their concerts. But though Ralph Towner has had occasion to play electric keyboards, he is committed to acoustic music in performance. It has to do with training, the processes through which his musical identity was formed.

"My commitment to acoustic music is not really a big romantic thing. I just was never interested in electric guitar. I didn't like the way it sounded; I never played with a pick, for example, because I just was never drawn to the sound of the electric guitar. I wasn't on the jazz scene until I got a classically oriented technique on the guitar. It's a matter of training, just the way it worked out for me. I've committed a lot of years to studying acoustic instruments, and I express myself very well on them. I do find them more sympathetic than electric instruments, but I find electric instruments fascinating too. I'm influenced a lot by them. I experiment a lot with imitating electronic sounds on acoustic instruments, for instance. There are also unique tunings that come about through electric instruments that I try to pick up, especially on the twelve-string—twelve-tone tunings. You have to keep your ears open for electric music."

Though Towner's playing on classical and twelve-string guitars, as well as piano, has matured to a great extent since the Weather Report recording, the style of that twelve-string sound on "The Moors" was unique starting with note one, as was Towner's music on *Road*. Part of the reason for the unusual texture is the technique Towner brings to his double-stringed axe. "The most noticeable thing is the twelve-string. I haven't heard a classically trained player play a twelve-string because it butchers your fingernails, which serve as your several picks. I developed a special way of plucking it that I use as well on the classical guitar. More sounds get drawn out with a much smaller stroke. I push the string down and let it roll up from my finger, more than I sweep it. It means that I'm not *brushing* the string as much as I'm really *pushing* it. It results in a lot of volume, plus my *finger* hits the strings before the finger*nail* does. The reason my finger hits first is that if you hit the vibrating string with something hard, you'll get what amounts to pick noise or (in this case) nail noise. With my technique, the sound produced by the vibrating string isn't shrouded as much in the sound made by its contact with the nail. It's a cleaner sound."

There are other elements that individualize Towner's playing. Aside from the physicality of sound production, there is Ralph's way of hearing the instrument in his musical mind: "In addition to my classically styled technique, the music that I'm playing is very keyboard-oriented. I treat the guitar quite often like a piano trio; if I'm playing alone, it's almost a one-man band approach. There'll be the melodist, the inner voices, and the bass voice. I seldom run these voices through really simultaneously, although that's the illusion. Each part of the music gets my attention as it's going by, which it does at quite a rapid rate. The illusion is created by setting up a focus of attention in the music. For example, if I play something melodically, I'll try to hang it over. If I start an inside voice beneath the melody, I'll hold the melody; I won't stop it and then start the inside voice. The melody gets hung over, and then I go to the next part. The attention of the listener or a player flows more easily; it's not shifted abruptly to what comes next.

"Also, I think of my playing approach as three-dimensional. It has levels of importance. I'll bring out or accent a note, and gradually work it back to a lesser volume level. I'm always concerned with the level of voicing, whether it's primary, secondary, or tertiary. It's a matter of controlling these things as far as the attention of the listener goes, as well as the importance of each voicing in the music. These tend to be very small discriminations, but they have important results."

The selection "Images Unseen" from Ralph's solo LP *Diary* offers the best opportunity to delineate Towner's voices and how he manipulates them. The piece is a textural improvisation on twelve-string guitar, with gong accompaniment for coloristic effect. Towner moves through the guitar's upper, lower, and middle registers freely, with furtive, dissonant, and abrupt power. Pure tones, lines, and colors emerge, rippling and melting into one another by means of diversified accents. Prominent in this piece also is a device frequently employed by Towner, the use of implied or "hidden" notes. Here the jumps between the voices that Towner described above are executed so swiftly that the transitional chords or lines are merely implied—that is, voiced at minute volume or not at all. This technique is evident in the twelve-string playing, but is especially prevalent in Ralph's classical guitar music, where the inherently quieter volume level allows the hidden notes to smooth the flow of the playing. For Towner, it all has to do with controlling the myriad voices to be found in his instruments.

"To take the example of the six-string guitar, your melody is on the first string, and the middle of your chord—the thirds, sevenths, and ninths—is occupying the next three strings, and you're probably playing the bass notes on the fifth and sixth. I don't necessarily have to play everything at once. I might do a figure on the bass, go up and play the melody for just a second—this is either an improvised line or a written melody—and leave that hang in the air, then move down again and play a lower voice or one of the inside (middle) voices, playing them a bit more quietly, so the attack doesn't drown out the focus of attention as if it were a primary voice. Then I'll return as quickly as I can to the initial melodic voice and pick it up where I left it hanging. But it's a matter of overlap, really; you don't just go through one-two-three steps.

"All good players seem to me to do that, whether they're aware of it or not. I mentioned this to Gary Burton, as a matter of fact—we play quite similarly, especially in solo situations—and even though it appears to me that he does the very same thing, he doesn't think that way. He considers the total instrument and the motion all over it. But also, the vibes are very visually oriented and the guitar isn't in the same way. The guitar can be more easily abstracted in its totality. It's very complicated, really; but it's the classical technique that allows me to make discriminations in volume, tone, and accent for individual notes and groups of notes within the total chord."

The usual canard about a "classical" approach to improvised music prattles on about a loss of spontaneity, a dry, sterile attitude. Towner's debunk: "To me, there's nothing to be uptight where a 'jazz' player's concerned about being classically trained or influenced. On the contrary, it's a technique, in a way, of being able to make really fine discriminations and articulation in playing." It represents Ralph's approach to the instrument, rather than a style, or a specific, limited way to sound.

Since Ralph's guitar playing is keyboard-oriented, it would be natural to assume that his musical start came on the ivories. It's only partially true. "My mother was a piano teacher," he explains, "so there was always a piano in the house. I was imitating classical things when I was three years old, I guess. I wasn't drawn to jazz and forms of improvisational music until I was twenty—very late. I studied cornet and trumpet until I was seventeen. That gave me my reading background."

Towner's musical development became two-pronged; he studied classical music on guitar and began to get into improvisational music —jazz—on the piano. "The Scott LaFaro–Bill Evans combination really hooked me into jazz, and I'm influenced quite a bit by bass players in my approach to the guitar, as well as by pianists. So I guess the trio concept has really been applied to my guitar style. I started strictly as a classical guitar player, however, without any real notion of improvising, at the same time I was playing jazz piano. I was, at one time, involved with imitating Bill to a T on piano. That had a rather devastating effect on my personality until I realized I was a lot more violent than Bill; then I was able to develop from that."

Ralph's keyboard debt to Evans is acknowledged on his first LP for ECM, a collaboration with Oregon bassist Glen Moore called *Trios/Solos*. Side 2 opens with a Towner reading of Evans's "Re: Person I Knew" (Bill's anagrammed tribute to producer Orrin Keepnews). It's a faithfully executed commentary on the Evans impressionistic style, but doesn't show Ralph as an original keyboard artist. Subsequent recordings on *Diary* and with Oregon show him less concerned with swinging *per se* than Evans, and inclined to establish a subtler sense of rhythmic flow. Ralph shares the Evans penchant for introspection, but without the moodiness that causes Bill's frequent idiosyncratic touches.

"I was drawn to the guitar, strictly as a student composer—from the classical end. I now practice classical music strictly because it gives me a guideline; if I just play what I want to play, I'll play what I can do. If it's a classical piece, it's going to be something I wouldn't ordinarily do with my fingers or musically. It's a vehicle that I can learn from, to control voices, and so forth.

"The result of all this technical talk," Ralph returned to the original subject of the conversation, "is hopefully to put more emotion in your playing. It's not something to be afraid of; 'technique' is a maligned word. It really gives me a greater vocabulary to be more emotional in my playing.

"When you're playing your music, it's too late then for you to think about your technique. You're just playing music. You can't say to yourself, 'Now I'm going to play this lovely short note here.' It's too late. Because if you think that way, it pulls you away, divides your attention. That internal dialogue has to stop when you really start to perform. In this sense, playing is really a form of meditation; the internal dialogue ceases. Any interruption of self-consciousness derails the piece, especially on guitar, because the margin of error is so great on the classical guitar. You can draw energy from a crowd, but you don't take conscious notice of them or what you're doing. Oregon's music is frequently referred to as spiritual, and it's spiritual insofar as any music is, in this sense that we've just been talking about."

Ralph picked up the twelve-string guitar almost by accident, and as the direct result of meeting and playing with Paul Winter. "Before I met Paul, working in New York, I was a jazz pianist, really; it was easy to hear my roots there. And as an improvising musician on the classical guitar, I was really into kind of a more stretched-out Baden-Powell thing, with a more complicated harmonic base. Really Brazilian in my approach, though. So I was a Brazilian-style guitarist and a jazz pianist, working mainly as a pianist because of the volume and acoustical problems of working with classical guitar and trap drums. I like trap drums, but unless you're in a recording studio, playing a classical guitar with them is impossible.

"When I first met Paul, he had a twelve-string and wanted me to try to play it. My first reaction was, 'My God, I'll break my fingernails off!' It was like playing a cheese grater, awful. But it was a wonderful guitar. An interesting thing about the Winter Consort was that they were avoiding any style I was capable of playing in, but it was quite an eclectic mixture that they were into. I really wanted to try and write some music for their format—trying perhaps to weld it into something more unified. Not making it a synthesis group, playing all kinds of music from all over the world with all kinds of instruments, but using those instruments to make *a* music."

A stylistic direction was what was needed, and Towner's music, heard on *Road* and the later *Icarus*, provided it to a considerable extent, leading the Winter Consort from its previous classico-Renaissance pretentions into a more thoroughly integrated modern chamber music. "I wanted to do something that really sounded good with all of the instruments, that wasn't this, that, or another thing. After I played awhile with the group, I got to know everyone's voices." The *Road* and *Icarus* albums are both models of enlightened early fusion music from the then rarely heard acoustic point of view, with only the best work of the British group Pentangle matching the craft of its blend. Eventually, however, it was musical differences of opinion and direction that led Towner, bassist Glen Moore (who appeared on *Road* but was replaced by Herb Bushler on *Icarus*), reed-player Paul McCandless and multi-instrumentalist Colin Walcott to defect and create Oregon, whose music has its seeds in these two LPs by the Winter Consort.

In any case, it was Paul Winter who led Ralph to the twelve-string, and Ralph credits the instrument with leading him out of "jazz" as a strict concept and into other areas. Even today, Ralph's relationship with the instrument is unusual. "Actually, I don't practice the twelve-string all that much, and the harmonic things I get into are actually simpler than the ones I use on the classical guitar. Some effects that the twelve-string creates are just great, but the more standard things that you'd try on a six-string just don't come off as well at all. The same voicings that sound well on the classical won't sound the same on the twelve, so I don't make any attempt to play the same way on the two instruments. The twelve-string has to be adapted to on its own. The new tunings I've tried didn't even come about until recently."

Asked to elaborate further on his uses for each guitar, Towner replied, "I haven't really figured out a way to express that in words yet. I find it's easier to play the classical guitar; it's a more flexible instrument. I can play more complicated lines on it. The interplay among the voices is really more pianistic than on the twelve-string. I can accent more unusual notes on the twelve-string, however. I can also create walls of things, really complex patterns in which the accents are always different. Every instant I'm trying to bring something else. I like to do a lot of polyrhythmic things on the twelve-string, just through accents. It's funkier too. I can bend strings. If I try that on a classical guitar, it sounds a little silly to me— sometimes I can do it." (An example of successful classical guitar string bending is on Towner's duet "The Rough Places Plain" with sitarist Colin Walcott, on the first Oregon album for Vanguard. Here Ralph mimics the notebending technique of the Indian instrument to great effect.)

Further exemplification of Towner's style on each guitar can be gleaned from his recordings. The influence of Indian music in Towner's twelve-string work is very strong, especially the rhythmic element, in the Winter Consort's two discs. "General Pudson's Entrance," a Towner composition from *Road*, demonstrates Ralph's predilection for breaking up tempos into polyrhythms. The guitar's rushed, agitated rhythmic strumming is set against evenly flowing lines. *Icarus*'s twelve-string/tabla duet with Walcott called "Juniper Bear" illustrates the point even further. Here the interplay between strings and percussion is truly stunning, as Towner applies his twelve-string techniques more directly to an Indian format. It's similar to his playing on "The Moors," only in a more rhythmically (albeit broadly) defined space. The jagged chording is still linked by dazzling multi-note runs and hidden notes, with more bent strings and ringing plucked notes adding more accent tension.

Another good introduction to Towner's twelve-string voices is the title tune from Oregon's *Distant Hills* album. In his short solo Ralph again explores the full range of voices and accents, this time in a more melodic, less purely textural piece than the solo album's "Unseen Images." On "Entry in a Diary" (from the ECM *Diary* LP), Towner's accents for the twelve-string are given full play; because he tends to play quieter passages more slowly and deliberately than on the classical, the diversification of ways to emphasize notes is especially apparent.

On selections like "Dark Spirit" (from the *Distant Hills* album), "Ode to a Fillmore Dressing Room" (from Winter's *Icarus*), and in several other places on Oregon's new album *Winter Light*, one can hear that Ralph's classical guitar work is more evenly flowing, dynamically and linearly. The touch is lighter and notes are perhaps struck more precisely than on the twelve-string. The six-string chording creates a blanketlike, coloristic base rather than serving as rhythmic punctuation. All in all, the approach is more traditional in surface style, but Towner's unique musical mind and way of hearing guitar music stamps the style with his own strong identity.

Our conversation turned to problems of amplification in acoustic music. Being heard correctly, especially in a live situation when one has to compete with traps and possibly reeds, is perhaps the most severe technical problem an acoustic guitarist has to face. "I did an album for ECM with Jan Garbarek and Jon Christensen, and we did a rock-and-roll type number where I tried a pickup on the twelve-string. It just didn't come off. You see, what's happening is that all the overtones are happening about a foot or two out from the guitar. They have to happen in space rather than through the wood. A pickup and contact mike are just picking up the initial vibrations, eliminating most of the exciting qualities of the twelve-string."

Those overtones are a key fixture in much of Towner's music on both guitars and piano. On his piece "Aurora" from Oregon's *Distant Hills*, for example, Towner overdubs piano and guitar, employing sustained chordal overtones to form a drone base. It's a totally acoustic effect, one that can't be duplicated on electric instruments. Towner thus can't endorse making the halfway step of amplification that the pickup provides between acoustic and solid-body electric. "I really haven't tried to find an acceptable method of picking up on acoustic that much. In one Oslo club with Garbarek and Christensen, I had to use a pickup because the sound system was bad and I couldn't be heard over the drum. I stuck on a Barcus Berry, plugged into an amp, and promptly drowned everyone out. It's like some kind of a zealot; I find that the worst offenders of drowning out other musicians are converted acoustic musicians. I played electric piano in jamming situations last year with Jan Hammer, and got off on playing just as loud as I could."

Ralph plays electric piano on two LPs by British reedman Clive Stevens. His tone on the electric keyboard leans to a high distortion level, but his style follows a pattern set by the acoustic work, as rapid single-note lines give way to blocks of chords. The effect isn't as unique as on his guitars or even on the acoustic piano; the electric work closely resembles George Duke and Herbie Hancock. *Atmospheres*, the first date with Stevens, is a fine LP, but Ralph is too often lost amidst the high electric mix of two guitars, Billy Cobham's traps, and amplified saxes. A wider coloristic range is shown in Towner's appearances on the second Stevens album, *Voyage to Uranus*.

Towner's increasingly prolific recording for ECM brought up the question of label chief Manfred Eicher's fondness for putting musicians in challenging situations, notably the solo concert and LP. "Not many musicians," begins Ralph, "can make a total concert on one instrument. I have to change instruments; I wouldn't think of doing an entire concert on the twelve-string. But it's not as frightening as you'd think. You have complete control over the intensity. You're not dealing with other musicians—when you play with others, you see, you're still playing just one piece of music. If the intensity drops, in a lot of situations you won't have a strong enough voice to bring it up again. If the group loses the thread, and you hear people shuffle, for instance, you know you've lost it. In the group situation there may not be a whole lot you can do to bring it back again. When you're by yourself, you can do complete about-faces if you want. There's complete control over your power. The sad thing, I find, is that when you're finished playing your concert, there's nobody to discuss it with; you're all alone. I find it to be an exciting effort, but after a while I get lonely doing it. I can't say it's as thrilling playing a solo concert that's good as playing a group concert that's good, providing you play well and get the same results in the group situation. But the main difference, really, is in the kind of control that you have."

The *Diary* solo LP was finished quickly. "We did every piece immediately; there was no laying down of one track and coming back the next day to overdub. The album took only two days to finish—one session of about four or five hours, another hour the next day, and then the mix. I discovered a really good technique for overdubbing. I didn't want a situation where one instrument was accompanying another. I wanted to have more of an improvised interplay between instruments. The music had to flow without one instrument stuck in a backup position. I would start a piece on one instrument, play it so far in a primary role, and then stop within the piece. Then I'd go back, pick up another instrument, playing it in the secondary role underneath the first instrumental voice. But then I'd go beyond the point where the first track stopped, bringing the secondary voice to a primary role. The flip-flop process gave me the opportunity to change roles on a single tune. So you lose a lot of the accompaniment-lead effect." It sounds, in fact, as if Towner is playing in a mirror much of the time, so sensitively is each voice reflected in the other.

"Psychologically," continued Ralph, "I also tried not to match the opposite track. I didn't play *with* it in the sense of watching it or thinking about it, any more than I would really think about another musician playing along. It was a feeling, and I played with the feeling. I seldom made plans about how long I was going to play, fixing bar lengths and so forth. A couple of the pieces had no bar lines. I trusted my feelings. When I felt like a section was coming to an end—going from a free section into a written section, for example—I would just *trust* after about four minutes, let's say, that 'we' were heading in the right direction. It was pretty uncanny, though. I don't even know if I could do it twice." Towner is still pleased with the album.

A stock interviewer's question when talking to an ECM artist is, How does Manfred Eicher do it? "He's something else, I'll tell you that. He always reacts differently. Whenever I think I can predict what Manfred's going to do, he'll do something else. He's very subtle and quiet, really dedicated to the music. It's the most unusual thing I've ever seen in a person who deals with a record company. On solo albums he'll make a lot of quiet suggestions about feelings and things, but he'll stay very busy with technical things that I don't really understand—things with the board, mike placement, engineering. He's so experienced and has such a natural gift for sensing what to do as far as production goes. But he seldom gives orders on solo LPs—he never told me to do this or that.

"On the record I just did with Garbarek and Christensen, he was much more aggressive. I intended to play much more piano on it, for example; he said that was ridiculous, that what I do that is so unusual is play the twelve-string. He didn't want a regular piano-bass-sax-drums quartet, even if I did play wonderful piano. He was right. I ended up playing the twelve-string differently than I've ever played it, and I made some important steps that kept me from getting bored with it. I do have periods where I don't play it. I leave it in its case and seldom practice it. But I don't intend to give it up, of course."

While touching again on this subject of his relationship with his twelve-string guitar, Ralph mentioned in passing that the guitar is an instrument more environmentally sensitive than others. I asked him to elaborate. "Acoustic guitar is always different, and that can be very frustrating. Some days, everything will be there—bass, treble, middle voices. Other days, something will be missing. On my guitar it'll be most often the bass, but every instrument's different. Mine likes damp weather. You have to adjust your playing technique to the state of the instrument every day, because you can't change its physical condition, short of taking the best possible care of it that you can.

"As far as nail noise is concerned, one thing about having a large tone is that you can place the mike farther away, and that's important. People with very small tones, who play with their fingers, or picks for that matter, will get a lot of string noise. On the left hand there are ways of minimizing that squeak that you'll always have on wound strings—fingering techniques, for example, and other steps to avoid it as much as you can. If you have a good enough acoustic sound, though, you can place the mike a bit farther away."

Ralph's increasing solo stature as an artist in no way detracts from his commitments to Oregon. The entire group attains steadily increasing recognition across the country. "The steady thing is Oregon," states Ralph, "the solo thing is planned six to seven months in advance, or that's the way I like to do it, at least. That becomes a vacation for everyone else. But it's a changing concern; we're getting more work with the group. I like to play solo concerts, but my main interest is in this unusual group."

Editor's Note

Since the above was written in 1975, Oregon and its members have continued to develop as innovators and mature musicians. Towner's career remains active. There have been a number of new albums, including two solo albums and one of duos with John Abercrombie. Together and apart, the musicians of Oregon have done a great deal to encourage both acoustic and non-Western music, have set new improvisatory standards, and have become role-models for many younger players from both the jazz and classical sides of the music that encompasses them both.

Acknowledgments

Introduction by James Sallis. Copyright © 1995, James Sallis.

"Four Jazz Choruses" by James Sallis originally appeared in *Karamu*. Copyright © 1989, James Sallis.

"The Guitar in Jazz" from *The Book of Jazz* by Leonard Feather. Copyright © 1957, 1965, reprinted by permission of Leonard Feather.

"Nick Lucas" by Jas Obrecht. Copyright © 1978 Miller Freeman, Inc. Reprinted by permission of *Guitar Player* magazine.

"Eddie Lang" adapted from *The Guitar Players* by James Sallis. Copyright © 1982, reprinted by permission of the author.

"From Blues to Jazz Guitar" by Dan Lambert. Copyright © 1984, reprinted by permission of the author.

"The Jazz Guitar Duet: A Fifty-Year History" by Richard Lieberson. Copyright © 1978, 1984 Miller Freeman, Inc. Reprinted by permission of *Guitar Player* magazine and the author.

"Charlie Christian" by Bill Simon from *The Jazz Makers*, ed. Nat Shapiro/Nat Hentoff. Copyright © 1957.

"Django's Blues" by Dan Lambert. Copyright © 1984, reprinted by permission of the author.

"Oscar Moore" and "Jazz Guitar and Western Swing" by Michael Price. Copyright © 1984, reprinted by permission of the author.

"Swing Guitar: The Acoustic Chordal Style" by Richard Lieberson. Copyright © 1984, reprinted by permission of the author.

"Middle Ground" by James Sallis. Copyright © 1984, reprinted by permission of the author.

"Joe Pass" reprinted by permission of Louisiana State University Press from *Jazz Spoken Here*, by Wayne Enstice and Paul Rubin. Copyright © 1992 by Louisiana State University Press.

Index

Wyble, Jimmy, 7, 45, 82, 83, 86–87, 138

Yazoo Records, 27
"You Go to My Head," 6
"You Have to Change Keys to Play These Blues" (Lang/Johnson), 20, 40–42
"You Look Good to Me" (Waller), 110
Young, Lee, 77

Young, Lester, 57, 58, 111, 116, 119, 125, 150, 157
"You Rascal You" (Reinhardt), 71–74
"Yours Truly Is Truly Yours" (Van Eps), 101

Zappa, Frank, 10
Zeigler Twins, 14
Zoller, Attila, 8, 116, 157